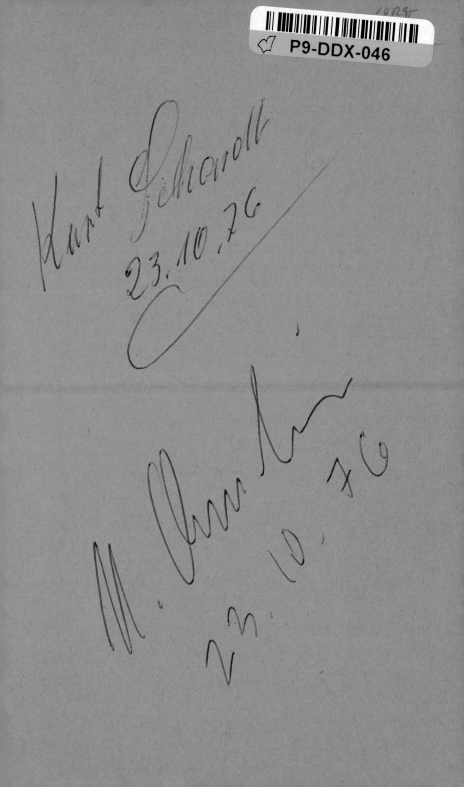

Where the Great German Wines Grow

Where the Great German Wines Grow

A Guide to the Leading Vineyards

by HANS AMBROSI

Translated by
GAVIN HAMILTON and THOM PRINGLE

HASTINGS HOUSE · PUBLISHERS

New York

The publishers are grateful to Diana Frese, William Leedom and Peter M. F. Sichel for their invaluable help in reviewing the original German edition and the translation.

Library of Congress Cataloging in Publication Data

Ambrosi, Hans, 1925–
   Where the great German wines grow.
   Translation of Wo grosse Weine wachsen.
   Bibliography: p.
   Includes index.
   1. Wine and wine making—Germany, West—Directories.
I. Title.
TP559.G3A615   641.2′2′0943   75-33726
ISBN 0-8038-8070-7

Published simultaneously in Canada by
Saunders of Toronto, Ltd., Don Mills, Ontario
Printed in the United States of America

Table of Contents

Foreword   vi
How to Use This Book   viii
An Introduction to German Wines   xiv

The Great German Wines Estates
    Ahr and Mittelrhein   1
    Moselle-Saar-Ruwer   7
    Nahe   39
    Rheingau   61
    Rheinhessen   105
    Rheinpfalz   137
    Baden   161
    Württemberg   175
    Franconia   191

Reference Section
    How to Read a German Wine Label   207
    German-English Dictionary of Wine-Appreciation Terms   214
    German-English Dictionary of Technical Wine Terms   219
    Wine Auctions   229
    Wine Festivals   230
    Useful Addresses   230

Index of Estates, Locations and Vineyards   233

Foreword

The author and publisher are delighted to present this first guide to West Germany's leading vineyards after lengthy preparation. It is designed for both the traveller and the wine lover who wants to appreciate the wines he drinks, to whom it gives pleasure to discover fine wines and to learn how they were made and their geographical and historical background.

In the following chapters you will read about the kind of soil and terrain on which the grapes for each particular wine grow, and about the cellars in which those wines are produced and aged. For those who plan to visit Germany's beautiful wine country there is detailed information on how to visit the individual estates and taste their wine. Of interest to all will be the histories of the estates and their owners, and notes about the many objects of interest which, along with the tasting rooms and cellars, are found at almost every estate. Descriptions of the labels present additional evidence of the rich, tradition-filled histories of the wine estates. A number of the labels are shown. Your knowledge and enjoyment of wine will be greatly enhanced by these introductory chapters and the thorough reference section at the back.

This book stands out among wine books with its clear systematic presentation of a vast quantity of detailed information. Though it emphasizes wine technology, the book should capture the reader's imagination with descriptions of the estates and their melodious monastic, aristocratic, and bourgeois names and histories, the vineyards in their idyllic settings, the estate buildings, the castles, the mansions, the old cellars and, certainly, the wines themselves. You will be inspired, I hope, to become better acquainted with German wines and to visit these regions someday.

In previous wine literature the large German wine estates have been treated only incidentally. This is a great oversight, for they have contributed so much to the international reputation of German wines. Today the discerning wine connoisseur needs all the information he can get to maintain his independent opinion against increasing conformity.

This information takes into account the new German wine law, which came into force in June 1971, providing for the consolidation of about 20,000 vineyards into 3,000. A few estates have requested that some old vineyard names be included because the new law is not yet fully implemented, and because many pre-1971 wines are still available. A full and complete list of all vineyard names can be found in my new German wine atlas, *Weinlagen-Atlas mit Wein Lexikon Deutschland* (Ceres-Verlag Rudolf-August Oetker KG, Bielefeld, West Germany, 1974).

Only when an estate made the figures available could the area of its vineyard be given. Also, because wines are affected by the vineyard, vintage, and even the bottling, it was often difficult to find characteristics common to all wines produced by one estate. Subjective opinion being of great value in assessing wine, each person must taste for himself.

In selecting the estates, I included those which have a vineyard area of more than 50 acres or which are important for their history or quality. With over 90 estates included, it was necessary to concentrate on only the most important facts. Preference was given to information which the estate itself felt was of major interest. We made our project known through the trade press to as many interested persons as possible, and continue to welcome comments and additional information.

Favored climatically and geographically, the estates described in this book form a kind of elite, but the owners do not conduct themselves as such. They prefer to give their total personal attention to the production of outstanding German wines. I hope this book helps to give recognition to their complete and unselfish devotion in an age of impersonal mass production.

Finally, I would like to thank the *Stabilisierungsfonds für Wein,* which carefully compiles useful and complete statistics about the German wine industry, for generously supplying material used in this book.

HANS AMBROSI

How to Use This Book

The delicate character that has made German wines so popular makes their description difficult. It is easy to appreciate the careful balance of sugar, acid, alcohol and flavor elements in a wine, but it is another matter to describe that balance with words—to communicate that taste sensation to someone else. Establishing uniform standards to guide vintners in producing such wines is even more difficult.

Germans have never been afraid to attempt the difficult, and after producing renowned wines for more than 1,000 years, the German wine industry recently devised new standards for wines that could be used and understood by wine makers and consumers as well.

The new classification system had to be detailed. Thus, the consumer must learn basic facts about the production and labeling of German wines. But in order to appreciate the wines of any well-organized wine country, one must know something about the country's wine-production standards. France's many appellations and producing areas, and Italy's denominazione concept, need to be carefully studied. Even in the United States, the words on a label mean more than the casual observer realizes. An American sparkling wine, for instance, that has been "fermented in the bottle" has not been processed in the same manner as a sparkling wine that has been "fermented in *this* bottle."

Explaining the structure and procedures of the German wine industry is a basic purpose of this book. The material is mainly concerned with wine produced after July 1971, when the new German wine law and regulations were put into effect. The new law covers most of the German wines that you will find for sale today, unless you are interested in rare old vintages. In those cases though, the estate descriptions and comments may still be relevant, as they often contain information pertaining to the years, even centuries, before 1971.

If you are not already acquainted with German wines, you will find four parts of this book to be especially helpful: this chapter, the following "Introduction to German wines," and the article on reading German wine labels and German-English wine-term dictionaries in the reference section. Anyone who has read the first three parts and refers to the dictionary section as necessary can acquire a basic understanding of German wines and the estate descriptions and comments that form the main part of the book.

Many specialized terms now used in the German wine industry have no convenient equivalents in English, so that wine experts the world over use the actual German terms in discussing German wines. Words such as Grosslage, Qualitätswein, and Auslese are not italicized in the text, but are used as English words. The reader can have a thorough working knowledge of German wines by looking up any unfamiliar term in the German-English dictionaries in the reference section. This is important to both novice and connoisseur, for wine lovers are constantly faced with German words on bottle labels, even when the wines are exported to English-speaking countries. People who visit West Germany will encounter still more.

The German names of the wine-producing regions have been retained in this book in order to eliminate confusion and to agree with the terms found on German wine labels. The two exceptions are Moselle and Franconia (known in German as Mosel and Franken), which are well known to most English-speaking people. English names, where used, refer to German geographical features and political areas, which is the common practice. The wine-producing regions are not always the same are the political areas, even though the names may be similar.

Names, regulations and categories are important in wine appreciation, but it is the colorful lore behind a wine that brings it to life. Was it produced by a prince? Is it the same kind of wine served in the White House? Did the grapes come from a vineyard established by the Romans? The real connoisseur will want to know how the wine was processed, what kind of soil the grapes grew on, if the wine was aged in wooden barrels . . . Even if an interested wine drinker cannot visit Germany in person he can tour the leading wine estates by reading this book.

The estate section describes more than 90 estates, most of which export their wines to English-speaking countries. When you purchase a high-quality German wine outside of Germany, there is a good chance it will be from one of these estates, and you will be able to read the story of the wine before you drink it. But you must identify the producer of the wine, not the vineyard name that is usually a prominent part of the label.

The official name of a wine's producer is often difficult to identify on a label. In the index at the back, you will find the names of the estates in this book and variations of those names, enabling you to identify a particular producer. We have listed all the vineyards, Grosslage names, and villages discussed in the estates section to help you determine which estates produce wine from a particular vineyard or area. When you have isolated the name of the producer, you can read in the particular section all about the history of the estate, its vineyards, grape varieties, soil and terrain, label design, and wine-production philosophy. *From my notebook,* included in the description of each estate, contains many inside facts and opinions gained through years of personal contact with the estates' owners.

For the wine lover who wants to confirm what he tastes, detailed information about the types of soil, terrain, and vineyard names is important, for grapes grown on one type of soil will taste different from the same kind of grapes grown on another type of soil. The slope of the land will also affect the way grapes mature by providing different degrees of water drainage and sunshine. The acreage figures tell how big the estate is, in which vineyards the estate has an interest, and where the estate owns only part of a vineyard, the vineyard name may be followed by a number in parentheses telling how many acres the estate owns in that vineyard. Some estates did not supply acreage figures, in other cases the size of the holdings was so small that acreage figures were deleted. If an estate owns the entire vineyard, the words "entire vineyard" will appear in parentheses after the vineyard name.

The *grape variety* is one of the first things a connoisseur wants to know about a wine, for it is basic to a wine's character. Some vintners endorse the old traditional varieties; others favor the newer varieties. This is a topic of much debate. You can learn about the wine philosophy of an estate by checking the varieties planted there. A conservative policy would favor a large percentage of the established varieties such as Riesling and Sylvaner; large percentages of relatively new varieties, such as Scheurebe and Morio-Muskat, indicate a more progressive policy. German names for the grape varieties, with the exception of Sylvaner, are used throughout the text to reduce confusion when the names are encountered on bottle labels. Most of the major varieties are explained in the reference section in the German-English Dictionary of Technical Wine Terms, along with their equivalent French or American names.

Estate specialties and *The wines* show the estate's wine philosophy even more clearly. The comments you read under these headings will tell you whether the wine you have is typical of the wines produced by the estate and will help you to put the wines and the estate itself into perspective. Some estates produce very special wines or wines from unusual grape varieties. It would be tragic to a real wine lover to consume a bottle of wine and only afterwards learn that it was a unique product.

Most labels on German wines are works of art, often with generations or centuries of history behind them. Some have been designed by renowned artists, many convey a special meaning, and many carry the family coat of arms and its reputation. Under the *Label* heading in each estate description you will learn the background of the estate's label, and the little extra meanings that certain estates have for their different bottle capsules and label colors.

Occasionally a label will have a picture of the estate or one of its buildings which helps those who cannot visit to at least visualize the estate. And when the wine lover does go there, it is a thrill to recognize the estate from the picture on the label. Tens of thousands do just that every year, enjoying one of the most picturesque areas in the world, the wine regions of Germany.

Many tourists want to see the Rheingau and Moselle scenery, but the serious wine lovers and members of the trade are anxious to learn all they can about German wine. There are special wine tours, in which all arrangements to visit estates and sample various wines are made. Others may prefer to be on their own or to attend a special wine seminar like that of the German Wine Academy.

The Academy's five day course in wine appreciation is repeated several times in summer. For advanced students and novices who really want to learn about German wines, the courses are taught in English by practicing experts from throughout the German wine industry. There are classes in technical subjects, classes in wine appreciation, visits to wine estates, daily tasting sessions, usually two or three per day, and there are social events. The Academy takes care of all arrangements including meals, lodging and transportation, leaving the student free to concentrate on wine.

A complete list of addresses and seminars is included in the reference section. The locations and visting policy given in the section on individual estates will allow independence to the person who wants to explore the wine country on his own. Also listed, in the *Points of interest* section of each estate's description, are many attractions that are worth seeing in their own right. Kloster Eberbach, a Hessian state winery and a magnificent secluded monastery, is an awe-inspiring sight.

The estates have three types of visiting policies: some accept no visitors, some accept members of the trade, and some welcome all visitors. Under *Visits and tastings* you can read about each estate's policy and whether English-speaking personnel are available.

When you wish to visit a particular estate you should call, or have your concierge call, to make an appointment. The estate should be informed which language you speak, the number of people in your group, and whether a tasting is desired. If you are a bona fide member of the wine industry involved in production, marketing or education and research, be sure to mention this as well as any special interest you may have. Someone interested in sales would want to speak with the sales manager. Also, keep in mind that at certain times, especially when everyone is busy with harvesting and crushing, smaller estates will have little time to pay attention to visitors. It is better to call a few days in advance than to write, as very few estates are eager correspondents or are able to schedule operations much in advance. As even large estates do not usually have English-speaking persons on their office staff, your hotel concierge should make the call if you do not speak German. If we have listed an estate as having English-speaking personnel available, you can expect someone to help with your visit, even if it is a local resident or the owner's son who may have learned English.

With your appointments made, you can start out: the only way for the avid wine lover is by car. To get to the many isolated estates, a rented automobile is the easiest way, but with two or more people sharing, it is also the most inexpensive. Remember Germany's extremely strict laws concerning drinking and driving, which are enforced for tourists and residents. If you're by yourself, go easy during the tastings. Groups can rotate drivers for different days and reward them for their abstinence with a free evening meal and a bottle of the best wine of the day.

To get to the estates, use a detailed road map along with the location and routing descriptions given in the estate section of this book. Distances given in the directions are given in metric measurements, as the odometers in European rental cars are calibrated in kilometers. Roads throughout Germany are generally well marked.

In your travels through Germany and through this book, you will encounter several "wine roads." These are routes established on existing roads, which lead through the most interesting and picturesque vineyards of a region. The best known is the German Wine Road (Deutsche Weinstrasse) a route that runs north-south through the Rheinpfalz region, along the Haardt Mountains from Grunstadt through Bad Durkheim and Neustadt to Schweigen. It was established in 1932 and is marked with signposts showing a bunch of grapes. In Baden Wine Road (Badische Weinstrasse) leads from Weinheim past the Kaiserstuhl and through the Markgräflerland to the Swiss border; it is marked with signposts showing grapes and the Baden coat of arms. The Nahe Wine Road (Naheweinstrasse) is a circle that starts and ends in Bad Kreuznach and is marked with signposts showing a "Römer" wine glass and a large "N." The Rheingau Riesling Route wanders through the Rheingau from Lorch to Hochheim and has been marked since 1973 with signs showing a wine glass with a crown. In Franconia there is a sort of Bocksbeutel Road (Bocksbeutelstrasse), but it is unofficial and not marked. It is hardly necessary to have marked wine roads along rivers, as in the Moselle Valley, where the vineyards are adjacent to the river, but in flat areas such as Württemberg, the wine-producing areas are less apparent.

Germans take the wine business very seriously, but they believe in enjoying the fruits of their labor, and the land is filled with wine festivals. With the exception of January, you can find a wine *Fest* someplace in Germany at almost any time of the year. During August and September there are so many festivals that you can find at least one of these rollicking events in any wine region. There have been as many as 30 to 40 festivals in one month in the Moselle-Saar-Ruwer region. To find your way to a festival, contact the German National Tourist Office, one of the wine promotion offices listed under "Useful Addresses" in the reference section, or write to Deutsche Wein-Information, 6500 Mainz, Fuststrasse 4, West Germany.

It would be a shame for any wine lover to wait when there is so much to do in Germany, so take a wine course, rent a car, wander through the countryside, go to a wine *Fest* and enjoy the wine. *Prosit!*

An Introduction to German Wines

In an attempt to create some order out of the chaos that existed among the various wine-producing countries in Europe, the European Economic Community has started to slowly standardize wine production. The most apparent effect has been the establishment of three quality levels for all colors (red, rosé, and white) of still table wines. The categories are: basic, intermediate, and highest quality.

Basic wines are intended to be wholesome and inexpensive. They are consumed regularly, usually daily, and are valued as refreshment. They must meet minimum standards, but these are not demanding, and the wines are rarely exceptional. A basic wine can be outstanding, but if it is, it may warrant a higher classification and a higher price.

Intermediate wines have some fine characteristics, but are moderately priced, and are appropriate for everyday consumption. They are rarely used indiscriminately and their standards are more demanding than those for basic wines. The wine usually has to be typical of wines of its region.

Highest quality wines are outstanding and usually have special characteristics. Intended for special occasions, these wines are not for regular everyday consumption. The standards are very demanding, and in some cases require unique conditions for the wine to qualify for the designation.

The quality categories are interpreted differently by various countries, but we are not really concerned here with the wines of France, Italy or Luxembourg. In the new wine law of 1971, the Germans have tried to be faithful to the spirit of the EEC wine policy, and the three categories of wine produced in West Germany are now called *Deutscher Tafelwein* (German Table wine) *Qualitätswein bestimmter Anbaugebiete* (quality wine from designated regions), and *Qualitätswein mit Prädikat* (quality wine with special attribute).

Tafelwein is rarely, if ever, exported from Germany. It may originate in any of five approved table-wine districts: Moselle (Mosel), Rhein, Main, Neckar, and Oberrhein, or it may be a mixture of different districts. If the producer wants to be more specific, he may use a sub-region or village name on the label, providing that 75% of the grapes came from the stated area, but he is not allowed to use a vineyard name on the label. Tafelwein can hardly be classed as a "great" wine, so we will not dwell on it in this book.

The higher quality categories, the Qualitätsweine represent the best wines that Germany produces and are the types of wines produced by the estates described in this book. A Qualitatswein must originate in one of the eleven designated regions, which have the following characteristics:

Ahr. Located along the Ahr River in the northwestern part of Germany's grape-growing section. It is famous for its red wine, and more than 50% of its 1,200 acres of grapes are devoted to red-wine varieties.

Mittelrhein. Located along the Rhine River in the northwestern part of Germany's grape-growing section. Produces white wines almost exclusively. Approximately 83% of the 2,200 acres of vineyards are planted with Riesling vines. Very few wines are exported.

Moselle-Saar-Ruwer. Located along the Moselle, Ruwer, and Saar rivers southwest of the Moselle-Rhine junction. One of Germany's most famous and picturesque regions. Almost 100% white wine. Total vineyard area is 28,000 acres, of which two thirds are planted with Riesling vines.

Rheingau. Located on the north side of the Rhine River just west of Frankfurt. One of Germany's most famous wine-producing regions. Produces 98% white wines. Almost 80% of the 7,000 acres of vineyards are planted with Riesling vines.

Nahe. Located at the intersection of the Nahe and Rhine rivers. About 11,000 acres of vines, one third Sylvaner and one third Müller-Thurgau. Approximately 90% white wine.

Rheinhessen. Locted directly south of Rheingau, on the opposite side of the Rhine River. More than 90% of the wines produced here are white; the main grape varieties are Sylvaner and Müller-Thurgau. Total vineyard acreage about 53,500 acres.

Hessische Bergstrasse. Located east of Rheinhessen and slightly east of the Rhine River. Germany's smallest wine-producing region, with about 672 acres of vineyards; more than 50% Riesling vines. Produces almost all white wine.

Franconia (Franken). Located along the Main River east of Frankfurt. The total vineyard acreage is about 7,500 acres, of which 41% is planted with Müller-Thurgau and 46% with Sylvaner vines. Famous for the unique "Bocksbeutel" bottle.

Rheinpfalz. Located on the western side of the Rhine River just below Rheinhessen. In vineyard area, the second-largest wine-producing region in Germany (50,000 acres). Approximately 87% white wine; 33% Sylvaner grapes; 23% Müller-Thurgau.

Baden. A long thin region extending along the eastern side of the Rhine River from the junction of the Neckar to the Bodensee. Produces 78% white wines. The main white-wine variety is the Müller-Thurgau. Total vineyard area is 30,000 acres.

Württemberg. Spread over a large area south of Franconia. Of the total 19,000 acres of vineyards, more than 50% are devoted to red-wine varieties, with the Trollinger being the most popular grape variety. The home of "Schillerwein." Very little wine is exported.

A Qualitätswein bestimmter Anbaugebiete may originate from a region (*Gebiet*), a subregion (*Bereich*), a vineyard group (*Grosslage*), or a single vineyard (*Einzellage*) and may also use community names for identification. A Qualitätswein mit Prädikat may have the same origins, but may not come from an area as large as a region; a subregion is the largest geographic origin allowed for a "Prädikatswein."

In addition, the Qualitätswein mit Prädikat category is broken into five classes: *Kabinett, Spätlese, Auslese, Beerenauslese,* and *Trockenbeerenauslese.* Kabinett wines are the most common and Trockenbeerenauslese wines are the most rare and the most costly of the five. Complete details concerning the requirements for each class are given in the reference section.

When you choose a high-quality German wine, there are six basic categories to consider (the Qualitätswein bestimmter Anbaugebiete and the five classes of Qualitätswein mit Prädikat) and eleven regions of origin. As you read this book, you will find descriptions of the leading producers of these wines, grouped according to wine region, and detailed comments on the types of wines they produce. The tasting and individual judging is up to you.

Ahr and Mittelrhein

Ahrweiler   Bad Neuenahr   Linz

Staatliche
Weinbau-
domäne
Kloster
Marienthal

RHEIN

AHR

Koblenz

MOSEL

RHEIN

Oberwesel

Weingut Heinrich Weiler

AHR

1971 er

Marienthaler
Klostergarten

Spätburgunder Beerenauslese

A. P. Nr. 1 791 295 10 72

Qualitätswein mit Prädikat

Staatliche Weinbaudomäne
Kloster Marienthal/Ahr
Erzeugerabfüllung

MITTEL- RHEIN

Oberweseler Römerkrug

Riesling - Spätlese

Erzeugerabfüllung

Qualitätswein mit Prädikat

A. P. Nr. 1 677 096 8 72

Weingut Heinrich Weiler · Oberwesel · am Rhein

WEITERER BESITZ IN KAUB UND ENGEHÖLL

SILBERNE KAMMERPREISMÜNZE

Weinprämiierung 1973   Landwirtschaftskammer Rheinland-Pfalz

Staatliche Weinbaudomäne Kloster Marienthal (Ahr)

Address: 5483 Bad Neuenahr-Ahrweiler, Walporzheimer Strasse
48 and 5481 Marienthal, Klosterstrasse
Telephone: (02641) 34590

Location: The offices and cellars are located in the buildings of the former Marienthal Convent, situated in idyllic countryside.

How to get there: Entering Marienthal from Bad Neuenahr-Ahrweiler or from Altenahr/Dernau, drive about 300 m. (275 yd.) up the street between the Marienthal Winzerverein and Hotel Klosterquelle.

Points of interest: The ruins of the convent (church and cloisters); the old cellars; the charming vineyards.

History: The Augustine convent of Marienthal was founded in 1136, dissolved in 1802, and was later owned by several proprietors. In 1910, it was acquired by the state-owned railways, and in 1925 by the Prussian government, which transformed the property into a wine estate serving as a model for the Ahr wine-growing region. It became the Rhineland-Palatinate State Domain in 1945 and was incorporated into the agricultural institute at Ahrweiler in 1952.

Terrain and soils: The total area devoted to vineyards is 50 acres, of which 80% is steeply sloping terrain. The soil is mainly schist with loess.

Vineyard names: Marienthaler Klostergarten (24 a.), Marienthaler Stiftsberg (18.33 a.), Walporzheimer Pfaffenberg (1 a.), Walporzheimer Himmelchen (0.54 a.), Walporzheimer Alte Lay (0.47 a.), Walporzheimer Kräuterberg (1.16 a.), Ahrweiler Rosenthal (2.35 a.), Ahrweiler Silberberg (1.56 a.).

The Grosslage name is Marienthaler Klosterberg.

Grape varieties: 58% Pinot Noir, 15% Portugieser, 5% Müller-Thurgau, 22% experimental red-wine varieties.

The wines: The red wines, all barrel aged, have the typical elegant, racy character of Ahr wines. The best wines are velvety with a delicate fruitiness.

Estate specialties: Ahr red wine at its most noble; a high proportion being of Auslese quality or better. The estate has gained many high state and national awards for individual wines and for outstanding achievements in viniculture.

Label: It shows the stylized Prussian eagle symbolizing state domains.

Marketing: Because the estate is close to the national capital and to the Ruhr area, there are many regular private customers. The estate wines are well represented on wine lists in German hotels.

Visits and tastings: By appointment, the convent ruins, cellars, and vineyards can be visited, and wine tastings can be arranged to suit individual preferences. English-speaking personnel available.

From my notebook: This wine estate, featuring only red wines, is situated in the most beautiful part of the romantic Ahr Valley. A visit is recommended to all lovers of red wine, who will be attended by knowledgeable personnel.

OBERWESEL (AM RHEIN)

Weingut Heinrich Weiler

Address: 6532 Oberwesel, Mainzer Strasse 2
Telephone: (06744) 323

Location: The estate buildings are situated in the center of the village at the foot of the Schönburg near the Liebfrauenkirche Church and opposite the Oberwesel railway station.
How to get there: Take route B-9 from Koblenz or Bingen.
Points of interest: The old German wine bar in the cellar of the building with its historic steins and candle sticks.
History: According to records, ancestors of the present wine estate proprietor have been engaged in viticulture in Oberwesel since 1607. The coat of arms of the family, which is widely represented in this region, is said to have originated in 1550.
Terrain and soils: The estate covers about 12 acres of steeply sloping, terraced terrain. The soil is slate with loess.
Vineyard names: Oberweseler Römerkrug (5.7 a.), Oberweseler St. Martinsberg (1.8 a.), Engehöller Goldemund (1.6 a.), Kauber Rosstein (3.2 a.).
Grape varieties: 85% Riesling, 8% Müller-Thurgau, 5% Sylvaner, 2% Ruländer.
The wines: As typical representatives of the Mittelrhein, they are full, robust, fruity wines characteristic of the slate soil.
Estate specialties: These wines have won many national and state awards, including bronze, silver, and gold medals.
Label: The pentagonal label shows medieval Oberwesel with a wine ship and the family coat of arms.
Marketing: Primarily direct sale supported by shipment through agents in Hamburg, Munich, and Frankfurt.
Visits and tastings: By appointment, the proprietor is happy to show visitors through the cellars and vineyards and conduct wine tastings. English-speaking personnel available.

From my notebook: Oberwesel has been called the most romantic and beautiful sanctuary on the Rhine. This could also be said about the estate tasting room, which is imaginatively decorated. The carefully made wines from this small but well-managed estate are typical of the Mittelrhein. The proprietor, Heinrich Weiler, is 70 years old and very active. He graciously conducts visitors on a most informative tour through the cellars.

Moselle-Saar-Ruwer

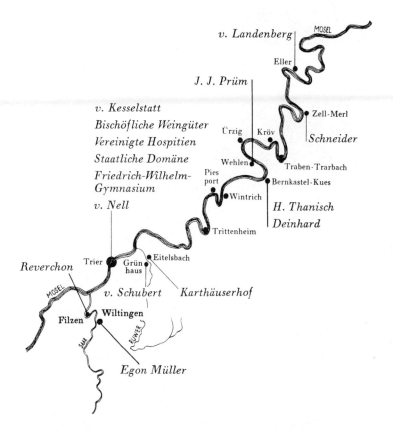

ELLER (AN DER MOSEL)

Weingut Freiherr von Landenberg

Address: 5591 Ediger-Eller 2, Moselstrasse 60
Telephone: (02675) 277

Location: The manor house and cellars are in the middle of Eller, which is picturesquely situated on the banks of the Moselle River.

How to get there: Coming from Koblenz, take the Koblenz-Trier autobahn, turn off at Kaisersesch, and drive through Cochem. Traveling from Trier, turn off at Ulmen. You can also drive the 57 km on route B-49 from Koblenz.

Points of interest: The manor house is typical of the Moselle area and formerly belonged to the Elector of Trier. It has a romantic tasting cellar and an interesting wine museum with old cooper's equipment and valuable books.

History: The Barons of Landenberg, whose ancestoral castle is in Turbenthal near Winterthur, were first recorded in 1177; the original coat of arms is dated 1250. The estate is an old family property. The proprietor is H. Trimborn von Landenberg.

Terrain and soils: The vineyards cover about 22 acres of steeply sloping terrain. The soil is mainly schist.

Vineyard names: Ellerer Calmont, Ellerer Pfirsichgarten, Ellerer Bienenlay, Ellerer Engelströpfchen, Ediger Elzogberg, Ediger Osterlämmchen, Senheimer Lay, Mesenicher Goldgrübchen.

Grape varieties: 99% Riesling, 1% experimental varieties.

The wines: The racy Moselle acidity is less noticeable because the wines are robust and full. The large number of cellared bottles indicates that careful bottle aging is considered important.

Estate specialties: The extensive wine list contains five vintages, the proportion of fine wines being very high. Single bottles of older vintages are still available.

9

Label: The various vineyards and qualities are denoted by different labels showing the coat of arms, the estate, and the landscape.

Marketing: Usually sold to regular private customers. Sample assortment and presentation packages are featured. The entire range of estate wines is also offered in the estate's pub (Alte Thorschenke) and hotel (Parkhotel Landenberg), both located in Cochem.

Visits and tastings: The cellars and tasting rooms can be visited by appointment and wines tasted. English-speaking personnel available.

From my notebook: Wine may be purchased in the interestingly decorated tasting rooms and cellars. The young proprietor has extensive knowledge of Moselle viticulture and its history.

ZELL-MERL (AN DER MOSEL)

Schneider'sche Weingüterverwaltung

Address: 5583 Zell-Merl, Merler Strasse 28
Telephone: (06542) 2054

Location: The offices and main cellars are near the church in the Merl section of Zell. New, larger cellars are being constructed in the "Auf dem Barl" business district. The firm's Machern estate, a former monastery, is located in Wehlen directly by the Zeltingen bridge.

How to get there: Take route B-55. Zell is about halfway between Koblenz and Trier. The Machern estate is 5 km. from the autobahn turn-off at Wittlich and can also be reached directly via route B-50.

Points of interest: The modern cellars in Marl; the contrast between the old terraced vineyards and the new, integrated, widespaced vineyards; the former Cistercian monastery of Machern situated in charming countryside in Wehlen.

History: The firm was founded in 1869, but experienced most of its growth during the last 25 years. The Machern estate was founded in 1238, secularized in 1803, and acquired by the firm in 1969. The firm's current proprietor is Franz Schneider.

Terrain and soils: The estate has 72 acres in Zell and Merl, and 39 acres in Wehlen and Zeltingen. Of the total 111 acres of vineyards, 50% are on gently sloping, 40% on steeply sloping, and 10% on flat terrain. The soil is mainly schist with loamy soil on the lower terraces.

Vineyard names: Merler Königslay-Terrassen (10 a.), Merler Adler (10 a.), Merler Klosterberg (10 a.), Zeller Burglay-Felsen (2.5 a.), Zeller Petersborn-Kabertchen (2.5 a.), Zeller Marienburger (entire vineyard—37 a.), Wehlener Klosterhofgut (entire vineyard—17.3 a.), Zeltinger Deutschherrenberg (2.5 a.)

The Grosslage names are Zeller Schwarze Katz and Wehlener Münzlay.

Grape varieties: 78% Riesling, 7% Müller-Thurgau, 15% experimental varieties.

The wines: Grapes grown on the steep slopes produce racy, elegant wines influenced by the slate soil. On the deeper soils, the grapes (especially new varieties) produce full, aromatic wines. In producing its wines, the estate attempts to preserve the individual varietal and vineyard characteristics. The majority of the wines are pleasant and fruity, in keeping with the current public taste preferences.

Estate specialties: Fine wines, which have won many national and international awards.

Label: Different labels are used depending on the orgin of the grapes used in the wine.

Marketing: Sold to the wholesale trade, hotels, restaurants, and to private persons in small quantities. Large export trade.

Visits and tastings: The vineyards and the Merl cellars may be visited. A permanent sales room has been established at the Machern estate in Wehlen where wine may be purchased by the glass. By appointment, informative and expert wine tasting can be arranged. Groups of up to 200 can be accommodated. English-speaking personnel available.

From my notebook: The Merl estate has developed into an impressive, modern winery mainly concerned with production and marketing. The Machern estate, with its salesroom and facilities for large parties, is well suited for visitors.

WEHLEN

Weingut Joh. Jos. Prüm

Address: 5554 Wehlen
Telephone: (06531) 291

Location: The winery, offices, and manor are in Wehlen on the bank of the Moselle River about 100m (110 yd) upstream from the bridge.

How to get there: Drive from Bernkastel-Kues on route B-50/53 for 4 km toward Wittlich. About 300 m (330 yd) after entering Wehlen, turn right to the bridge over the Moselle River.

Points of interest: The stately manor house; the extensive vaulted cellars, parts of which are centuries old, with long rows of barrels and a rare-wine library; the view across the vineyards stretching from Bernkastel to Zeltingen, with the "Wehlener Sonnenuhr" (Wehlen sundial), imparts the impression of a grandiose, natural ampitheater.

History: The first person recorded as bearing the name of Prüm was Herhardus Hermann Prüm who lived from 1169 to 1229. The family has been in viticulture in Wehlen for centuries, and an ancestor, Jodocus Prüm, constructed the Wehlen and Zeltingen sundials in 1842 to facilitate time keeping for the vintners who, in those days, were without pocket watches. The estate is named for Joh. Jos. Prüm (1873–1944). His son, Seb. Prüm (1902–1969) was honored by the state government in 1967 with the title "Economic Counselor" for special services in maintaining quality standards.

Terrain and soils: Of the 34.6 acres of vineyards, 90% are on steeply sloping terrain. The soil is mainly schist.

Vineyard names: Wehlener Sonnenuhr (the largest proprietor with 11.1 a.), Wehlener Rosenberg, Wehlener Klosterberg, Wehlener Nonnenberg, Graacher Himmelreich, Graacher Domprobst, Zeltinger Sonnenuhr, Bernkasteler Bratenhöfchen, Bernkasteler Lay.

Grape varieties: 94% Riesling, 6% Müller-Thurgau and new
varieties.

The wines: The elegant, racy Moselle Riesling type is very prominent. Not only the very finest wines, but the Kabinett wines,
too, retain a stimulating, lively character after several years of
storage because of their fruit and acidity.

Estate specialties: A high proportion of Auslese and Beerenauslese
wines. Single bottles of interesting vintages dating back to the
turn of the century are kept in the rare-wine library. At an
auction of fine wines held in April 1974 in Wiesbaden, a bottle
of 1949 Wehlener Sonnenuhr Trockenbeerenauslese was sold
for $600.

Label: It features a panoramic view of the vineyards of Bernkastel-
Zeltingen which lie on the opposite bank of the Moselle from
the manor. Most of the estate's vineyards are located there.

Marketing: Almost exclusively to the trade and wine brokers.
Wines are regularly put up for sale at wine auctions in Trier.

Visits and tastings: By appointment.

From my notebook: A family establishment, carefully managed by
Dr. Manfred Prüm, with an impressive background and a high
reputation for its current Riesling wine production.

BERNKASTEL-KUES

Gutsverwaltung Deinhard

Address: 5550 Bernkastel-Kues, Martertal
Telephone: (06531) 493

Location: In Kues near the railway station.

How to get there: Drive through the Moselle Valley or take the
Hunsrück highway.

History: It was acquired in 1900 from Mayor Kunz by Julius
Wegeler, who paid 100 gold marks per square meter for the

Bernkasteler Doctor vineyard. By purchasing neighboring vineyards in Bernkastel and Graach, the estate was extended to almost 25 acres by 1906, and cellars for 300 barrels were built. The Bernkasteler Doctor vineyard has the highest value per acre of any vineyard in Germany.

Terrain and soils: Of the 27 acres of vineyards, 80% are on steeply sloping and 20% on gently sloping terrain. The soil is mainly schist.

Vineyard names: Bernkasteler Doctor (3 a.), Bernkasteler Graben (4.75 a.), Bernkasteler Bratenhöfchen (7.7 a.), Bernkasteler Lay (2.5 a.), Bernkasteler Schlossberg (0.25 a.), Bernkasteler Matheisbildchen (2.5 a.), Bernkasteler Johannisbrünnchen (2.5 a.), Graacher Domprobst (1.25 a.), Graacher Himmelreich (1.25 a.), Graacher Abtsberg (1.25 a.).

Grape varieties: 98% Riesling, 2% miscellaneous.

The wines: Fine, racy, clean Riesling wines. Typical of the area.

Estate specialties: Bernkasteler Doctor wine, from what is probably the most famous vineyard in Germany.

Label: It features the Wegeler family coat of arms.

Marketing: Joint sales of the wines from the Deinhard wine estates exclusively to the trade and high-class restaurants. No sales to private consumers. Export through Deinhard & Co. in Koblenz.

Visits: Possible for groups of experts by previous appointment. No wine tastings.

From my notebook: The majority of wines from this estate are exported because of the Deinhard Company's active export operation. The estate administration is managed by Karl Felix Wegeler, as is the wine estate Geheimrat J. Wegeler Erben located in Oestrich (Rheingau), which is also owned by Deinhard.

BERNKASTEL-KUES

Weingut Wwe. Dr. H. Thanisch

Address: 5550 Bernkastel-Kues, Saarallee 31
Telephone: (06531) 282

Location: The manor and estate buildings are on Saarallee on the west bank of the Moselle River; the Doktor-Keller is on the Bernkastel side of the town on Hinter dem Graben, not far from the market place.

How to get there: Take the Hunsrück highway, the Koblenz-Trier autobahn (turning off at Wittlich), or route B-53 along the Moselle River.

Points of interest: The Doktor-Keller, a cellar hewn out of rock with an impressive row of barrels and wrought-iron work; the legend of the doctor illustrated on the cellar gate; the Bernkasteler Doktor vineyard located above the cellar.

History: The Thanisch family, first recorded in Bernkastel in 1636, was described in 1800 as "the largest property owners in the community of Bernkastel and producers of noble wines." Ernst Anton Hugo Thanisch (1853–1895), the grandfather of Mrs.

Mechthild M. G. Thanisch, the present proprietor, was a doctor of philosophy, a member of Parliament, and a local politician. It was during his proprietorship that the estate's wines became famous because of their spectacular successes at early wine auctions. After his death, the estate continued to build its reputation under the proprietorship of his widow.

Terrain and soils: The 32 acres of vineyards are located on steeply sloping terrain with schist soil.

Vineyard names: Bernkasteler Doktor, Bernkasteler Graben, Bernkasteler Lay, Bernkasteler Schlossberg, Brauneberger Juffer Sonnenuhr, Wehlener Sonnenuhr, Graacher Himmelreich.

The Grosslage names are Bernkasteler Badstube and Bernkasteler Kurfürstlay.

Grape varieties: 93% Riesling, 7% experimental varieties.

The wines: Individual aging in wood and careful bottling are used here to produce the classical Moselle wine at its finest and most elegant.

Estate specialties: Bernkasteler Doktor is only marketed as a Prädikat wine. Was also known as Doktor und Graben from 1884 to 1971, especially at auctions. Fine wines of vintages back to 1921 are still available.

Label: It features a lithograph in "Art Nouveau" showing Bernkastel, the Doktor vineyards, and the manor. Wines from the Doktor vineyard have a special cork brand and capsule.

Marketing: The estate auctions its wines at the auctions of the Trier Association of Wine Estate Owners of the Moselle, Saar, and Ruwer, e.V. (main group). The wines are then distributed worldwide by wholesalers.

Visits and tastings: Possible by appointment. Tours are expertly guided by the manager, Helmut Bauer. English-speaking personnel available.

From my notebook: A family business with an old tradition in which the world reputation of the Bernkasteler Doktor is maintained in a dignified manner. At $25,000 per acre, this vineyard, registered prior to 1971 as being 3.5 acres (Thanisch with 1.5 a., Deinhard 1.75 a., and Lauerberg 0.25 a.), has the highest value per acre of any vineyard in West Germany. According to legend, it received its name from the Trier Elector, Boemund II

(1354–1362), who became ill, and after being told by his doctors that he was going to die, drank himself back to health on this wine.

During the course of vineyard consolidation in 1971, the Bernkasteler Doktor vineyard was extended to about 9.9 acres by including parts of the Bernkasteler Graben vineyard, which is equal in quality (the Thanisch portion of Graben is about 5.2 a.). At the time of publication this particular consolidation had not been completed.

TRIER-EITELSBACH

Karthäuserhof Eitelsbach

Address: 5500 Trier-Eitelsbach, Postfach 40
Telephone: (0651) 5131

Location: The Karthäuserhof is idyllically situated in a sheltered tributary valley of the lower Ruwer River in the Eitelsbach section of Trier. The vineyards are directly adjacent to the manor house.

How to get there: Drive from the center of Ruwer (located at the junction of the Moselle and Ruwer Rivers) toward Eitelsbach. In Eitelsbach, turn left by the village fountain into the drive to the Karthäuserhof.

Points of interest: The English park with its centuries-old trees, preserved as an area of natural beauty; the manor complex with its former moated castle (twelfth century) and house; the stables with their Trakehner thoroughbreds and extensive buildings; the well-tended cellars and vineyards on the slopes of the Karthäuserhofberg.

History: About 1200, the property of the Electors and Archbishops of Trier. From 1335 until its secularization in 1803, it was farmed by the Carthusian monks. In 1811, an ancestor of Mrs.

Tyrell acquired the property at an auction in Paris. The present owner, Werner Tyrell, is the chairman of the Trier Moselle-Saar-Ruwer Wine Estate Owners Association, and has also been the president of the German Vintners Association since 1964.

Terrain and soils: Of the 45 acres of vineyards, 70% are on gently sloping and 30% on steeply sloping terrain. The soil is mainly schist.

Vineyard names: (These vineyards are all completely owned by this estate) Eitelsbacher Karthäuserhofberg Kronenberg, Eitelsbacher Karthäuserhofberg Burgberg, Eitelsbacher Karthäuserhofberg Sang, Eitelsbacher Karthäuserhofberg Orthsberg, Eitelsbacher Karthäuserhofberg Stirn.

Grape varieties: 100% Riesling.

The wines: A classical Moselle-Ruwer Riesling in produced here. The wines, individually aged in wood, tend to be robust and *spritzig;* most are dry. With their fruity acidity, they can be stored for long periods without loss of freshness.

Estate specialties: In addition to the last three vintages, the wine list contains a limited number of older vintages. Single bottles of vintages back to 1921 are available, but are sold only in very limited quantities.

Label: The main label is a neck label from the nineteenth century, a unique feature in the German wine industry. Its motif symbolizes the history of the estate: miter, cross, and staff for the first owner, the Archbishop of Trier; the long-tailed monkey for the Carthusian monks; the wagon wheel and "C" for St. Catherine, who was venerated in Eitelsbach as a patron saint.

Marketing: The wine is sold through brokers, the trade, good restaurants, and at auctions. Large quantities are exported.

Visits and tastings: By previous appointment, the estate, cellars, and vineyards can be visited and wine tastings arranged.

From my notebook: This estate is situated in idyllic landscape near Germany's oldest city. As Mr. Tyrell is extremely busy with his duties as president of the German Vintners Association, visitors should make arrangements well in advance. A tasting conducted by the estate manager, secretary, or cellar master, however, is also very informative.

GRÜNHAUS

C. von Schubert'sche Gutsverwaltung

Address: 5501 Grünhaus-Mertesdorf
Telephone: (0651) 5111

Location: The estate is on the Moselle River, 2 km above the junction with the Ruwer River, near the village of Mertesdorf. The estate buildings are near the railway station. The independent section of the community of Maximin Grünhaus and the old monastery, now the home of the proprietor, are just up the hill.

How to get there: Take route B-52 for 7 km from Trier through Ruwer.

Points of interest: The old monastery buildings of the former Benedictine abbey of St. Maximin, built in the tenth century; the cellars, part of which are of Roman origin; the Roman aqueduct in the park.

History: First recorded on January 7, 966, in a deed signed by Otto I to the Abbey of St. Maximin (preserved in the French National Library in Paris). Also cited in documents in 1135, 1277, and 1579. It was secularized in 1803, and in 1811 passed into the possession of Baron von Handel, a minister to the Prince of Nassau-Saarbrücken. Friedrich Wilhelm III granted it the status of a manor estate in 1822. About 1850, it passed into the possession of Baron von Solemacher and was acquired in 1882 by Baron von Stumm-Halberg, the great-grandfather of the present owner, Andreas von Schubert.

Terrain and soils: The 51.5 acres of vineyards are all on a single hillside, 30% of which is steeply sloping terrain. About 95% of the vines are trained on wires; a rarity in the Moselle-Saar-Ruwer region.

Vineyard names: Maximin Grünhäuser Bruderberg (6.2 a.), Maximin Grünhäuser Herrenberg (21 a.), Maximin Grünhäuser Abtsberg (24.2 a.).

Grape varieties: 95% Riesling, 5% Müller-Thurgau.

The wines: Fine, fruity, well-balanced wines with a racy, elegant acidity. Because the vineyards are located in a tributary valley, considerable Botrytis cinerea (noble rot) occurs. Fine wines make up a large portion of the production.

Estate specialties: The Bruderberg, Herrenberg, and Abtsberg vineyards stem from the monastic period and are known for their quality. As the name "Maximin Grünhaus" implies, they are entirely owned by the Schubert family. The estate's wines win awards regularly.

Label: The label shows a view of the vineyard with the old monastery buildings and the family coat of arms. The bottle also has a neck label indicating if the wine is Kabinett, Spätlese, Auslese, or Beerenauslese.

Marketing: The wines are sold to a wide circle of regular clients in the wine, hotel, and restaurant trades, as well as to private customers. Ten per cent of the production is exported.

Visits and tastings: By appointment, a limited number of people can visit the estate and taste wines in the cellar. English-speaking personnel available.

From my notebook: The Maximin Grünhaus wines are racy, fruity Ruwer wines with much character. The fully consolidated vineyards, the 235 acres devoted to dairy cattle, the orchards, and the 200 acres of game-filled woods make this estate a jewel of extreme charm.

TRIER

Reichsgraf von Kesselstatt

Address: 5500 Trier, Palais Kesselstatt, Liebfrauenstr. 9
Telephone: (0651) 73727 and 72578

Location: The main offices and cellars are in the middle of Trier opposite the cathedral and the Liebfrauenkirche (church), next to the public parking lot. The four estates are on the middle Moselle, Saar, and Ruwer Rivers, each with its own buildings.

Points of interest: The Kesselstatt Palace, a gem of baroque architecture; the extensive cellar with wooden barrels; the historic Josephshof vineyard in Graach, situated in a singularly beautiful portion of the valley.

History: The family of the Counts of Kesselstatt is documented as having resided on the Moselle River since the thirteenth century, and is closely connected with the history of the Electorate of Trier. The majority of the vineyards have been in the family for 600 years, with the exception of the Josephshof which was acquired in 1856. In the eighteenth century, the Imperial Court of Kesselstatt personally promoted local viticulture by extending the planting of Riesling vines. The Kesselstatt Palace, built in 1496, was burned during the war but has been completely restored. The Föhren Castle, located in the Eifel, has been the

Maximin **Grünhäuser** Herrenberg

1971er   1971er

QUALITÄTSWEIN mit PRÄDIKAT
der C. von Schubert'schen SCHLOSSKELLEREI - GRÜNHAUS
vormals Freiherr von Stumm-Halberg

MOSEL — SAAR — RUWER
A. P. Nr. 3 536 014 8 72

MOSEL-SAAR-RUWER
WEINGUT „DER JOSEPHSHOF"

1971er Josephshöfer Auslese

Qualitätswein mit Prädikat - A. P. Nr. 3 561 077-43-72

Reichsgraf von Kesselstatt, Trier

MOSEL-SAAR-RUWER
QUALITÄTSWEIN MIT PRÄDIKAT
A. P. Nr. 3 561 012 1 672

1971er

Trittenheimer Apotheke

Spätlese

ERZEUGERABFÜLLUNG
BISCHÖFLICHES PRIESTERSEMINAR · TRIER

seat of the family since 1438. The current estate owner is Count Franz Eugen von Kesselstatt.

Terrain and soils: The vineyards all have schist soil, and are mainly on steeply sloping and gently sloping terrain. They are distributed on the four estates as follows: Josephshof in Graach (25 a.), Domklausenhof in Piesport (30 a.), St. Irminenhof in Kasel/Ruwer (27 a.), and Oberemmeler Abteihof in Oberemmel/Saar (67 a.). The total area is 149 acres.

Vineyard names: Josephshöfer, Graacher Himmelreich, Graacher Domprobst, Piesporter Goldtröpfchen, Piesporter Grafenberg, Piesporter Domherr, Kaseler Herrenberg, Kaseler Kehrnagel, Kaseler Hitzlay, Kaseler Nieschen, Oberemmeler Karlsberg, Oberemmeler Altenberg, Oberemmeler Rosenberg, Oberemmeler Raul, Oberemmeler Agritiusberg, Niedermenniger Herrenberg, Niedermenniger Euchariusberg, Wiltinger, Braunfels, Scharzhofberger.

Grape varieties: 98% Riesling, 2% experimental varieties.

The wines: The classical Riesling wines of the Moselle-Saar-Ruwer region are produced here. Individually aged in barrels, they are racy, with a fruity elegance, and have a delicate Riesling acidity.

Estate specialties: A high proportion of award-winning wines. The wine price list usually contains four or five vintages, including many Auslese and Beerenauslese wines. Very dry wines suitable for diabetics are also produced.

Label: The label shows the family coat of arms. The color of the vine-leaf decoration depends on the estate: Josephshof = red, Domklausenhof = gold, St. Irminenhof = blue, Oberemmeler Abteihof = green.

Marketing: Sales to the trade and high-class restaurants through brokers and representatives.

Visits and tastings: The palace and cellars can be visited by appointment, and wine tastings can be arranged.

From my notebook: This is the largest private wine estate in the Moselle-Saar-Ruwer region and it has the longest tradition. Visitors should not fail to make arrangements in advance. Arrangements for visiting Josephshof, in Graach, can also be made at the Trier offices. The extensive family archives are housed in their own department at the city library in Trier.

TRIER

Verwaltung der Bischöflichen Weingüter

Address: 5500 Trier Gervasiusstrasse 1
Telephone: (0651) 72352

Location: The main offices and cellars are in the center of the city
near the cathedral. The vineyards are on the Moselle, Saar, and
Ruwer Rivers, and are administered by 9 local stations. The
grapes are pressed at these locations, and the grape-must is then
taken to the main cellars in Trier.

How to get there: In Trier, take Südallee to the city library, located
on Weberbacherstrasse, then turn into Rahnenstrasse.

Points of interest: The recently enlarged, extensive cellars, parts of
which are 400 years old; the impressive long rows of barrels.

History: On January 1, 1966, three wine estates, previously independent and with different histories, were joined together under
the common administration and cellaring facilities of this organization. They are as follows:

Bischöfliches Priesterseminar Trier (Trier Episcopal Seminary).
The vineyard property goes back to a donation of the Elector
Clemens Wenzeslaus in 1773. The estates were confiscated in
1794, but returned to the seminary in 1809.

Bischöfliches Konvikt Trier (Trier Episcopal Hostel). The majority of the estate stems from bequests by Elector (and Archbishop) Philipp Christoph von Sötern (1623–1652), to mention
but one benefactor, and passed into the hands of the Trier
Cathedral Chapel in 1653. After secularization, it was acquired
by a prelate, Johannes Endres. He was the director of the Episcopal Hostel from 1860 to 1892. He gave the estates to this institution with the stipulation that education be provided for
needy scholars at the school.

Hohe Domkirche Trier (Trier Cathedral). Parts of the wine estate
were originally monastic property, such as Scharzhof (near

Wiltingen). Other parts, such as Avelsbach, were privately owned.

Terrain and soils: The vineyards are on steeply sloping terrain and have schist soil. The vineyard areas of the estates are: Episcopal Seminary, 76 a.; Episcopal Hostel, 101 a.; Cathedral, 53 a. The total area is 230 acres.

Vineyard names: Episcopal Seminary estate (Bischöfliches Priesterseminar): Ürziger Würzgarten (3.7 a.), Erdener Treppchen (3.7 a.), Trittenheimer Apotheke (6.2 a.), Trittenheimer Altärchen (2.1 a.), Kaseler Nieschen (5 a.), Kaseler Kehrnagel (7.4 a.), Kanzemer Altenberg (22.5 a.), Wiltinger Kupp (12.8 a.), Ayler Kupp (7.4 a.).

Episcopal Hostel estate (Bischöfliches Konvikt): Piesporter Goldtröpfchen (6.2 a.), Eitelsbacher Marienholz (50 a.), Kaseler Nieschen (7.4 a.), Kaseler Kehrnagel (5 a.), Avelsbacher Herrenberg (7.4 a.), Ayler Herrenberger (19.75 a.), Ayler Kupp (9.9 a.).

Cathedral estate (Hohe Domkirche): Avelsbacher Altenberg (21 a.), Avelsbacher Herrenberg (5 a.), Scharzhofberger (19.75 a.), Wiltinger Braunfels (1.7 a.), Wiltinger Rosenberg (5.7 a.).

Grape varieties: 95% Riesling, 5% new varieties.

The wines: The wines are aged exclusively in oak barrels. Great care is taken to produce typical Riesling wines with a fine, fruity acidity.

Estate specialties: Various wines have won high awards. The rare-wine cellar contains a good assortment of vintages from recent decades. A high proportion of very dry wines with the diabetic seal of the DLG are offered.

Label: The same labels are used for all three estates. Only the different coats of arms in the upper left corner and the estate name printed at the bottom indicate the origin.

Marketing: Two price lists are issued, one for the trade and one for private customers. The winery is an important supplier of sacramental wine.

Visits and tastings: The main cellars can be visited by appointment. Wine tastings in the cellar, for up to 100 persons, or in two modern tasting rooms can be arranged. English-speaking personnel available.

From my notebook: An exemplary winery with modern large-scale cellars and an old tradition. Tours conducted by the director of the estates, Dr. Thiel, or by members of his staff are very instructive. A map on the wine price list shows the location of the vineyards of the Estate.

TRIER

Güterverwaltung Vereinigte Hospitien Trier

Address: 5500 Trier, Krahnenufer 19
Telephone: (0651) 76051

Location: The offices and cellars are in the center of the city on the eastern bank of the Moselle River and midway between the two historic bridges. The seven estates are on the banks of the Moselle and Saar Rivers.

Points of interest: Probably the oldest wine cellar in Germany with foundations and walls once part of the Roman Horrea, the greatest Roman storehouse north of the Alps; the Roman Hall in the St. Irminen hospice.

History: The Vereinigte Hospitien (United Hospitals) evolved from the Trier hospitals founded in the Middle Ages and secularized in 1794. Today the foundation is a non-profit corporation. The revenues from the estates (covering 3,460 acres) are used to provide for about 600 invalids and patients.

Terrain and soils: Of the 988 acres of vineyards, 70% are on steeply sloping and 30% on gently sloping terrain. The soil is mainly schist; the Trier Augenscheiner vineyard has red sandstone soil.

Vineyard names: Serriger Vogelsang, Serriger Schloss, Saarfelser Schlossberg, Wiltinger Hölle (entire vineyard), Wiltinger Kupp, Wiltinger Braune Kupp, Wiltinger Rosenberg, Wiltinger Braunfels, Scharzhofberger, Kanzemer Altenberg, Trierer Deutsch-

herrenberg, Trierer St. Maximiner Kreuzberg, Trierer Augenscheiner (entire vineyard), Trierer Thiergarten, Piesporter
Goldtröpfchen, Piesporter Schubertslay im Goldtröpfchen (entire
vineyard).

Grape varieties: 95% Riesling, 3% Müller-Thurgau, 1% Ruländer.

The wines: Typical Moselle and Saar Riesling wines of fruity elegance and racy acidity are produced.

Estate specialties: The proportion of fine wines on the price list is
surprising high. Four vintages, including wine, suitable for
diabetics are offered.

Label: It features St. Jacobus, patron saint of the Trier St.
Jacobus Hospital. This hospital was incorporated into a foundation with six other secularized hospitals by Napoleon.

Marketing: Wines are sold to the wholesale trade and to small-
quantity purchasers. They are well represented in Trier restaurants. A member of the Trier Moselle-Saar-Ruwer Wine Estate
Owners Association.

Visits and tastings: By appointment, the cellars can be visited.
Tastings can be arranged in the cellar, in the tasting room (up
to 12 persons), in the conference room (up to 25 persons), and
as an exception, in the Roman Hall (up to 150 persons). Parking space is available in the courtyard. English-speaking personnel available.

From my notebook: Despite the size of the winery, individual attention is given to clients. The publicly owned agricultural and
forest property is administered by the hospital's director, Dr.
Pilgram. The viticulture enterprise is directed by Mr. Ziebell.
Intriguing vineyard names, well-made wines, charitable activ-
ities, and the striking label featuring St. Jacobus make this a very
special Moselle wine estate.

TRIER

Verwaltung der Staatlichen Weinbaudomänen

Address: 5500 Trier, Deworastrasse 1
Telephone: (0651) 75946

Location: The main offices and cellars are in the center of the
city. The three completely consolidated wine estates are in
Avelsbach (near Trier), Ockfen, and Serrig (near Saarburg).
How to get there: Drive from the main railway station via Ostallee
to the entrance at Sichelstrasse 6. Parking space is available in
the large courtyard.
Points of interest: The huge vaulted cellar with 600 barrels; the
tasting room in the cellar vaults with a rare-wine library; the
domain vineyards.
History: In 1896 the Ockfen estate was founded at the instigation
of the President of the Prussian government and the senior forester, Mr. Hoepp (later, viticulture director). Oak woodlands
on southwestern and southern sites were converted into vineyards. A short time later the Serrig and Avelsbach estates were
acquired and the winery was built. A combination of experimental and practical viticulture is the major work of the domains.
Terrain and soils: Of the 200 total acres, 80% are on steeply sloping and 20% on gently sloping terrain. The soil is mainly schist.
The vineyard areas of the estates are: Avelsbach, 80 a.; Ockfen,
35 a.; Serrig, 85 a.
Vineyard names: Avelsbacher Hammerstein, Avelsbacher Kupp,
Avelsbacher Rotlay, Ockfener Bockstein, Ockfener Herrenberg,
Ockfener Heppenstein, Serriger Vogelsang, Serriger Heiligen-
born, Serriger Hoeppslei.
Grape varieties: 85% Riesling, 3% Müller-Thurgau, 1% Ruländer,
1% Spätburgunder, 10% miscellaneous.
The wines: Because the wines are individually barrel-aged, they

retain the character of Saar wines. Racy, wholesome beverage wines are aged, just as are valuable Trockenbeerenauslese wines with the finest nuances of acidity.

Estate specialties: The cellars contain treasures with vintage dates as old as 1920. The 1921 Trockenbeerenauslese, with 290° Öchsle and 0.16% acidity, is still an excellent wine today. These rarities survived the war because they were stored during the last years of the war in a sister estate in Eltville. The old wines demonstrate the longevity of the Saar wines. At an auction of old wines in 1972, a 1921 Trockenbeerenauslese from Serrig was sold for $300 per bottle.

Label: As royal Prussian domains, the estates sported the Prussian eagle on the label, which was stylized to its present form during the 1930s. The rhomboid label with the coat of arms of the Rhineland Palatinate is retained for special wines.

Marketing: Sales by brokers to the wholesale trade; also to private customers. The domain administration encourages trade by holding wine tastings in its Trier cellars.

Visits and tastings: By appointment, the wine estates and cellars can be visited. Wine tastings are organized by prior appointment. The discussion on wine is lead by the director, Dr. Sambale, or one of the cellar masters, and held in the romantic wine cellar. During the summer the stone tasting table in Ockfen, high above the magnificent Saar Valley, is most inviting. In Avelsbach, there are excellent examples of today's widespread experimentation which tries to wed the appropriate grape variety to the soil. The Serrig estate offers a ride through the vine-clad slopes in a small vineyard train, giving the visitor an impression of the heavy work done by the vintner on the steep slopes.

From my notebook: The large areas of the consolidated wine-growing estates on steep sites are adapted for mechanical cultivation through an ingenious road system, still considered to be ahead of its time. This and the outstanding organization are unique. Every guest is given expert replies to his questions on the wines by managers and cellar masters. In the tasting room, covered with cellar mold, visitors sit comfortably around rustic barrel tables. Sufficient time should be allowed for this instructive winery.

TRIER

Stiftung Staatliches Friedrich-Wilhelm-Gymnasium

Address: 5500 Trier Weberbachstrasse 75
Telephone: (0651) 73849

Location: The estate offices and main cellars are in the middle of Trier with six wine estates on the Moselle and Saar Rivers.

Points of interest: The cellar and vineyards.

History: The Friedrich-Wilhelm School Foundation is a corporate body which must support itself financially. Its roots are in the school established by the Jesuits in 1563, and its fortunes comprise endowments by the then-ruling prince, the city, the aristocracy, and many private benefactors. When the Jesuit Order was dissolved in 1773, the school retained its property under the original charter.

Terrain and soils: Of the 104 acres of vineyards, 65% are on steeply sloping, 20% on gently sloping, and 15% on flat terrain. The soil is mainly schist.

Vineyard names: Falkensteiner Hofberg, Pellinger Jesuitengarten (entire vineyard), Oberemmeler Scharzberg, Ockfener Geisberg, Mehringer Blattenberg, Mehringer Goldkupp, Mehringer Zellerberg, Trittenheimer Apotheke, Trittenheimer Altärchen, Neumagener Rosengärtchen, Dhroner Hofberger, Graacher Domprobst, Graacher Himmelreich, Zeltinger Sonnenuhr, Zeltinger Schossberg, Bernkasteler Bratenhöfchen, Bernkasteler Graben.

Grape Varieties: 88% Riesling, 10% Müller-Thurgau, 2% new varieties.

The wines: The classical Moselle Riesling with its prickly and fragrant character is produced. Individual barrel aging is practiced. A somewhat too racy acidity is skillfully balanced with residual sweetness. The Saar wines are particularly racy, and typical of the region.

Estate specialties: Four vintages are offered. With its 60 items, the list is extensive. Single bottles of older vintages are available.

Label: The coat of arms of the Jesuit college is shown, indicating the origin of the foundation.

Marketing: Mainly sold to the trade, hotels, and restaurants. Some sales to private customers.

Visits and tastings: By appointment, the cellars and vineyards can be visited. Tastings can be arranged for up to 40 persons in the cellar; seated tastings for up to 25 persons in the tasting room.

From my notebook: A wine estate rich in tradition. There is a map on the wine price list showing the location of the six estates and their vineyards on the middle Moselle and Saar Rivers. The estate's director, Mr. Engel, is an acknowledged expert on Moselle-Saar-Ruwer viticulture. The tastings he conducts are particularly instructive.

TRIER

Weingut Thiergarten Georg Fritz von Nell

Address: 5500 Trier, Im Thiergarten 12
Telephone: (0651) 32397

Location: The estate buildings stand alone in Olewig on the southwestern edge of Trier.

How to get there: In Trier, drive from the Kaiserthermen to the ampitheater, then take the first road to the right and follow the sign.

Points of interest: The attractive manor in the middle of the vineyards; the barrel cellar.

History: The estate was the property of the St. Mathias Benedictine monastery, and after secularization in 1803, was purchased and enlarged by Christoph von Nell. The name of the estate comes from one of its vineyards in a tributary valley of the

Moselle River not far from the ampitheater. During the Roman period, there were enclosures on the estate for the animals that were used in the ampitheater games.

Terrain and soils: Of the 40 acres of vineyards, 70% are on steeply sloping and 30% on gently sloping terrain. The soil is schist.

Vineyard names: Trierer Benediktinerberg (entire vineyard, 12.4 a.), Trierer Kurfürstenhofberg (entire vineyard, 12.4 a.), Trierer Thiergarten Unterm Kreuz (9.9 a.), Ayler Kupp, Wiltinger Klosterberg.

The Grosslage names are Trierer Römerlay and Scharzberg.

Grape varieties: 70% Riesling, 10% Müller-Thurgau, 20% new varieties.

The wines: They are individually aged in barrels, particular attention being paid to preserving the character of the vintage and vineyard. A wide assortment is produced, ranging from dry wines to the full, ripe 1971 vintage.

Estate specialties: The estate regularly submits wines to compete for state and national awards. It also participates in international exhibitions.

Label: It shows the family coat of arms of the von Nells.

Marketing: Sold to the trade and private clients.

Visits and tastings: By appointment, the cellars and vineyards near the manor can be visited. Wine tastings can be arranged in the cellar by candlelight, or in the tasting room for up to 60 persons. English-speaking personnel available.

From my notebook: A pleasant, family business in which the family of the young proprietor, Georg Fritz von Nell, is personally involved. Interesting wines. The tours and tastings are very informative.

Mosel – Saar – Ruwer

Amtl. Prüfungs-Nr.
3 561 024 12 72

Qualitätswein mit Prädikat
1971er
Trittenheimer Apotheke Auslese
Erzeugerabfüllung
Friedrich-Wilhelm-Gymnasium, Trier

Wir besitzen Lagen
von Weltruf:

Trierer
Kurfürstenhofberg
Trierer
Benediktinerberg
Trierer St. Petrusberg
Trierer Thiergarten
unterm Kreuz
Trierer Thiergarten
Felsköpfchen
Trierer Römerlay
Ayler Kupp
Wiltinger Klosterberg
Wiltinger Braunfels
Wiltinger Scharzberg
Bernkasteler Graben
Bernkasteler Badstube

MOSEL SAAR RUWER

Qualitätswein

1973er
Trierer Kurfürstenhofberg
A. P. Nr. 3 561 067 11 74 · Erzeugerabfüllung

Georg Fritz v. Nell, Trier-Thiergarten

MOSEL·SAAR·RUWER

1973er
Filzener Herrenberg

Weingut im Familienbesitz seit 1685

KABINETT
Qualitätswein mit Prädikat

ERZEUGERABFÜLLUNG   A. P. Nr. 3525018/14/74

WEINGUT·EDMUND·REVERCHON·FILZEN/SAAR

FILZEN

Weingut Edmund Reverchon

Address: 5503 Konz-Filzen, Saartalstr. 3
Telephone: (06501) 2109

Location: The offices, winery, and manor are on the north edge of
Filzen.
How to get there: Drive from Trier through Konz along the Saar
River.
Points of interest: The attractive, red manor house with its dig-
nified furnishings; the park; the vaulted cellar with its barrels;
the steep vineyards in the Saar countryside.
History: The estate, with the vineyards, was first noted in records
in 1685. In 1787, it became the residence of the Huguenot
family Reverchon, which originated in France (Franche
Comté) and at that time was involved in banking in Trier.
After the bank was given up in 1916, the estate was developed
independently and is today run by Eddie Reverchon and his
family.
Terrain and soils: Of the 44.5 acres of vineyards, 50% are on
gently sloping, 40% on steeply sloping, and 10% on flat ter-
rain. The soil is mainly schist.
Vineyard names: Filzener Herrenberg (entire vineyard, 19.8 a.),
Filzener Steinberger (7.4 a.), Ockfener Bockstein (7.4 a.),
Ockfener Geisberg (7.4 a.), Ockfener Kupp (2.5 a.).
Grape varieties: 80% Riesling, 10% Müller-Thurgau, 10% ex-
perimental varieties.
The wines: Light, *spritzig* Saar wines without much residual sugar;
exclusively barrel aged.
Estate specialties: The racy, elegant Saar Rieslings with a surpris-
ingly delicate, fruity acidity.
Label: The family coat of arms on a white background.

Marketing: Almost exclusively by direct sales. In order to be able to offer a wide assortment of Saar wines, wines bottled by other producers in the neighborhood are offered together with the estate wines.

Visits and tastings: The cellars and vineyards are gladly shown. Wine tastings are conducted by appointment in the parlor of the manor in an attractive atmosphere.

From my notebook: Anybody interested in Saar wines has an excellent opportunity here to have an assortment assembled to suit his own taste. Clients are encouraged to visit and cordially treated by the establishment. The view from the Filzener Herrenberg vineyard across the surrounding vineyards and along the winding Saar Valley is beautiful.

WILTINGEN

Egon Müller—Scharzhof

Address: 5511 Scharzhof bei Wiltingen
Telephone: (06501) 2432

Location: The Scharzhof is in a tributary valley of the Saar River about halfway between Wiltingen and Oberemmel at the foot of the Scharzhofberg hill.

How to get there: Drive from Trier through Konz to Wiltingen and turn off toward Oberemmel. The Scharzhof is 2 km outside the village on route L-138.

Points of interest: The dignified manor surrounded by fields and groups of trees, with its barrel cellar and outbuildings; the neighboring Scharzhofberg vineyard.

History: The Scharzhof name is of Roman origin. In 1030, Archbishop Poppo, a native of Badenberg, bestowed the estate on the Benedictine monastery of "St. Marien ad martyres" in Trier. During the French revolution in 1796, it was secularized and auctioned on "11 Thermidor de l'an V" (July 7, 1797) when it was acquired by the great-great-grandfather of Egon Müller, the present proprietor. Part of it passed into other hands through inheritance.

Terrain and soils: Of the 23.5 acres of vineyards, 63% are on steeply sloping and 37% on gently sloping terrain. The soil is schist.

Vineyard names: Scharzhofberg (independent section of the community), Wiltinger braune Kupp, Wiltinger Klosterberg, Wiltinger Braunfels.

Grape varieties: 96% Riesling, 4% experimental varieties.

The wines: These elegant, racy Saar Rieslings, cleanly aged in wood, are of perfect character. With their Saar-Riesling acidity and early bottling, the wines retain their freshness for years—indeed, they require 4 or 5 years of storage to reach their peak.

Estate specialties: The Scharzhofberg Kabinett wines are light and animated; the Spätlese and Auslese wines offer the overall fullness and finesse of this leading vineyard. Fine wines of vintages back to 1921 are available.

Label: The word "Scharzhofberger" is printed diagonally in black and gold on a white background with a view of the manor and part of the vineyard with a gold vine leaf surrounding it. A gold capsule is used for the finest Ausleses and Beerenausleses; white is used for other qualities.

Marketing: Through the trade and auctions; no price lists. A high proportion of exports.

Visits and tastings: By appointment, a limited number of persons can be accommodated.

From my notebook: On this estate, situated in a beautiful country setting, quality and tradition are important. Only award-winning wines are bottled. There is no price list, and the old, established trade connections are maintained with success—as the auction prices demonstrate. Mr. Egon Müller also runs the wine estate "La Gallais" in Kanzem. The wines from that estate are marketed under a special label.

Nahe

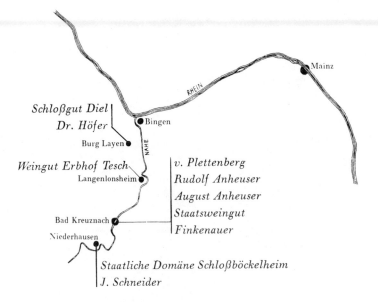

Schloßgut Diel
Dr. Höfer

Burg Layen

Weingut Erbhof Tesch
Langenlonsheim

Bad Kreuznach

Niederhausen

Bingen

NAHE

RHEIN

Mainz

v. Plettenberg
Rudolf Anheuser
August Anheuser
Staatsweingut
Finkenauer

Staatliche Domäne Schloßböckelheim
J. Schneider

Weingut Jakob Schneider

Address: 6551 Niederhausen, Winzerstr. 15
Telephone: (06758) 6701

Location: In the center of the village.

How to get there: Drive along the Nahe River from Bad Kreuznach through Bad Münster and Norheim.

Points of interest: The farm buildings with open cattle sheds; the vaulted cellar; the tasting room; the automatic sprinkler system in the Niederhäuser Hermannshöhle vineyard.

History: The wine estate has been in the possession of the family for 400 years.

Terrain and soils: In addition to 74 acres of mixed agricultural land, there are 31 acres of vineyards; 80% are on steeply sloping and 20% are on gently sloping terrain. The soils are red schist and sandstone.

Vineyard names: Niederhäuser Hermannshöhle (7.4 a.), Niederhäuser Rosenheck (7.4 a.), Niederhäuser Klamm (5 a.), Niederhäuser Steinwingert (3.7 a.), Niederhäuser Rosenberg (2.5 a.), Norheimer Kirschheck (5 a.).

Grape varieties: 90% Riesling, 6% Müller-Thurgau, 2% Traminer, 2% Sylvaner.

The wines: Organic fertilization of the vineyards, extremely late harvesting, individual barrel aging, and controlled-temperature fermentation produce exceptionally spicy, elegant wines containing a high extract percentage. The wines also have well-balanced sweetness and acidity. The difference between the more manly growths from schist soils, and the softer, spicier growths from volcanic soils is interesting.

Estate specialties: Nahe Riesling wines typical of vintage and vineyard, bearing the influence of the stony hillside soils.

Label: It features the family coat of arms dated 1575.

Marketing: Typical family distribution with regular private customers.

Visits and tastings: Visitors are cordially treated. By appointment, wines can be tasted by up to 40 persons in the tasting room.

From my notebook: Of particular interest to those who would like to see mixed viticulture and cattle farming in a classical form rarely found in Germany today. Jacob Schneider, the senior partner and a well traveled man with many interests, introduces the estate wines to visitors in a warm, friendly fashion.

NIEDERHAUSEN

Staatlichen Weinbaudomänen Niederhausen-Schlossböckelheim

Address: 6551 Oberhausen
Telephone: (06758) 6215

Location: The offices, estate buildings, and cellars dominate the vineyards from a hill with a wonderful view of the valley.

How to get there: Drive 15 km from Bad Kreuznach through Bad Münster, Norheim, and Niederhausen.

Points of interest: The exceptionally well-tended, completely integrated wine estate set in an idyllic landscape; the partially automatic irrigation system; the modern cellar, partially furnished with a cooling system.

History: Established by the Prussian state government in 1902 during the general promotion of viticulture. Today it is the property of the Rhineland-Palatinate state government.

Terrain and soils: The total area of 100 acres is divided among three estates: Niederhausen-Schlossböckelheim, Münster-Sarmsheim, and Altenbamberg in the Alsenztal. The terrain is all steeply sloping with grades of 25 to 60 degrees. The soils are schist, sandstone, and magmatite.

Vineyard names: Schlossböckelheimer Kupfergrube, Schlossböckelheimer Felsenberg, Niederhäuser Steinberg, Niederhäuser Hermannsberg, Niederhäuser Hermannshöhle, Niederhäuser Kerz, Münsterer Kapellenberg, Münsterer Dautenpflänzer, Münsterer Pittersberg, Dorsheimer Burgberg, Dorsheimer Goldloch, Altenbamberger Rotenberg, Traisener Bastei, Ebernburger Schlossberg.

Grape varieties: 90% Riesling, 3% Sylvaner, 3% Müller-Thurgau, 4% experimental varieties.

The wines: As dictated by the geographical location of the estates, the Riesling wines are similar to Moselle Rieslings with their racy, but delicate acidity, and to Rheingau wines in their floweriness and elegance. With modern cooling techniques, very fragrant wines can be produced. The wines have little residual sweetness.

Estate specialties: An elegant type of Riesling is produced here and fine wines are well represented. The wines are only submitted for awards to compare achievements, and any awards won are not indicated on the bottle label. Single bottles of older vintages are still available.

Label: It shows the stylized Prussian eagle.

Marketing: Principally through wine brokers to all branches of the trade; special terms of sale available to the wine trade and wholesalers. Auctions in Bad Kreuznach.

From my notebook: The estate is very charming, as are the castle of Ebernburg (Hutten and Franz von Sickingen) and the castle ruins of Schlossböckelheim, where Henry VI was once imprisoned by his son. Both castles are situated on the Nahe Wine Route.

BAD KREUZNACH

Reichsgräflich von Plettenberg'sche Verwaltung

Address: 6550 Bad Kreuznach Winzenheimer Strasse, Postfach 825
Telephone: (0671) 28357

Location: The offices and cellars are situated on the northeast
edge of Bad Kreuznach on an open slope surrounded by vineyards. The property, containing many small parcels of land, is
worked from two farms.

How to get there: Drive 2 km from the middle of Bad Kreuznach
to Winzenheim, or take the Bad Kreuznach north by-pass. The
newly built winery can be seen from the road. Signs indicate
the entrance.

Points of interest: The exceptionally modern winery with the
charming wine tasting room for 30 persons; the nearby vineyards with interesting comparison tests between various grape
varieties; the view of the Nahe Valley and Bad Kreuznach.

History: "The Hunter from the Palatinate," famed in song, was
actually Friedrich Wilhelm Utsch, and besides his occupation
as hereditary electoral forester, he tended his own vineyard
which passed through marriage into the possession of the
Puricelli-Count Plettenberg family. The two proprietors, Counts
Egbert and Wolfgang von Plettenberg, now manage the establishment.

Terrain and soils: The 100 acres of vineyards are located in various communities; 58% are on gently sloping, 29% on steeply
sloping, and 13% on flat terrain. The various types of soils
include red sandstone, acid magmatite, loam, clay, and gravel.

Vineyard names: Winzenheimer Rosenheck, Kreuznacher Brückes,
Kreuznacher Kahlenberg, Kreuznacher Kapellenpfad, Kreuz-
nacher Forst, Kreuznacher Hinkelstein, Kreuznacher Osterhöll,
Bretzenheimer Vogelsang, Bretzenheimer Pastorei, Roxheimer

Höllenpfad, Schlossböckelheimer Kupfergrube, Schlossböckelheimer Felsenberg, Norheimer Götzenfels.

The Grosslage names are Kreuznacher Kronenberg and Schlossböckelheimer Burgweg.

Grape varieties: 60% Riesling, 18% Müller-Thurgau, 7% Ruländer, 5% Sylvaner, 10% miscellaneous, mainly experimental
varieties.

The wines: An impressive number of wines is offered from four
vintages. Well-made, clean, and flowery wines are produced in
the modern cellars. Characteristics of the grape variety, soil, and
vineyard are carefully retained, and the wines have well-
balanced residual sweetness.

Estate specialties: The price list contains numerous fine wines,
many of which have gained high awards. The cellar still contains single bottles of treasured older vintages.

Label: It shows the coat of arms of the Counts of Plettenberg. The
qualities are further indicated by a vertical, wide, colored stripe
on the label: Qualitätswein bestimmter Anbaugebiete = olive;
Kabinett = light blue; Spätlese = gray; Auslese, Beerenauslese,
and Trockenbeerenauslese = gold.

Marketing: Primarily through wholesalers and export representatives. The wines are well represented in high-class restaurants
and hotels.

Visits and tastings: By appointment, the winery and vineyards can
be visited. Wine tastings can also be arranged and are individually planned to meet the visitor's interests. The tastings are
conducted by the proprietors and by Mr. Koch. English-speaking
personnel available.

From my notebook: Currently, these are the most modern estate
cellars on the Nahe. The efficient winery, the well-tended vineyards, and last but not least, the ample parking make this estate
particularly attractive to visitors. Tastings are informative and
expertly conducted.

BAD KREUZNACH

Rudolf Anheuser'sche Weingutsverwaltung

Address: 6550 Bad Kreuznach Strombergerstrasse 15-19 Postfach 106
Telephone: (0671) 28748

Location: The cellars and offices are in the northern section of Bad Kreuznach. The vineyards are worked from stations in Bad Kreuznach and in Schlossböckelheim (Heimberger Hof).

How to get there: It is best to ask in Bad Kreuznach. Accurate inquiries are necessary, as confusion with other Anheuser wine estates is possible.

History: The Anheusers have been active in Bad Kreuznach viticulture since 1630. Rudolf Anheuser founded the estates, which are named after him, in 1888 and developed them into a model operation. Paul Anheuser inherited the majority of the estate and marketed his wines under his own name. His son, Rudolf Peter Anheuser, took over the estate in 1969.

Terrain and soils: The total area amounts to 161 acres (133.5 acres of vineyards), which is distributed in various communities on the Nahe and on the banks of the Rhine near Oppenheim. Because the vineyards are wide-spread, they contain various type of soil; 50% of the vineyards are on steeply sloping, 30% on gently sloping, and 20% on flat terrain.

Vineyard names: Kreuznacher Krötenpfuhl (14.8 a.), Kreuznacher Mönchberg (7.4 a.), Kreuznacher Kahlenberg (5 a.), Kreuznacher Hinkelstein (14.8 a.), Kreuznacher Narrenkappe (7.4 a.), Kreuznacher St. Martin, Schlossböckelheimer Königsfels (27.2 a.), Schlossböckelheimer In den Felsen (12.4 a.), Schlossböckelheimer Heimberg (9.9 a.), Schlossböckelheimer Mühlberg, Niederhäuser Felsensteyer (12.4 a.), Niederhäuser Pfingstweide (7.4 a.), Norheimer Kafels, Altenbamberger Kehrenberg, Altenbamberger Schlossberg, Monzinger Gabelstich, Roxheimer Höllenpfad, Oppenheimer Herrenweiher, Dienheimer Tafelstein, Dienheimer Falkenberg.

Grape varieties: 76% Riesling, 12% Müller-Thurgau, 7% Sylvaner, 3% Ruländer, 2% Weissburgunder and Scheurebe.

The wines: The varietal, vineyard, and vintage characteristics are emphasized by individual barrel aging. The cooling technique used during fermenting and aging produces an attractive fruitiness in the wines.

Estate specialties: Five vintages are offered. The proportion of Auslese wines is considerable. The range of wines is extensive, beginning with wines suitable for diabetics and extending to robust Ruländer.

Label: The name Paul Anheuser is inscribed on the label in large red letters. The wines of the Rudolf Anheuser'sche Weingutsverwaltung are marketed under this name, as is noted at the bottom of the label. The Anheuser coat of arms, dating from the sixteenth century, is at the bottom left.

Marketing: Sold through commissioned agents, mainly to the wholesale trade. Private purchase at the cellars is possible. Member of the First Auction Association of the Nahe Wine Estates at Bad Kreuznach.

Visits and tastings: By appointment, the cellars and vineyards can be visited. Tastings can be arranged in the cellar. English-speaking personnel available.

From my notebook: An old family business with interesting Nahe wines. The young owner, Rudolf Peter Anheuser, is personally involved in the business and discusses his wines and the problems of his business with expertise and a refreshing unconventionality.

BAD KREUZNACH

Weingut August Anheuser

Address: 6550 Bad Kreuznach Brücken 53
Telephone: (0671) 33109

Location: The offices and cellars are on the north edge of the town
and the vineyards are located in six different communities.

How to get there: Take route B-48 to Bingen. The winery is visible
at the edge of Bad Kreuznach.

Points of interest: The cellar hewn out of rock, with beautiful oak
barrels and an immense quantity of cellared bottles; the model
vineyards.

History: The name Anheuser has been connected with viticulture
in Bad Kreuznach for centuries. Today there are various Anheuser wine establishments. This company was founded in its
present form by August Anheuser in 1896 and it is named after
him. The present proprietor is Egon Anheuser.

Terrain and soils: The 141 acres of vineyards, distributed in various communities, are 50% on gently sloping, 35% on steeply
sloping, and 15% on flat terrain. Many types of soil are represented, including acid and basic magmatite, gravel, loess-loam,
and red sandstone.

Vineyard names: The estate controls property in 24 vineyards. The
most important are: Kreuznacher Brückes (17.3 a.), Kreuznacher Narrenkappe (29.7 a.), Kreuznacher St. Martin (22.2
a.), Kreuznacher Krötenpfuhl, Kreuznacher Mönchberg, Kreuznacher Hofgarten, Norheimer Kafels, Norheimer Dellchen,
Niederhäuser Hermannshöhle, Schlossböckelheimer Felsenberg,
Schlossböckelheimer Königsfels, Schossböckelheimer Mühlberg.

Grape varieties: 70% Riesling, 13% Sylvaner, 10% Müller-
Thurgau, 4% Ruländer, 3% miscellaneous.

The wines: Individual barrel aging is used to emphasize the
varietal, vineyard, and vintage characteristics. The wines are

well-balanced and fruity; particular attention is paid to the classic Riesling type. The 181 wines offered in the price list of May, 1972 were appropriately and correctly characterized as ranging from charming and mild to steely and dry.

Estate specialties: A wide assortment of 181 wines is offered. This is a singular opportunity for wine lovers to obtain mature wines which, otherwise, are usually hard to find. Dozens of wines from the 1960s, for example, are still available.

Label: The Anheuser coat of arms dating from 1627 is shown. The quality groups are additionally designated on the label by different colors: Qualitätswein bestimmter Anbaugebiete— white, Kabinett and Spätlese—cream. A special label with a gold edge is used for Auslese or better.

Marketing: Sold to the trade through commissioned agents and wholesale distributors. As a member of the First Auction Association of the Nahe Wine Estates, the estate regularly sends wines to auction.

Visits and tastings: By appointment, the cellar and vineyards can be visited. Wine tastings are individually planned by previous arrangement.

From my notebook: The whole establishment exudes tradition and dignity, from the sales room, decorated with medals, to the tasting room in the cellar. This is an opportunity for lovers of older wines to enjoy rarities at reasonable prices.

BAD KREUZNACH

Staatsweingut Weinbaulehranstadt Bad Kreuznach

Address: 6550 Bad Kreuznach, Rüdesheimer Strasse 68
Telephone: (0671) 2057

Location: The offices, cellars, and shipping office are on the institution's property at the west exit of Bad Kreuznach, at the foot of the Kahlenberg vineyards.

How to get there: It is best to ask in Bad Kreuznach.

Points of interest: The large, modern instructional and experimental plantings in the vineyards.

History: Founded in 1900 as the provincial viticultural school. Today it is a state instructional and experimental institute with the wine estate providing excellently trained young oenologists for the German wine industry, as well as promoting and influencing viticulture on the Nahe. Owned by the Rhineland-Palatinate state government.

Terrain and soils: Of the 74 acres of vineyards, 40% are on gently sloping, 20% on steeply sloping, and 38% on flat terrain. The remaining 2% are on terraced sites. The soils are schist, sandstone, and loam.

Vineyard names: Kreuznacher Forst (7.4 a.), Kreuznacher Hinkelstein (9 a.), Kreuznacher Kahlenberg (12.4 a.), Kreuznacher Mollenbrunnen (5.7 a.), Kreuznacher Vogelsang (7.9 a.), Kreuznacher Steinweg (5.4 a.), Kreuznacher Monhard, Kreuznacher Kapellenpfad, Norheimer Kafels (6.2 a.), Norheimer Dellchen, Norheimer Kirschheck.

Grape varieties: 47% Riesling, 15.4% Müller-Thurgau, 12% Sylvaner, 9% Scheurebe, 3.7% Ruländer, 12.9% miscellaneous, including 48 experimental varieties that have been under test since 1961.

The wines: Importance is placed on retaining the characteristics of the grape varieties. Due to individual barrel aging, the wines are elegant, with well-balanced fruitiness and delicate acidity (characteristics midway between a Moselle and a Rhine wine).

Estate specialties: Despite active experimental work with new varieties, the Riesling is still the main variety offered for sale. Wines are regularly sent to competitive tastings. In the past 12 years, 116 wines produced by the estates have gained high awards. All wines sold since 1958 bear the German wine seal.

Label: The narrow label features the coat of arms of the Rhineland-Palatinate.

Marketing: Sold to the trade, restaurants, hotels, and private customers. Member of the First Auction Association of the Nahe Wine Estates at Bad Kreuznach.

Visits and tastings: By appointment, the cellar and vineyards can be visited. Wine tastings can be arranged for groups of visitors of up to 120 persons. A stylish new tasting room with projection facilities is available for groups of up to 40 persons.

From my notebook: This estate is one of the leading estates in the Nahe region. The high quality of the wines draws regular customers. The director, Dr. Röder, has rendered great services in the development of the Bad Kreuznach Institute and the DLG Bundesweinprämierung (national wine judging). The method of using pressurized carbon dioxide to ferment grape-must, known in the wine industry as controlled fermentation, has found its way from the Bad Kreuznach Institute to wineries all over the world.

BAD KREUZNACH

Weingut Carl Finkenauer

Address: 6550 Bad Kreuznach Salinenstrasse 60
Telephone: (0671) 28771

Location: The offices and cellars are in the center of the town opposite the *Landesratamt* offices. The majority of the vineyards are within the Bad Kreuznach city limits.

How to get there: Proceed from the train station and Kreuzkirche (a church) toward Bad Münster.

Points of interest: The well-tended estate buildings; the vaulted cellar.

History: The Finkenauer family has been established in Bad Kreuznach since 1792, and is documented as being in viticulture since 1828.

Terrain and soils: Of the 88.5 acres of vineyards, 65% are on gently sloping, 15% on steeply sloping and 20% on flat terrain. The various soils include loess-loam, gravel, sandy loam, and loamy clay.

Vineyard names: Kreuznacher Gutental, Kreuznacher Breitenweg, Kreuznacher Osterhöll, Kreuznacher Mollenbrunnen, Kreuznacher Hinkelstein, Kreuznacher Forst, Kreuznacher Narrenkappe, Kreuznacher Mönchberg, Kreuznacher Kapellenpfad, Kreuznacher Krötenpfuhl, Kreuznacher Brückes, Kreuznacher Kanzenberg, Kreuznacher Rosenberg, Schlossböckelheimer Königsfels, Schlossböckelheimer Mühlberg, Winzenheimer Rosenheck, Roxheimer Mühlenberg, Roxheimer Sonnenberg, Bosenheimer Paradies.

The Grosslage name is Kreuznacher Kronenberg.

Grape Varieties: 60% Riesling, 15% Müller-Thurgau, 10% Sylvaner, 15% Scheurebe, Spätburgunder, Ruländer, and miscellaneous varieties.

The wines: In view of the various grape varieties, vineyard locations, and individual barrel aging, there are many different wines. In general, they are vigorous and robust, but still fine and elegant. The Riesling is fruity and the Müller-Thurgau rich in bouquet.

Estate specialties: Dry wines suited for diabetics are indicated on the price list. The rosé produced here is more delicate than those produced in Württemberg and Baden. The Spätburgunder is velvety and soft.

Label: It features the name Carl Finkenauer (1875–1948) and the family coat of arms. It is assumed that the ancestors lived in wooded country full of finches (*Finken*) and the two finches on the emblem are a play on the name.

Marketing: Sold to better restaurants, the trade, and private customers.

Visits and tastings: By appointment, the cellar and vineyards can be visited. Two tasting rooms, one for 15 persons and one for 40 persons, are available. English-speaking personnel available.

From my notebook: A friendly, family business. The wines I tasted were well-balanced and mellow. The estate buildings near the park offer good parking facilities.

LANGENLONSHEIM

Weingut Erbhof Tesch

Address: 6536 Langenlonsheim, Naheweinstrasse 99
Telephone: (06704) 611

Location: The estate buildings, tasting room, and cellar are at the market place.

How to get there: Drive 8 km on route B-48 from Bingen-Bingerbrück toward Bad Kreuznach.

Points of interest: The modern winery with a three-tier tank cellar and a traditional barrel cellar; the modern, well-tended vineyards.

History: The wine estate of the Langenlonsheimer-Tesch ancestors was first recorded in an inheritance register in 1723, and was handed down in the family for nine generations. Twice there were no male heirs, and heiresses married outside the family. In 1769, Johann Martin Müller married an heiress, and in 1905, Johann Tesch, whose family has been established in Traisen since 1487, married the second heiress. After handing over the estate to his son-in-law, Johann Tesch, Martin Müller became the first wine inspector for the Bad Kreuznach rural district in 1909. The estate was handed over to Kurt Tesch, the father of the present proprietor, in 1937. By increasing the vineyard area and extending the winery, he contributed greatly to the estate's development. Today, with its 225 acres, the estate is considered the largest family viticultural and agricultural business on the Nahe.

Terrain and soils: Of the 95 acres of vineyards, 74% are on gently sloping, 7.5% on steeply sloping, and 18.5% on flat terrain. The soils are red schist, red sandstone, gravel, and loess.

Vineyard names: Langenlonsheimer St. Antoniusweg (8.6 a.), Langenlonsheimer Steinchen (17.5 a.), Langenlonsheimer Königsschild (8.2 a.), Langenlonsheimer Löhrer Berg (15.3 a), Langenlonsheimer Bergborn (7.4 a.), Laubenheimer Hörnchen (2 a.), Laubenheimer Karthäuser (13.6 a.), Laubenheimer St. Remigiusberg (7.7 a.), Laubenheimer Krone (9.9 a.), Dorsheimer Goldloch (4.7 a.).

Grape varieties: 58% Riesling, 14% Müller-Thurgau, 10% Sylvaner, 5% Ruländer, 5% Weissburgunder, 4% Spätburgunder, 2% Gewürztraminer, 1% Scheurebe, 1% experimental varieties.

The wines: They are well-balanced, fruity, and elegant, with a delicate sweetness.

Estate specialties: Numerous award-winning wines. Particular importance is placed on maintaining the characteristics of the grape varieties. The diverse vineyards, located in three communities, yield wines of varied character.

Label: The portrait on the label is of Martin Müller, the owner of the estate from 1835 to 1858. The neck label bears the coat of arms of the Tesch family, dating from 1487. The individual qualities of the wines are distinguished by various colored stripes on the label.

Marketing: The majority of the sales are to private clients.

Visits and tastings: By making an appointment with Mr. Kurt Tesch, Sr., visits and tastings can be arranged.

From my notebook: A modern, progressive, family business, taken over recently by Mr. Hartmut Tesch, a trained oenologist, while the senior Mr. Tesch looks after visitors.

BURG LAYEN

Schlossgut Diel auf Berg Layen

Address: 6531 Burg Layen
Telephone: (06721) 32333 and 33311

Location: In the center of the village.

How to get there: Drive from Bingen on route B-36 through Münster-Sarmsheim toward Bad Kreuznach, turning off to the right into Trollbachtal (7 km), or take the Bingen Koblenz autobahn, turning off at Dorsheim (0.5 km).

Points of interest: The extensive cellar hewn out of rock; the manor, which was remodeled in 1970; the wine bar in the Ostturm (East Tower).

History: Burg Layen was mentioned in records as early as the twelfth century. In the seventeenth century the emperor elevated the owners of the castle of Layen to Imperial Barons. The castle was destroyed in 1689. The Diel family, here as tenants, purchased the castle, manor, and vineyards in 1806.

Terrain and soils: Of the 47 acres of vineyards, ⅓ are on steeply sloping, ⅓ on gently sloping, and ⅓ on flat terrain. There are various types of soils.

Vineyard names: Burg Layer Schlossberg, Burg Layer Rotenberg, Burg Layer Johannisberg, Dorsheimer Klosterpfad, Dorsheimer Goldloch, Dorsheimer Pittermännchen, Münsterer Königsschloss.

Grape varieties: 50% Riesling, 10% Müller-Thurgau, 5% Traminer, 5% Ruländer, 30% experimental varieties.

The wines: In both variety and vintage, the assortment is large. The wines all have a clean, elegant character; the lesser vintages are noticeably *spritzig,* and the riper vintages are full with well-balanced sweetness.

Estate specialties: The large list contains interesting older vintages, a selection of dry wines, red and rosé wines, and various assort-

Weingut Erbhof Tesch

LANGENLONSHEIM · NAHE

Seit Anno 1723 *Familienbesitz*

Langenlonsheimer Löhrer Berg

RIESLING SPÄTLESE

QUALITÄTSWEIN MIT PRÄDIKAT

Amtliche Prüfungsnummer 1 738 166 8 72

NAHE- WEIN

SEIT
1775

BURG LAYER

Qualitätswein mit Prädikat

AUSLESE

Erzeugerabfüllung

A. P. Nr. 1 763 034 6 74

WEINGUT DR. JOSEF HÖFER, SCHLOSSMÜHLE

BURG-LAYEN BEI BINGEN AM RHEIN

NAHE

SITZ DER FAMILIE DIEL
SEIT ÜBER
300 JAHREN

Schloßgut Diel auf Burg-Layen·Bingen·Rh.

Dorsheimer Goldloch Riesling

Kabinett

Qualitätswein mit Prädikat – A. P. Nr. 1 763 019 7 74

Erzeuger-Abfüllung

ments. The rarities list is a treasure of wines which have become rare, and are available for reasonable prices. The owner
considers his rosé Qualitätswein mit Prädikat to be a particular
specialty.

Label: It features the castle coat of arms and a view of the estate
taken from an old etching. The color of a diagonal stripe below the coat of arms and the color of the capsule differ according to the quality of the wine.

Marketing: Direct sale to the trade, hotels, and private customers.

Visits and tastings: By appointment, visits and tastings can be arranged. The stylish rooms are excellent for group wine tastings.

From my notebook: The manor, carefully renovated in 1970, and
the remains of the castle are worth a visit, even for those who
are not interested in wine. The present proprietor, Dr. Ingo Diel,
an agronomist, is considered to be a pioneer in the introduction
of new grape varieties. Comparison tastings of wines from the
extensive experimental plantings are held each year and are
highly recommended. Interested parties can receive invitations
on application.

BURG LAYEN

Weingut Dr. Josef Höfer Schlossmühle

Address: 6531 Burg Layen
Telephone: (06721) 2209

Location: At the southern approach to Burg Layen.

How to get there: Drive from Bingen through Münster-Sarmsheim
toward Bad Kreuznach and turn right at Trollbachtal, or take
the Bingen-Koblenz autobahn, turning off at Dorsheim.

Points of interest: The ruins and well-preserved tower of the old
castle of Layen which dominates the property; parts of the
former castle cellar, with walls six to nine feet thick, are today

incorporated in the wine cellar; the sixteenth century Madonna, carved from wood; pewter drinking vessels and Rhine Noppen glasses on display in the tasting room.

History: The wine estate has been in the family since 1775, as is shown in a document of that year regarding the castle mill belonging to the hereditary Count zu Eltz. This document was signed by Count Anselm zu Eltz Kempenich, known as Faust von (Fist of) Strumberg. The fief was purchased by the family in 1806.

Terrain and soils: Of the 86.5 acres of vineyards, 50% are on gently sloping, 20% on steeply sloping, and 30% on flat terrain. The soils are schist, sandstone, gravel, and loess.

Vineyard names: Burg Layer Hölle (3.5 a.), Burg Layer Schlossberg (3.7 a.), Burg Layer Rothenberg (3 a.), Burg Layer Johannisberg (4.2 a.), Dorsheimer Honigberg (1.7 a.), Dorsheimer Goldloch (1.5 a.), Dorsheimer Trollberg (6.2 a.), Dorsheimer Klosterpfad (8.2 a.), Dorsheimer Laurenziweg (0.25 a.), Münster-Sarmsheimer Königsschloss (12.6 a.), Münster-Sarmsheiser Trollberg (1 a.), Laubenheimer Karthäuser (2 a.), Bretzenheimer Hofgut (2 a.), Bretzenheimer Pastorei (2.2 a.), Guldentaler Honigberg (5.2 a.), Winzenheimer In den

17 Morgen (6.7 a.), Winzenheimer Honigberg (3.2 a.) Winzenheimer Berg (7.2 a.), Winzenheimer Rosenheck (2.2 a.), Kreuznacher Hungriger Wolf (1.7 a.) and others.

Grape varieties: 40% Sylvaner, 18% Müller-Thurgau, 15% Riesling, 17% Ruländer, Weissburgunder, Sieger, Freisamer, Morio-Muskat, and other varieties.

The wines: The goal is to produce a mild, elegant wine that is not too dry. The 1971's are particularly mellow and fruity with a delicate, mature sweetness.

Estate specialties: The fruity, new varieties.

Label: It shows the old estate coat of arms of the castle mill.

Marketing: Wines are sold through representatives and directly to private persons.

Visits and tastings: By appointment, the estate buildings and cellar can be visited. Wine tastings are individually planned by arrangement.

From my notebook: An attractively situated estate with interesting wines. Mrs. Maria Höfer took charge after the death of her husband, Dr. Josef Höfer, and now runs the estate expertly and energetically, supported by a staff comprised mainly of women.

Rheingau

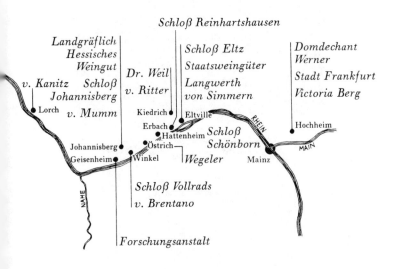

Schloß Reinhartshausen

Landgräflich
Hessisches
Weingut

Schloß Eltz
Staatsweingüter
Langwerth
von Simmern

Domdechant
Werner
Stadt Frankfurt
Victoria Berg

Dr. Weil
v. Ritter

v. Kanitz   Schloß
Johannisberg

v. Mumm

Lorch

Kiedrich

Eltville

RHEIN

Hochheim

Erbach
Hattenheim

Schloß
Schönborn

MAIN

Johannisberg
Östrich
Geisenheim   Winkel

Wegeler

Mainz

NAHE

Schloß Vollrads

v. Brentano

Forschungsanstalt

RHEINGAU

1971er
JOHANNISBERGER KLAUS
RIESLING AUSLESE
AP Nr. 260 230 11 72

ERZEUGERABFÜLLUNG

LANDGRÄFLICH
HESSISCHES WEINGUT
JOHANNISBERG/RHG.
QUALITÄTSWEIN MIT PRÄDIKAT

QUALITÄTSWEIN
MIT
PRÄDIKAT
RHEINGAU
A. P. Nr. 26026 001 72

1971er
Schloss Johannisberger.
Grünlack
SPÄTLESE

Erzeuger-Abfüllung
Fürst von Metternich
Domäne Schloß Johannisberg

G. H. v. Mumm'sches Weingut

RHEIN-GAU

JOHANNISBERG IM RHEINGAU

Johannisberger Hansenberg
Riesling Kabinett
Qualitätswein mit Prädikat
Erzeuger-Abfüllung   A. P. Nr. 26032 018 74

LORCH

Gräflich von Kanitz'sche Weingutsverwaltung

Address: 6223 Lorch
Telephone: (06726) 346

Location: The offices and cellars are in the center of the village next to the historic Hilchenhaus.

How to get there: Take the Köln-Frankfurt autobahn and turn off at Dernbacher Dreieck. Continue on to Bendorf and then a further 50 km on route B-42 to Lorch. An alternate method is to drive 42 km from Wiesbaden on the Rheingau Riesling Route (some of which is route B-42).

Points of interest: The barrel cellar; the Hilchenhaus, which is the most beautiful Renaissance building on the middle Rhine, dating from 1546. You can buy wine by the glass in the Hilchenhaus throughout the year (closed on Fridays).

History: The wine estate was in the possession of the von Staffel family from the thirteenth century onward. In the sixteenth century it was inherited by the Barons vom Stein. The present proprietor, Count von Kanitz, inherited the estate from the last imperial baron, Heinrich Friedrich Karl vom und zum Stein, a Prussian minister and political reformer.

Terrain and soils: All of the 47.6 acres of vineyards are on steeply sloping terrain. The soils include sandy loam, schist, and quartzite.

Vineyard names: Lorcher Schlossberg, Lorcher Kapellenberg, Lorcher Krone, Lorcher Pfaffenwies, Lorcher Bodental-Steinberg.

Grape varieties: 84.2% Riesling, 5.4% Müller-Thurgau, 3.8% Sylvaner, 2.9% Gewürztraminer, 3.7% miscellaneous varieties.

The wines: The wines are individually aged and have a subtle residual sweetness. They appear fuller and softer than the original

type of Rheingau wines, the slate giving them a delicate fruitiness.

Estate specialties: All the wines sold have attained high awards at
state and national wine judgings.

Label: It shows the coat of arms of Count von Kanitz.

Marketing: Through wine brokers to the trade and at the auctions
at Kloster Eberbach. Also sold to regular customers and private
consumers, as well as by the glass in the Hilchenhaus.

Visits and tastings: By appointment, the cellars and vineyards can
be visited. Wine tastings are given in the wine room in the Hilchenhaus for groups up to 30 persons.

From my notebook: This wine estate, located where the Rheingau
and the Mittlerhein meet, is worthy of a visit because of the
spectacular landscape, the impressive architecture of the estate
buildings, and the well-made wines. Cold food is served in the
Hilchenhaus.

GEISENHEIM

Hessische Forschungsanstalt fur Wein-, Obst- und Gartenbau

Address: 6222 Geisenheim, von Lade Strasse 1
Telephone: (06722) 8016

Location: The main buildings and offices are in the park that contains the research center.

How to get there: Take route B-42 from Wiesbaden toward Rüdesheim, turning off at Gymnasiumstrasse, or take the Rheingau Riesling Route.

Points of interest: The experimental center receives most of its visitors during the summer. Included in the center are the faculties of wine and beverage technology, and the departments of horticulture and agriculture of the Wiesbaden Technical School with its park, shrub garden, and experimental gardens for flowers. There are also extensive experimental plantings for viniculture, viticulture, and horticulture. In addition to the research work, the institute has an interesting wine cellar containing many sculptured casks.

History: Founded in 1872 as a royal Prussian training institute, its assignment read: the advancement of viticulture and horticulture through research, instruction, and counsel. Scientific stations, established as departments of the institute later became world-famous. The original two-year course has been extended to three years. Today the staff has about 50 scientists, 50 technicians, and 200 other co-workers. The total area of experimental plantings is 200 acres.

Terrain and soils: Of the 101 acres planted with vines, 31 are run by the vine breeding and grafting department, and 70 are run by the viticulture department. The soils include schist, quartzite, loess, loess-loam, clay, and marl.

Vineyard names: Geisenheimer Rothenberg (2 a.), Geisenheimer Kläuserweg (8.6 a.), Geisenheimer Mäuerchen (13.6 a.), Geisenheimer Fuchsberg (55.1 a.), Rüdesheimer Magdalenenkreuz (6.7 a.), Rüdesheimer Klosterberg (5 a.), and others.

The Grosslage names are Rüdesheimer Burgweg and Johannisberger Erntebringer.

Grape varieties: 50% Riesling, 10% Müller-Thurgau, 10% Ruländer, 10% Spätburgunder, 6% Weissburgunder, 5% Gewürztraminer, 9% miscellaneous and experimental varieties. The plots belonging to the vine breeding and grafting department are planted with American-rootstock mother plants, as well as the results of crosses and clone selections of various European vine varieties.

The wines: Although the vine research department has its own cellar available for processing the harvests from the experimental plots, the grapes from the viticulture department are taken by the wine and process technology department, which produces the wines and markets them.

The experimental vineyards in the communities of Geisenheim and Rüdesheim produce fruity, fine wines of different characters because of the vineyards' different terrains and soils. Wines are aged in tanks and wooden barrels, and are always true to the character of the grape variety.

Estate specialties: A small quantity of the regular wines and of the wines from experimental plantings are kept in a special cellar to enable their development to be observed. The oldest wine in this library is dated 1896.

Label: It shows the coat of arms of the state of Hesse.

Marketing: Sales to the trade and private consumers. An annual price list is issued for bottled wines. The wine and process technology department (Institute für Kellerwirtschaft und Verfahrenstechnik, Blaubachstrasse 19, telephone 8016) is responsible for sales.

Visits and tastings: It is possible for people interested in viniculture and viticulture to arrange visits, but advance application must be made in writing. Special arrangements are required for wine tastings. English-speaking personnel available.

From my notebook: This large German technical school and research institute for viticulture, fruit-farming, and horticulture is not only visited by scientists from all over the world, but also by producers who want to learn the latest methods. Many wine lovers have become acquainted with the institute through the Rheingau wine seminars. These five-day courses and holiday seminars, entitled "Relaxation with Wine," are recommended for wine connoisseurs, as well as those new to the pleasures of fine wines. (See the reference section of this book for further details.)

JOHANNISBERG

Landgräflich Hessisches Weingut

Address: 6225 Johannisberg, Im Grund 1
Telephone: (06722) 8172

Location: At the southern entrance to the village of Johannisberg.
How to get there: Take the Wiesbaden autobahn, turning off onto route B-42 toward Rüdesheim. Between Winkel and Geisenheim, turn north for about 2 km. The estate buildings are on the left at the entrance of Johannisberg.
Points of interest: The cellar; the nearby vineyards.
History: In 1956, the Princes and Counts of Hesse acquired the wine estate from Counselor Krayer. The vineyards have been extended to their present size by additional purchases, and the old vaulted cellars have been modernized. In 1972, new estate buildings were constructed.
Terrain and soils: Of the 74 acres of vineyards, 80% are on gently sloping, 10% on steeply sloping, and 10% on flat terrain. The estate controls many scattered vineyards with different types of soil. Included are: schist, loess, loess-loam, clay, and marl.

Vineyard names: Johannisberger Klaus, Johannisberger Hölle, Johannisberger Goldatzel, Johannisberger Vogelsang, Geisenheimer Kläuserweg, Winkeler Jesuitengarten, Winkeler Gutenberg, Winkeler Hasensprung, Winkeler Dachsberg.

The Grosslage name is Johannisberger Erntebringer.

Grape varieties: 80% Riesling, 10% Müller-Thurgau, 5% Scheurebe, 5% experimental varieties.

The wines: The various soils yield wines with a wide range of characteristics. Three or four vintages are usually on the price list.

Estate specialties: Single bottles of older vintages are available. A sparkling wine under the trade name "Kurhessen" is manufactured from wines produced by the estate. Excellent Auslese wines are made from the Scheurebe grape.

Label: For both still and sparkling wines, the label shows the coat of arms of the Count of Hesse.

Marketing: Through wine brokers, at the Kloster Eberbach fair and wine auction, and by direct sale. Only one price list is issued, but the trade is given quantity discounts of up to 30%.

Visits and tastings: By appointment, visitors are welcome. Tastings can be arranged in advance.

From my notebook: The different wines are interesting, and some of them are not the original, dry, Rheingau Riesling type. Heinz Scheu, a trained agronomist who managed the estate until 1969, successfully introduced the Scheurebe grape (developed by his father) into the Rheingau. The Prince of Hesse lives in Schloss Friedrichshof, near Kronberg in the Taunus region. The manager of the estate, Karl Heinz Glock, attentively looks after guests and conducts interesting wine tastings.

JOHANNISBERG

Fürst von Metternich Winneburg'sches Domäne Rentamt, Schloss Johannisberg

Address: 6225 Johannisberg, Schloss
Telephone: (06722) 8027

Location: The mansion (*Schloss*) is situated on a commanding
  hill in the middle of the Rheingau between Winkel and Geisen-
  heim.
How to get there: Take the Wiesbaden autobahn and turn onto
  route B-42 in the direction of Rüdesheim. Between Winkel and
  Geisenheim, turn north and follow the green signs to Schloss
  Johannisberg. You can also follow the Rheingau Riesling Route.
Points of interest: The magnificent view from the terrace over the
  "blessed plains and vine-clad countryside" (Goethe) of the
  Rheingau, extending to Mainz, Rheinhesse, and into the Nahe
  Valley; the romantic abbey church (consecrated in 1130), which
  is now the estate (and community) church of St. John the Bap-
  tist; the abbey cellar (900 years old); the Schloss cellar, a gigantic barrel vault dated 1721 containing the "Bibliotheca subterranea" (underground library); old wine presses; the "Christus
  in der Kelter" chapel; the equestrian statue of the Spätlese messenger; the marker indicating 50° latitude; wayside shrines.
History: Viticulture was mentioned as early as 871 in a document
  of Ludwig the Pious. The monastery, the oldest one in the
  Rheingau, was founded by the Mainz Benedictine monks about
  1100, destroyed in 1525 and 1552, rebuilt in 1563, pledged
  against a loan in 1641, and refounded by the Abbey of Fulda
  as a priory in 1716, when the present buildings, with the exception of the church, were constructed. Rieslings have always
  been planted here and have set a noble example (thus, the name
  "Johannisberg Riesling" was borrowed in California, Brazil,

etc.). The wine world benefited greatly from the accidental discovery in 1755 of noble rot (Botrytis cinerea) and Spätlese.
The equestrian statue of the Spätlese messenger that stands near
the mansion commemorates this discovery: In 1755 the autumn
harvest-messenger, who was carrying the customary permission
to harvest from the Prince-Abbot of Fulda, arrived at the
Schloss after considerable delay. The grapes had rotted, but this
late picking (Spätlese) produced magnificent wines. After secularization, the Estate passed into the possession of the Prince
of Orange, then to the Emperor Napoleon and his marshal,
Kellermann. At the Vienna Congress it was granted to Emperor
Franz I of Austria, who presented it to Prince Clemens von
Metternich for his services in the reorganization of Europe. A
covenant, still honored, gives a tenth of the yearly yield to the
House of Hapsburg. The proprietor today is Prince Paul-Alfons
von Metternich-Winneburg, a grandnephew of Prince Clemens.

Terrain and soils: Of the 86.5 acres of vineyards, 50% are on
gently sloping, 25% on steeply sloping, and 25% on flat terrain. The soils include schist, quartzite, loess, and loess-loam.
The estate is fully consolidated.

Vineyard names: Schloss Johannisberg is, in the terms of the 1971
wine law, an independent section of the community. Therefore,
the only designation is Schloss Johannisberg.

Grape varieties: About 97% Riesling. The rest are experimental
varieties.

The wines: The very pronounced fruitiness of the Riesling character is unmistakable. Flavor and quality variations are indicated by different capsule colors. Until 1969, only unsugared
wines were produced; starting in 1970, small quantities of
Qualitätswein bestimmter Anbaugebiete have been made. Since
1864, all acid-rich, racy wines have been used to produce the
sparkling wine "Fürst von Metternich" that is made and sold
by Söhnlein-Rheingold in Wiesbaden.

Estate specialties: In the "Bibliotheca subterranea" (underground
library) there is still a bottle of 1784 wine from the monastic
period, and samples of all good vintages back to 1842 are kept.
Some older wines (25–30 years old) can be bought in the estate

wine café. High international, national, and state awards have been won.

Label: There are two labels. One, which was formerly used for estate-bottled wines, shows the Metternich coat of arms. The other, formerly used for Kabinett wines, has a picture of the estate. Since 1830, all labels have borne the signature of the *Rentmeister* (manager). For 150 years the color of the bottle capsules has indicated the quality of the wine in the bottle. According to the new wine law, these are now as follows for the coat-of-arms label: Kabinett = red, Spätlese = white, Auslese = rose, Beerenauslese = rose/gold. For the picture label they are: Kabinett = orange, Spätlese = white, Auslese = light blue, Beerenauslese =blue/gold, Trockenbeerenauslese = gold. A Qualitätswein bestimmter Anbaugebiete is indicated by a yellow capsule.

Marketing: Sold by brokers to the wholesale and export trade, as well as direct sale to consumers in small quantities at higher prices. Bottles with the picture label, formerly the Kabinett series, are sold only through a single company: currently Söhnlein-Rheingold of Wiesbaden.

Visits and tastings: The church, terrace, and vineyards are open at all times. The cellar can be visited, with or without tasting by appointment, on working days. There is tasting room for 50 persons.

From my notebook: One of the most famous German wine estates, with a long clerical and wine history. Tours and tastings conducted by the estate counselor, Josef Staab, and his staff are very instructive. The estate café, situated on the terrace, serves cold dishes and is open daily from 12:30 p.m. until 10:00 p.m., from Good Friday until All Saints Day (November 1). The café telephone number is (06722) 8538.

JOHANNISBERG

G. H. von Mumm'sches Weingut

Address: 6225 Johannisberg, Schulstrasse 30
Telephone: (06722) 8257 Telex: 042142

Location: The offices and cellars are at the edge of Johannisberg toward Winkel on the Rheingau Riesling Route.

How to get there: Take the autobahn from Wiesbaden, and then route B-42 toward Rüdesheim. In Winkel turn north and drive for 3 km.

Points of interest: The large wine cellar with a capacity of 211,000 gallons and 600,000 bottles; the 140-year-old wine press in the park; two wayside shrines in the vineyard; the castle of Burg Schwartzenstein, built in 1876, overlooking Johannisberg (wine can be purchased by the glass); the distant view of Mainz and Bingen.

History: The wine merchant Mumm, from Frankfurt, bought the grapes on the vine in the early summer of 1811 without dreaming what a high profit that unique comet vintage would bring

him. The receipts from that venture formed the basis on which
he built his wine estate. In 1957, the estate was acquired by
Rudolph August Oetker, of Bielefeld, and he extended it to its
present size by additional purchases.

Terrain and soils: The total vineyard area of 111 acres includes
74 acres in Johannisberg, 24.7 acres in Rüdesheim, 6.2 acres in
Geisenheim, and 6.2 acres in Winkel. The vineyard terrain is
40% steeply sloping, 30% gently sloping, and 30% flat. The
soils include schist, quartzite, loess, and loess-loam.

Vineyard names: Johannisberger Schwarzenstein (9.9 a.), Johannisberger Vogelsang (13.6 a.), Johannisberger Hölle
(8.6 a.), Johannisberger Mittelhölle (14.8 a.), Johannisberger
Hansenberg (9.9 a.), Johannisberger Goldatzel (13.6 a.), Johannisberger Klaus (3.7 a.), Rüdesheimer Berg Schlossberg
(1.2 a.), Rüdesheimer Berg Roseneck (8.6 a.), Rüdesheimer
Berg Rottland (3.7 a.), Rüdesheimer Bischofsberg (5 a.),
Rüdesheimer Drachenstein (6.2 a.), Winkeler Dachsberg (5
a.), Winkeler Hasensprung (1.2 a.), Geisenheimer Mönchspfad
(3.7 a.), Geisenheimer Kilzberg (1.2 a.), Geisenheimer Kläuserweg (1.2 a.).

The Grosslage names are Johannisberger Erntebringer, Rüdesheimer Burgweg, and Winkeler Honigberg.

Grape varieties: 86% Riesling, 8% Müller-Thurgau, 3% Ruländer,
2% Spätburgunder, 1% miscellaneous.

The wines: The wines are aged in wooden barrels and then trans-
ferred to tanks. A delicate acidity is retained in order to give
the wine longevity. Fruity wines, with subtle sweetness and
piquant acidity. The Riesling character is retained.

Estate specialties: Riesling wines are predominant. Single bottles of
all good vintages back to 1934 are kept in the rarities cellar.
Interesting Eisweins were obtained in 1965 and 1970. Annual
participation in state and natural wine competitions. Many international awards have been won.

Label: It shows the coat of arms of the wine estate. There is also
a picture of the Rüdesheimer Hill on a white background for the
Rüdesheimer wines. The wine qualities are indicated by colored
bottle capsules and label edges, which are as follows: Qualitätswein bestimmter Anbaugebiete = white; Kabinett = green;

Auslese, Beerenauslese, Trockenbeerenauslese = red; Eiswein = blue.

Marketing: Principally sold to good restaurants and the trade; considerable exports. Also sold in bottles and by the glass to private consumers on the estate.

Visits and tastings: By appointment, the vineyards and cellars can be visited. Wine tastings for up to 30 persons can be held in the rustic tasting room in the estate buildings, and for up to 55 persons in the castle of Burg Schwarzenstein. The wine tastings conducted by the estate manager, Mr. Wolf, are particularly instructive. English-speaking personnel available.

From my notebook: The restaurant "Burg Schwarzenstein," above the offices and surrounded by vineyards, is highly recommended for excursions. There is a wonderful view over the Rheingau, large parking lots, and paths in the vineyards and Taunus Woods. Guests should also note the wine carousel in the restaurant. Six different wines in qualities up to Beerenauslese are offered for tasting in small glasses—up the scale and down again on a rotating stand.

WINKEL

Schloss Vollrads

Address: 6227 Winkel
Telephone: (06723) 3314

Location: The castle is picturesquely situated 2 km above Winkel
   at the point where the vineyards merge into the Taunus Woods.
How to get there: Take the autobahn from Wiesbaden and then
   route B-42 toward Rüdesheim. In the middle of Winkel, turn
   north at the sign marked "Schloss Vollrads." From the edge of
   the village you will see the castle halfway up the hill. The old
   trees in the famous avenue were felled and replaced with new
   ones in 1973.
Points of interest: The historic buildings, especially the water
   tower; the castle garden; the old main cellar.
History: As early as 1100, the Knights of Greiffenclau and the later
   Imperial Barons of Grieffenclau lived in the Grau Haus (Gray
   House) in Winkel, which is still preserved. About 1300, they
   built the Schloss Vollrads castle and increased the size of their
   vineyard holdings in the course of time. The cellar invoices have
   been preserved in the tower archives since 1600. In 1846, the
   last Baroness of Grieffenclau married Count Hugo Matuschka.
   Since then, the name Matuschka-Greiflenclau and the combined
   insignias of both families have been used. Probably the oldest
   noble family in the Rheingau involved in viticulture.
Terrain and soils: Of the 91.5 acres of vineyards, 20% are on
   steeply sloping, 60% on gently sloping, and 20% on flat terrain.
   The soil is deep and retains water well. A large portion of the
   vineyards are planted in the wide-spaced rows of vines.
Vineyard names: The majority of the vineyards are near the castle
   in the community of Winkel, but there are also some plots in
   the communities of Mittelheim and Hattenheim. Schloss Vollrads

is the only name used on the label, however, because the new wine law classifies this as an independent section of the community.

Grape varieties: 90% Riesling, 5% Müller-Thurgau, 5% miscellaneous.

The wines: The type of Rheingau Riesling handed down from the past is still planted here, and this means that the wines have relatively little residual sweetness and a delicate, racy acidity.

Estate specialties: The fine wines are world famous. One bottle of Schloss Vollrads 1865 was sold for $150 at the rare-wine auction of the Rheingauer Weinkonvents in Kloster Eberbach in 1971. Single bottles of older vintages are preserved in a small wine museum. Little value is placed on awards because it is felt that the estate name guarantees quality.

Label: It shows the family coat of arms and is the same in design and color for all qualities. The colors of the bottle capsules, however, are different.

From 1971, (new wine law) the following capsule color code has been used: Qualitätswein bestimmter Anbaugebiete (two qualities) = green and green with gold stripes; Kabinett (two qualities) = blue and blue with gold stripes; Spätlese (two qualities) = rose and rose with gold stripes; Auslese (two qualities) = white and white with gold stripes; Beerenauslese = gold; Trockenbeerenauslese = gold with neck label. Prior to 1970 (old wine law), the capsule color code was: estate bottled without quality designation = green; Schloss bottled (three qualities) = red, red with silver stripes, and red with gold stripes: Kabinett (equivalent to Spätlese, three qualities) = blue, blue with silver stripes, and blue with gold stripes; Auslese (three qualities) = rose, rose with silver stripes, and rose with gold stripes; Beerenauslese = white; Trockenbeerenauslese = white with gold stripes and a neck label.

Marketing: almost exclusively through wine brokers and at the Kloster Eberbach wine auctions. Some wine is sold in barrels to the Rheingau regional vintners association. A high amount is exported, mainly to the United States, Great Britain, and Japan.

Visits and tastings: The courtyard, some of the garden, and the

VERBAND DEUTSCHER
PRÄDIKATS-
WEINGÜTER E.V.

Unsere Mitglieder besitzen
Lagen von Weltruf!

V
D P

VEREINIGUNG
RHEINGAUER
WEINGÜTER E.V.

A. P. Nr.

27 074 015 74

RHEINGAU
QUALITÄTSWEIN MIT PRÄDIKAT

1973er AUSLESE
SCHLOSS VOLLRADS

Erzeuger-Abfüllung

Graf Matuschka-Greiffenclau'sche Gutsverwaltung

RHEINGAU
1971er Winkeler Hasensprung Riesling Auslese
Qualitätswein mit Prädikat

A. P.-Nr. 27 017 010 72
Erzeuger-Abfüllung der
A. von Brentano'schen
Gutsverwaltung Winkel i. Rheingau

RHEINGAU
Schloss Schönborn

1971er

Erbacher Marcobrunn
Riesling
TROCKENBEERENAUSLESE

Domänenrat

A. P. Nr. 31 052, 024. 72
Erzeugerabfüllung der Gräflich von Schönborn'schen Cellerei Hattenheim
QUALITÄTSWEIN MIT PRÄDIKAT

vineyards are open to visitors, but the rooms in the castle are not, because they are still occupied. Groups may visit the winery by appointment. Prospective customers, willing to be billed for the cost, may arrange for wine tastings.

From my notebook: These carefully made, racy Riesling wines, with little residual sweetness, maintain their freshness for many years because of their abundant fruitiness. Schloss Vollrads is considered to be one of the most beautifully situated wine estates in Germany. The buildings of the Middle Ages, the gardens, and the vaulted cellars have an atmosphere that commands respect. Count Richard Matuschka-Greiffenclau, father of the current proprietor (Count Erwein Matuschka-Greiffenclau), was president of the German Vintners Association for 15 years after the war. He died at the age of 82 on January 4, 1975, highly esteemed by all.

WINKEL

A. von Brentano'sche Gutsverwaltung

Address: 6227 Winkel, Brentanohaus, Hauptstrasse 89
Telephone: (06723) 2068

Location: The "Brentanohaus," estate buildings, and cellars are in the center of Winkel on the Rheingau Riesling Route.
How to get there: Take the autobahn from Wiesbaden and then route B-42 toward Rüdesheim.
Points of interest: The Brentanohaus, which is preserved as a historic monument and some of which is a museum, contains items in good condition from the time of Goethe, as well as Clemens and Bettina Brentano; the gardens; the old barrel cellar; the Italian terrace.
History: The basket used for carrying harvested grapes, shown in the family coat of arms, indicates the origin of the name. The small son of one of the ancestors is said to have been rescued in

a grape basket (*brentano,* in Italian) during the siege and storm-
ing of the ancestral castle in upper Italy. The Brentanohaus of
today was built in 1751 and extended in 1782. The owner is
Achim von Brentano, who personally manages the estate.

Terrain and soils: The 19.8 acres of vineyards are split into many
plots, which are located on the gently sloping hills in the community of Winkel. The soils are loess and loess-loam; the ability
of the soil to hold water in dry weather produces rich harvests.

Vineyard names: Winkeler Hasensprung (9.9 a.), Winkeler Gutenberg (2.5 a.), Winkeler Jesuitengarten (2.5 a.).

The Grosslage name is Winkeler Honigberg.

Grape varieties: 100% Riesling.

The wines: Mellow, mature wines that clearly express their origin
in the deep loess soils of the lower Rheingau. Traditional barrel
aging and individual bottling are still practiced.

Estate specialties: To commemorate the 200th birthday of Goethe,
the 1949 Winkeler Hasensprung Riesling bore the special stamp
"Goethewein" for the first time. Goethe was often a guest of the
Brentanos, and wrote of their wine, "Unforgettable is the deli-
cious taste of the Eilfer Hasensprung of 1811."

Label: It shows an historic view of the estate buildings and surroundings. The family coat of arms is at the bottom left, below
the Goethe seal, which is registered. The seal, in blue relief, is
also applied to the bottle neck as an oval label instead of the
normal neck label.

Marketing: Through the wine trade and brokers, as well as at the
Kloster Eberbach auctions and wine fairs.

Visits and tastings: By appointment, the historic rooms in the
house and the barrel cellar may be visited. Wine tastings in the
appealing tasting room are individually planned by arrangement.

From my notebook: This combination of living history and original
Brentano Riesling wines can be a unique experience for ad-
mirers of Goethe and the early romantic period. The tours are
interesting, for the proprietor or his wife usually conduct the
guests. The historic rooms, which were largely unchanged
through the ages are still lived in by the Brentano family. Visits
should, as far as possible, be limited to small groups. Do not
forget to make an appointment in advance.

OESTRICH

Gutsverwaltung Geh. Rat Julius Wegeler Erben

Address: 6227 Oestrich-Winkel, Postfach 1105
Telephone: (06723) 3071

Location: In the center of Oestrich at the Friedensplatz square.
How to get there: Take the autobahn from Wiesbaden, then route
   B-42 toward Rüdesheim. The Rheingau Riesling Route may
   also be taken.
Points of interest: The progressive winery; the interesting experimental plantings.
History: in 1882, Privy Councilor Julius Wegeler purchased some of
   the best vineyards on the Rüdesheimer Hill. In 1894, the company of Deinhard (Koblenz), in which Wegeler was a co-
   partner, acquired the Oestrich estate and other vineyards in the
   Rüdesheim, Geisenheim, and Hallgarten areas. Today this establishment is one of the largest wine estates in the Rheingau
   and is administered by Karl-Felix Wegeler.
Terrain and soils: Of the 138 acres of vineyards, 42% are on
   gently sloping, 25% on steeply sloping, and 33% on flat terrain.
   The soils include loam, clay, marl, loess, and loess-loam.
Vineyard names: Hallgartener Schönhell (2.5 a.), Oestricher
   Doosberg (12.6 a.), Oestricher Lenchen (21.25 a.), Oestricher
   Klosterberg (6.4 a.), Mittelheimer Edelmann (12.4 a.), Mittel-
   heimer St. Nikolaus (12.4 a.), Mittelheimer Goldberg (1.2 a.),
   Winkeler Hasensprung (7.4 a.), Winkeler Gutenberg (1.2 a.),
   Winkeler Dachsberg (1 a.), Johannisberger Hölle (1.2 a.),
   Johannisberger Vogelsang (0.75 a.), Geisenheimer Rothenberg
   (18.3 a.), Geisenheimer Kläuserweg (4 a.), Geisenheimer
   Schlossgarten (16.8 a.), Rüdesheimer Berg Rottland (8.9 a.),
   Rüdesheimer Berg Roseneck (3.2 a.), Rüdesheimer Berg
   Schlossberg (5.4 a.), Rüdesheimer Bischofsberg (1.2 a.),
   Rüdesheimer Magdalenenkreuz (3.5 a.).

Grape varieties: 86% Riesling, 6% Müller-Thurgau, 2% Scheurebe, 1.5% Ruländer, 1.5% Gewürztraminer, 3% miscellaneous.

The wines: Clean, racy Rieslings are produced. Particular attention is paid to retaining the character of the grape variety.

Estate specialties: Riesling wines are emphasized. The estate's outstanding vineyards are responsible for the above-average number of fine wines.

Label: It shows the Wegeler coat of arms.

Marketing: Through the trade and to high-class restaurants. Sale in small quantities to private clients. Export sales through Deinhard and Co. in Koblenz.

Wine tastings: Expert wine tastings are given by arrangement.

From my notebook: A viniculturally and viticulturally progressive establishment, principally suited for visits by groups of experts. The estate wines are well represented on the English market.

HATTENHEIM

Domänenweingut Schloss Schönborn

Address: 6229 Hattenheim, Hauptstrasse 53
Telephone: (06723) 2007

Location: The offices and cellars are at the end of the village, above the Pfaffenberg vineyards, with an open view over the Rhine Valley. The large estate is scattered over 13 communities, from Hochheim to Lorchhausen.

How to get there: Coming from Wiesbaden, take route B-42 and turn onto the Rheingau Riesling Route.

Points of interest: The cruciform-vaulted cellar, more than 500 years old; the wooden barrels with carved ends; the pleasant wine tasting room.

History: The von Schönborn family in Winkel was recorded in 1349 as vineyard owners. In the course of time this developed into the largest private wine estate in the Rheingau. The Counts von Schönborn enjoyed, and still enjoy, an important reputation in official and cultural life. The clerical and temporal princes and bishops of the House of Schönborn were important patrons of the south-German baroque, as evidenced by the grandiose mansions and buildings in Würzburg, Bamberg, Mainz, Trier, Koblenz, Bruchsal, and one of the most important of the Schönborn mansions, Pommersfelden. Today the owners are Count Karl von Schönborn-Wiesentheid and Count Rudolf von Schönborn-Wiesentheid.

Terrain and soils: The total estate holdings amount to 200 acres, but only 148 acres are currently being cultivated. Of that amount, 58% are on gently sloping, 8% on steeply sloping, and 34% on flat terrain. The soils are schist, quartzite, loam, clay, marl, loess, and loess-loam.

Vineyard names: Hattenheimer Pfaffenberg (14.8 a.—entire vineyard), Hattenheimer Nussbrunnen (5 a.), Hattenheimer Wisselbrunnen (2.5 a.), Hattenheimer Engelmannsberg, Hattenheimer Schützenhaus, Erbacher Marcobrunn (5 a.), Rauenthaler Wülfen, Rauenthaler Baiken, Rauenthaler Rothenberg, Hallgartener Würzgarten (2.5 a.), Hallgartener Jungfer (5 a.), Oestricher Doosberg (32 a.—largest owner in this vineyard), Mittelheimer St. Nikolaus (3.7 a.), Johannisberger Klaus (9.9 a.), Winkeler Hasensprung (7.4 a.), Winkeler Jesuitengarten (2.5 a.), Winkeler Dachsberg (5 a.), Winkeler Gutenberg (5 a.), Geisenheimer Mönchspfad, Geisenheimer Mäuerchen (2.5 a.), Geisenheimer Schlossgarten (19.8 a.—largest proprietor in this vineyard), Geisenheimer Rothenberg, Rüdesheimer Berg Schlossberg (2.5 a.), Rüdesheimer Berg Rottland (3.7 a.), Rüdesheimer Bischofsberg, Lorcher Krone (2.5 a.), Lorcher Schlossberg, Lorcher Kapellenberg, Lorcher Pfaffenwies, Lorchhausener Seligmacher, Hochheimer Domdechaney (3.7 a.), Hochheimer Kirchenstück (6.2 a.) Hochheimer Hölle (7.4 a.), Hochheimer Stein, Hochheimer Sommerheil, Hochheimer Hofmeister.

The Grosslage names are Rüdesheimer Burgweg, Johannisberger

Erntebringer, Winkeler Honigberg, Oestricher Gottesthal, Hallgartener Mehrhölzchen, Hattenheimer Deutelsberg, Rauenthaler Steinmächer, Hochheimer Daubhaus.

Grape varieties: 91% Riesling, 4% Müller-Thurgau, 0.5% Spätburgunder, 4.5% experimental varieties.

The wines: The wines of the estate are individually barrel aged according to vineyard and quality. The goal is to produce clean Rieslings that are rich in extract. The estate considers bottle aging important.

Estate specialties: The Rheingau Riesling tradition is strongly maintained here. A high proportion of fine wines. A specialty of the estate are the sparkling wines "Schloss Schönborn" and "Graf von Schönborn" produced from estate Riesling wines. They are winey, robust, and retain their flavor long in the mouth. They are wines which do, indeed, sparkle.

Label: It shows the coat of arms of the Count of Schönborn, and has borne the signature and title of the estate manager for more than 100 years.

Marketing: The wine is largely sold through wine brokers to the trade, high-class restaurants and hotels, as well as at the Kloster Eberbach auctions and wine fairs. The first-class Schönborn hotels (Forsthaus Gravenbruch, located between Frankfurt and the Rhein-Main Airport; the Daxberg, in Spessart; Burg Rabenstein, in Franconia) and the Schönborn restaurants (Schloss Hallburg, in Franconia; Ilmbach, in the Steigerwald) offer the estate wines.

Visits and tastings: By appointment, visits to the cellars and vineyards are possible. Wine tastings for up to 20 persons are conducted in the historically furnished tasting room.

From my notebook: A look at the comprehensive eight-year sales program of this estate, the largest private wine producer in the Rheingau, shows that less emphasis is placed on systematic mass production than on maintaining the tradition of Rheingau wine. A wine tasting at this establishment, especially when it is conducted by the estate manager, Robert Englert, is highly recommended.

ERBACH

Schloss Reinhartshausen

Address: 6229 Erbach
Telephone: (06123) 4009

Location: The estate offices and hotel are situated in idyllic sur-
    roundings at the west side of the village of Erbach on the
    Rheingau Riesling Route.
How to get there: Take route B-42 west from Wiesbaden for 14 km
    to Erbach.
Points of interest: The well-tended mansion with its charming view
    over wooded areas and vine-clad hills to the Rhine Valley; the
    hotel with valuable pictures from the collection of Princess
    Marianne of Prussia.
History: The core of the estate was once the seat of the Knights of
    Erbach, and records of the estate date back to the twelfth
    century. The knights were followed by barons, counts, and
    princes. Princess Marianne of Prussia, a daughter-in-law of
    Kaiser Wilhelm I, inherited the mansion from the last of the
    counts and princes of Westphalia. The estate was much im-
    proved under her management. After her death in 1883, the
    property went to her son, Prince Albrecht of Prussia, Regent of
    Brunswick (Braunschweig), and was then inherited in 1906 by
    his eldest son, Prince Friedrich Heinrich of Prussia, who tended
    Schloss Reinhartshausen with great interest and loving care
    through the years. He was followed by the youngest son of the
    last German crown prince, Prince Friedrich of Prussia. This
    prince, highly regarded by all, left Schloss Reinhartshausen to
    his sons in 1966.
Terrain and soils: The majority of the vineyards lie on southern
    slopes running down to the Rhine River between the wine-
    producing villages of Erbach and Hattenheim. Of the 99 acres

of vineyards, 80% are on gently sloping and 20% on steeply sloping terrain. The soils are schist, quartzite, loam, clay, marl, and loess-loam.

Vineyard names: Erbacher Marcobrunn, Erbacher Schlossberg (entire vineyard), Erbacher Siegelsberg, Erbacher Hohenrain, Erbacher Honigberg, Erbacher Rheinhell, Hattenheimer Wisselbrunnen, Hattenheimer Nussbrunnen, Kiedricher Sandgrub, Rauenthaler Wülfen, Rüdesheimer Bischofsberg.

Grape varieties: 90% Riesling, 5% Weissburgunder, 3% Spätburgunder, 2% Traminer.

The wines: They are of very high quality, well-balanced, ripe, and fruity.

Estate specialties: Single bottles of older vintages back to 1861 are carefully treasured in the cellar. Particular attention is given to maintaining the character of the Rheingau Riesling.

Label: It has been the same for more than 100 years. Its design originates in the history of the estate; it contains the orange, white, and blue colors of Princess Marianne, and the eagle of the Princes of Prussia.

Marketing: Through wine brokers to the trade and restaurants. Exclusive agent in the United States is Heublein International Wine Company, Hartford, Connecticut.

Visits: By appointment, the estate and cellars may be visited.

From my notebook: A magnificent estate of many facets. The good vineyards supply distinguished wines, and the Rheininsel Mariannenau supplies aromatic, high-quality fruit and farm products for the hotel (Schloss Reinhartshausen). The wines accompanied by traditional food of the area can also be tasted in the *Schloss* cellar.

KIEDRICH

Weingut Dr. Weil

Address: 6229 Kiedrich, Mühlberg 5
Telephone: (06123) 2308

Location: The estate buildings are directly below the gothic St.
    Valentine's Church (Sankt-Valentinus-Kirche) which overlooks
    the village.
How to get there: Take the autobahn from Wiesbaden and turn
    onto route B-42 toward Rüdesheim. At the west side of Eltville,
    on the Rheingau Riesling Route, turn north.
Points of interest: The manor, in English country-house style with
    a lovely garden; the view from the buildings of leading Kiedrich
    sights and the ruins of Scharfenstein; the historic tasting room;
    the collection of wine lists and menus from the imperial courts.
History: The first vineyards were purchased by Dr. R. Weil in
    1867. In 1979, he acquired the manor, the central section of
    which was built by an English nobleman, Baron Sutton.
Terrain and soils: Of the 44.5 acres of vineyards, 80% are on
    gently sloping, 10% on steeply sloping, and 10% on flat terrain.
    The soils are acid magmatite, schist, loam, loess, loess-loam, and
    marl.
Vineyard names: Kiedricher Gräfenberg (7.4 a.), Kiedricher
    Wasserrose (18.5 a.), Kiedricher Sandgrub (13.6 a.), Kied-
    richer Klosterberg (5 a.).
The Grosslage name is Kiedricher Heiligenstock.
Grape varieties: 94% Riesling, 4% Müller-Thurgau, 2% Spät-
    burgunder.
The wines: A wide assortment, ranging from very dry, barrel-aged
    Rieslings of original character to more flavorful wines catering
    to modern tastes. Four or five vintages are usually offered.
Estate specialties: Single bottles of older vintages are available.

RHEINGAU
Qualitätswein mit Prädikat
A. P. Nr. 34 003 009 72
1971er Kiedricher Gräfenberg
Riesling Spätlese
Erzeugerabfüllung aus dem Weingut des
Dr R. Weil, Kiedrich (Rheingau)

REICHSFREIHERR VON RITTER ZU GROENESTEYN

ERZEUGER- ABFÜLLUNG

SCHLOSS GROENESTEYN

1973er Spätlese
Rüdesheimer Berg Rottland Riesling

Qualitätswein mit Prädikat Amtliche Prüfungsnummer 5/016 009 74

Weingut des Freiherr von Ritter'schen Rentamtes Rüdesheim am Rhein
RHEINGAU

SCHLOSS ELTZ

Gräflich Eltz'sche Güterverwaltung Eltville a/Rh.

AMTLICHE
PRÜFUNGSNUMMER
067

DEUTSCHER
MIT
PRÄDIKAT
QUALITÄTSWEIN

Erzeuger- Abfüllung

1971er Schloss Eltz
Auslese
Rauenthaler Baiken Riesling

R H E I N G A U

Label: It bears a map of the Kiedrich area, the Kiedrich coat of arms, and a picture of the castle ruins of Scharfenstein.

Marketing: Principally through wine brokers. Two price lists are issued, one for the trade and one for individual consumers. Large quantities are exported.

Visits and tastings: By appointment, the estate buildings, cellar, and vineyards can be visited. Wine tastings are given with a flair and they take into account guests' preferences regarding the type and scope of the tastings. English-speaking personnel available.

From my notebook: An interesting assortment of vintages and flavors are to be found here. Individual aging in small casks is still practiced. The estate buildings and the tasting room radiate an historic atmosphere. The guests are individually greeted by the proprietor, Robert Weil, and tastings and tours are instructive and informative.

KIEDRICH

Schloss Groenesteyn, Weingut des Reichsfreiherrn von Ritter zu Groenesteyn

Address: Offices: 6229 Kiedrich, Postfach 9
Winery: 6220 Rüdesheim, Oberstrasse 19
Telephone: Offices, (06123) 2492; winery, (06722) 2521

Location: The offices are in Schloss Groenesteyn in the center of Kiedrich. The winery, in which the Kiedrich harvest is processed, is in the west section of Rüdesheim.

How to get there: Drive from Wiesbaden through Eltville on the Rheingau Riesling Route.

Points of interest: The winery in Rüdesheim; the baroque mansion in Kiedrich with valuable plaster ceilings from the first half of the eighteenth century.

History: The wine estate, Schloss Groenesteyn, once the Schwalbacher Hof, dates from the fourteenth century. Since 1640, it
has been in the possession of the Barons von Ritter. The owner
today is Baron Heinrich von Ritter zu Groenesteyn.

Terrain and soils: Of the 37 acres of vineyards in the community of
Kiedrich, 60% are on gently sloping, 30% on steeply sloping,
and 10% on flat terrain. Of the 44.5 acres of vineyards in the
community of Rüdesheim, 55% are on steeply sloping and 45%
on gently sloping terrain. The soils are gravel, schist, quartzite,
loess, and loess-loam.

Vineyard names: Kiedricher Gräfenberg, Kiedricher Wasserrose,
Kiedricher Sandgrub, Kiedricher Klosterberg, Rüdesheimer Berg
Rottland, Rüdesheimer Berg Roseneck, Rüdesheimer Berg
Schlossberg, Rüdesheimer Bischofsberg, Rüdesheimer Kirchen-
pfad, Rüdesheimer Klosterlay, Rüdesheimer Magdalenenkreuz.
The Grosslage names are Kiedricher Heiligenstock and Rüde-
sheimer Burgweg.

Grape varieties: 92% Riesling, 8% Müller-Thurgau.

The wines: Typical Rheingau Riesling wines are made here. The
estate's goal is to produce well-balanced wines with a delicate
trace of natural sweetness and an elegant acidity. Individual
barrel aging provides nuances. The Rüdesheimer wines are attractive and spicy; the Kiedricher wines delicate and flowery.

Estate specialties: Single bottles of older vintages are still available.
The wine list contains a high proportion of fine wines and
award-winning wines.

Label: It bears the family coat of arms.

Marketing: Through wine brokers at the Kloster Eberbach wine
fair and wine auction. A list is issued for the trade and private
customers; the trade is granted considerable discounts.

Visits and tastings: By appointment, visits and seated tastings are
possible. English-speaking personnel available.

From my notebook: A Rheingau wine estate with old family tradi-
tions and well-made Riesling wines. Because Schloss Groenesteyn is a residence, it is rarely available for visits. The estate
plans to hold wine tastings for large parties in the Rüdesheim
winery.

ELTVILLE

Schloss Eltz, Gräflich Eltz'sche Güterverwaltung

Address: 6228 Eltville, Eltzer Hof, Rosenstrasse
Telephone: (06123) 4084

Location: On the riverfront in Eltville, right next to the community church.
How to get there: In the village, drive toward the Rhine. The building is easily recognized by its long Renaissance facade.

Points of interest: The estate buildings and mansion, parts dating from the sixteenth and seventeenth centuries; the period wine cellar.

History: The ancestral seat of the Counts of Eltz is the 1000-year-old Castle Eltz on the Moselle River. In 1744, the provost of Mainz Cathedral, Hugo Franz zu Eltz, repurchased the house in Eltville, which had been in the family from 1633 to 1671. The selection of Eltville as the family seat was not only determined by the quality of the vineyards, but also by its proximity to the residence of the imperial chancellor and electors of Mainz, whose political policies were greatly influenced by the family.

Terrain and soils: The vineyards cover 98 acres, of which 80% are on gently sloping, 4% on steeply sloping, and 16% on flat terrain. The soils are schist, quartzite, gravel, loess, loess-loam, and marl.

Vineyard names: Eltviller Taubenberg, Eltviller Langenstück, Eltviller Sonnenberg, Kiedricher Sandgrub, Rauenthaler Baiken, Rauenthaler Gehrn, Rauenthaler Wülfen, Rauenthaler Rothenberg, Rauenthaler Langenstück, Rüdesheimer Berg Roseneck, Rüdesheimer Bischofsberg.

Grape varieties: 88.4% Riesling, 9.1% Müller-Thurgau, 1.3% Scheurebe, 1.2% experimental varieties.

The wines: The wines are modern Rheingau Riesling types rather than the traditional Riesling types. They are appealing, elegant, and smooth. The distinguished Riesling fruitiness is emphasized. The Spätlese wines have a mature sweetness.

Estate specialties: The number of wines is about average. Auslese, Beerenauslese, and Trockenbeerenauslese wines are among the most distinguished representatives of the Rheingau Rieslings. Single bottles of older vintages are still available. The number of award-winning wines is very high; in the past six years, six special awards were received from the state government, and seven special awards were received from the federal government.

Label: It shows the coat of arms used by the family since the twelfth century. It is red and silver with the upper section of a golden lion rampant. The family colors of red and yellow are derived from the coat of arms and are used on the Eltz wine labels. The second label has a view of the mansion and was discontinued in 1971, having previously been used to indicate "sugared" or "enriched" wines.

Marketing: Sales made through wine brokers at the Kloster Eberbach wine fair and wine auction. A single price list is also issued. Discounts of up to 30% are granted to the trade; considerable quantities are exported.

Visits and tastings: By appointment, the estate buildings and cellars can be visited. The vineyards are not in the vicinity of the buildings. Wine tastings can be arranged; the scope and type of the tasting will be individually planned. English-speaking personnel available.

From my notebook: Elegant, well-balanced wines to meet modern tastes are produced here. The imposing buildings have a dignified atmosphere. The Rhine River on one side and the town center of Eltville (dating from the Middle Ages) on the other are very impressive. With the well-made wines, the traditional surroundings, and expert interpretation by members of the estate staff, the tastings are always worthwhile. The proprietor, Count Jakob zu Eltz, is extraordinarily well-versed in languages and viticulture. He is the president of the Rheingau Vintner Association.

ELTVILLE

Verwaltung der Staatsweingüter Eltville

Address: 6228 Eltville Schwalbacherstrasse 56–62, Postfach 169
Telephone: (06123) 4155 and 4156

Location: The offices and central winery are at the north edge of Eltville; seven separate estates are located between Assmannshausen, in the lower Rheingau, and Bensheim, on the (Hessische) Bergstrasse.

How to get there: Take the Wiesbaden-Rüdesheim autobahn to its end, driving through Martinsthal on the Rheingau Riesling Route, and enter Eltville from the north via Schwalbacher Strasse.

Points of interest: Kloster Eberbach, the former Cistercian monastery near Hattenheim, founded in 1135, an almost perfectly preserved medieval monastery; the monastery's *Kabinett* cellar and hospital cellar; the collection of old wine presses in the former lay-brothers refectory; the 79-acre Steinberg vineyard (2 km from Kloster Eberbach), laid out by the monks in the twelfth century—it is all of one piece and still surrounded by a high wall; the ruins of Ehrenfels Castle on the most beautiful part of Rüdesheim Hill (the steep Rüdesheimer Berg Schossberg vineyard) above the Binger Loch; the red-wine winery at the wine estate in Assmannshausen, with a vaulted barrel cellar; the impressive, steep Assmannshäuser Höllenberg vineyard; the Schloss Hochheim wine estate, with historic buildings and model plantings in the Hochheimer Domdechaney vineyards; the Bensheim/Heppenheim wine estate, with cellars in Bensheim and experimental plantings in Heppenheim.

History: The majority of the vineyards date from the monastic period (some of them from the twelfth century). They were ceded to the Duke of Nassau when secularized in 1803 and acquired in 1866 by the royal Prussian domain administration. Today the seven wine estates in the Rheingau and on the Bergstrasse, as well as the former monastery of Eberbach, are administered from Eltville and are subordinate to the Hessian Ministry of Agriculture and Environment, in Wiesbaden. Kloster Eberbach is now a state winery. Here wine auctions, wine fairs, state and federal wine judgings and the harvest thanksgiving of the Rheingau Vintners Association take place. The German Wine Academy and the Rheingau Weinkonvent meet here. During the summer months there are concerts of classical music.

Terrain and soils: With 482 acres (6 acres are planted with rootstock mother plants, and 8.2 acres are used for a vine nursery), the seven wine estates are, as a group, the largest wine producer in Germany. Almost two thirds of the area is gently sloping, about one third is steeply sloping, and a small portion is flat.

The soils vary from blue shale, in Assmannshausen, to loess-loam, on the Bergstrasse. The estates are: Assmannshausen (53.4 a.), Rüdesheim (58 a.), Hattenheim (35 a.), Steinberg (86.7 a.), Rauenthal (114.2), Schloss Hochheim (41.3 a), Bensheim/Heppenheim (77.6 a.), and Rebschule Insel Lorch (1.8 a.).

Vineyard names: Assmannshausen estate: Assmannshäuser Höllenberg (50.9 a.) and others.

Rüdesheim estate: Rüdesheimer Berg Schlossberg (21.3 a.), Rüdesheimer Berg Rottland (20 a.), Rüdesheimer Berg Roseneck (4.7 a.), Rüdesheimer Bishofsberg (5 a.), and others.

Hattenheim estate: Hattenheimer Engelmannsberg (21 a.), Hattenheimer Mannberg (3 a.), Erbacher Marcobrunn (8.9 a.), and others.

Steinberg estate: Steinberger (entire vineyard, 79.3 a.) and others.

Rauenthal estate: Rauenthaler Baiken (24.5 a.), Rauenthaler Gehrn (33.4 a.), Rauenthaler Wülfen (9.1 a.), Rauenthaler Langenstück (12.1 a.), Kiedricher Gräfenberg (3.5 a.), Eltviller Sonnenberg (2.5 a.), Eltviller Taubenberg (13.8 a.), and others.

Schloss Hochheim estate: Hochheimer Domdechaney (13.6 a.), Hochheimer Kirchenstück (7.4 a.), Hochheimer Stein (7.4 a.), Hochheimer Berg (3 a.), and others.

Bensheim/Heppenheim estate: Bensheimer Streichling (8.4 a.), Bensheimer Kalkgasse (5.2 a.), Schönberger Herrnwingert (entire vineyard, 20.3 a.), Heppenheimer Centgericht (entire vineyard, 36.6 a.), Heppenheimer Steinkopf (6.2 a.), and others.

The Grosslage names are Rüdesheimer Burgweg, Hattenheimer Deutelsberg, Rauenthaler Steinmächer, and Hochheimer Daubhaus.

Grape varieties: 74.6% Riesling, 10.5% Pinot Noir, 8.4% Müller-Thurgau, 6.5% miscellaneous.

The wines: The goal is to produce well-balanced and elegant wines that are mellow and exhibit the delicate Riesling fruit and acidity. As Rheingau wines, they have a great deal of backbone and body, and are suitable for lengthy storage. The range of characteristics is large, including spicy, flowery wines from Rüdesheim, full-bodied wines from Hochheim and Hattenheim, elegant and racy ones from Steinberg, fruity wines of Rauenthal, and fragrant, vigorous wines from the Bergstrasse.

Estate specialties: The ruby red Assmannshäuser Höllenberg Spätburgunder, with its slightly almond flavor and velvety elegance, is considered by the winery to be the aristocrat of the red wines and is a specialty of the establishment. The wide assortment of fine wines offered for auction at Kloster Eberbach is an impressive achievement of the seven estates. The 1970–71 Hochheimer Domdechaney Epiphany Eiswein brought $85 per bottle at auction, and an original bottle of 1895 Steinberger from the royal Prussian domain was sold for $1100. Single bottles of older vintages are treasured in the Kloster Eberbach cellar and are probably the greatest of their type in Germany. Wines of the latest five to seven vintages are offered in the price list and at the auction.

Label: The same version of the stylized domain eagle that dates back to Prussian times is used for all qualities. Wines auctioned at Kloster Eberbach have a special circular design on the label, with the words "Ersteigert im Kloster Eberbach."

Marketing: Through brokers at the Kloster Eberbach fair (in April) and wine auctions (in April and November). Also direct sales to consumers. There is only one price list; discounts are granted to the trade, restaurants, and wholesalers. The shipping costs, prepaid to the station of destination, are included in the prices shown on the list.

Visits and tastings: The Kloster Eberbach monastery can be visited from April to October between 10 A.M. and 5 P.M. By appointment, the Kloster Eberbach winery (telephone 06723-4228) will conduct seated tastings with 10 to 12 wines in the historic tasting room (up to 24 persons), the refectory (up to 120 persons), or the lay brothers' dormitory (up to 350 persons). Tastings of three wines can be held in the *Kabinett* cellar. The wineries at Assmannshausen (telephone 06722-2272) and Bensheim (telephone 06251-3107) and all estates will be pleased to receive visitors. English-speaking personnel available.

From my notebook: This wine domain, the largest in Germany, gives visitors interesting wines, information, and demonstrations, and also sponsors the famous Kloster Eberbach wine fairs and wine auctions. The monastery is a jewel set in magnificent country setting, and even the Rheingau visitor with little time should make a point to see it. In the two Kloster Eberbach wine restaurants, Pfortengaststätte and Klosterschänke (the manager is Tino Pfaff, telephone 06723-2821), excellent Steinberger wine may be ordered by the glass. An instructional and demonstration vineyard was recently opened.

RHEINGAU
Qualitätswein mit Prädikat
1971er
Steinberger
Riesling
AUSLESE
Erzeuger-Abfüllung – Amtl. Prüf.-Nr. 33050 003 72
Verwaltung der Staatsweingüter, Eltville

Qualitätswein RHEINGAU mit Prädikat
Freiherr Langwerth von Simmern Eltville
Hattenheimer Nussbrunnen
Erzeuger-Abfüllung
Riesling 1971er Riesling
A. P. Nr. 33045 005 72

VERBAND
DEUTSCHER
PRÄDIKATSWEIN-
VERSTEIGERER E.V.
Unsere Mitglieder besitzen
Lagen von Weltruf!

V
D   P
V

QUALITÄTSWEIN
MIT PRÄDIKAT
aus eigener Erzeugung eines
unserer Mitgliedsbetriebe.
A.P.Nr.
40 083 002 72

Domdechant Wernersches Weingut
seit 1780 im Familienbesitz
1971er
Hochheimer Domdechaney
Riesling Spätlese
ERZEUGERABFÜLLUNG
R H E I N G A U

ELTVILLE

Freiherrlich Langwerth von Simmern'sches Rentamt

Address: 6228 Eltville, Langwerther Hof, Postfach 15
Telephone: (06123) 2497

Location: The offices and cellars are in the oldest part of Eltville, charmingly situated near the Rhine River, the electoral castle, and the Eltviller Rheinberg vineyard.

How to get there: Take the autobahn from Wiesbaden and then route B-42 toward Rüdesheim.

Points of interest: The pleasant estate buildings in a well-tended park; the Renaissance manor; the Gothic-style Stockheimer Hof; various half-timbered houses; an old wine press dated 1775; the well; the imaginative tasting room; the barrel cellar.

History: Since 1464 the wine estate has been in the possession of the Barons Langwerth von Simmern. The Hattenheimer Castle, today a part of the estate, dates from 1118.

Terrain and soils: The 93.9 acres of vineyards are mostly on gently sloping terrain; 10% are on steeply sloping terrain. The soils include gravel, schist, quartzite, loess, loess-loam, clay, and marl.

Vineyard names: Eltviller Sonnenberg (14.9 a.), Eltviller Taubenberg (2.5 a.), Eltviller Langenstück (6.2 a.), Eltviller Rheinberg (2.5 a.), Rauenthaler Baiken (3.7 a.), Rauenthaler Rothenberg (1.2 a.), Erbacher Marcobrunn (3.7 a.), Hattenheimer Schützenhaus (24.7 a.), Hattenheimer Mannberg (14.8 a.), Hattenheimer Nussbrunnen (16 a.), Hochheimer Reichesthal (3.7 a.).

Grape varieties: 90% Riesling, 7% Müller-Thurgau and Scheurebe, 3% new varieties.

The wines: The wines are produced with robust character to increase their longevity, and they have well-balanced acidity. In-

dividual barrel aging makes the assortment particularly interest-ing. Thanks to progressive cellar technology, the wines are clean and well-made.

Estate specialties: Rheingau Riesling at its very best. A high pro-portion of fine and award-winning wines. Single bottles·of older vintages for particular occasions are still available.

Label: The unusual label design is more than 100 years old. In the midst of rich decoration, it features the family coat of arms. Qualities are also indicated by the neck label and the capsule.

Marketing: At the Kloster Eberbach wine-sales fairs and wine auc-tions, as well as through brokers and by direct sale. There is one price list; the trade is granted discounts.

Visits and tastings: The estate buildings and cellar can be visited by appointment. Tastings in the tasting hall (decorated with Delft tiles) can be arranged for up to 30 persons. English-speaking personnel available.

From my notebook: The Langwerther Hof is a gem in the medi-eval center of Eltville. One of the oldest wine estates in the Rheingau region, where tradition and modern technical thinking are combined. The longevity of those wines speaks for itself: the 1961, 1962, and 1963 vintages are still fresh and vigorous.

HOCHHEIM

Domdechant Werner'sches Weingut

Address: 6203 Hochheim, Rathausstrasse 30
Telephone: (06146) 2008

Location: The manor, visible from afar, is on the edge of the vine covered hills of Hochheim at the village entrance in the direction of Mainz.

How to get there: Take the Wiesbaden-Darmstadt autobahn, turning off at Hochheim, and drive 500 m (547 yd) to the edge of the village.

Points of interest: The wide vista from the manor overlooking the entire Rhine-Main area toward the town of Mainz, the Odenwald, Rheinhessen, Hunsrück, and Taunus.

History: In 1780, a Mainz merchant, Johann Baptista Werner, bought the Hochheim vineyard from Count York. After his death it was inherited by his son, the famous dean of the Mainz Cathedral, Dr. Franz Werner. Under his name it is owned today by the seventh generation of the Michel family. Complete estate records covering the wine harvests since 1780 mention the first wine auction in 1795.

Terrain and soils: The 32 acres of vineyard are all on southern slopes, which contain different types of soil because of the former river terraces. The soils include gravel, loamy sand, clay, and limestone.

Vineyard names: Hochheimer Domdechaney, Hochheimer Kirchenstück, Hochheimer Stielweg, Hochheimer Hölle, Hochheimer Sommerheil, Hochheimer Stein, Hochheimer Hofmeister, Hochheimer Reichesthal, Hochheimer Berg.

Grape varieties: 90% Riesling, 8% Müller-Thurgau, 2% Ruländer.

The wines: Thanks to the deep soils, the wines have a distinctive character with much fruitiness and ripeness.

Estate specialties: Special attention is given to the production of Auslese wines; a record-breaking Trockenbeerenauslese was produced in 1951, which had an Öchsle rating of 247° (the minimum Öchsle rating for a Trockenbeerenauslese is 150°). Numerous awards have been won at state and national wine judgings. Dry wines and wines suitable for diabetics are also included in the list.

Label: Since the beginning of the century the label with the estate coat of arms has remained unaltered.

Marketing: Through brokers at auctions of the Rheingau Wine Estates Association in Kloster Eberbach. There is also a price list for small sales to private clients. Considerable exports.

Visits and tastings: Because this is purely a family business, visits and wine tastings are possible only in special cases and by appointment. English-speaking personnel available.

From my notebook: Individual barrel and small-cask aging is still practiced in this well-managed family establishment. A series of wines is offered for a diversity of tastes and of various vintages. There is a high proportion of fine wines.

HOCHHEIM

Weingut der Stadt Frankfurt am Main

Address: 6203 Hochheim, Aichgasse 11
Telephone: (06146) 2374

Location: The buildings are at the south edge of town, directly above the most famous vineyards in Hochheim.

How to get there: Drive on the autobahn from Wiesbaden toward Darmstadt and turn off at Hochheim.

Points of interest: The impressive view of the unbroken rows of vineyards in front of the buildings.

History: Originally a six-acre wine estate belonging to the Carmelite convent in Frankfurt. It was ceded to the city of Frankfurt during secularization in 1803. Since 1904, additional purchases of vineyards have extended the estate to its current size.

Terrain and soils: The 60.5 acres of vineyards have wide row spacing and are on gently sloping terrain. The soils are loess, loess-loam, clay, and marl.

Vineyard names: Hochheimer Domdechaney (2.5 a.), Hochheimer Kirchenstück (7.4 a.), Hochheimer Stielweg (12.4 a.), Hochheimer Hölle (9.9 a.), Hochheimer Stein (7.4 a.), Hochheimer Hofmeister (7.4 a.), Hochheimer Reichesthal (5 a.), Hochheimer Sommerheil (2.5 a.), Hochheimer Berg (2.5 a.), Frankfurter Lohrberger Hang (3 a.).

The Grosslage name is Hochheimer Daubhaus.

Grape varieties: 83% Riesling, 8% Müller-Thurgau, 9% miscellaneous.

The wines: Mainly Hochheim wines, meaning they are well-rounded, full Riesling wines with a smokiness to the flavor that delicately emphasizes the subtle Riesling aroma.

Estate specialties: Spicy, surprisingly elegant Gewürztraminer and Morio-Muscat wines. The Frankfurt Lohrberg vineyard, located between the suburb of Seckbach and the northeast boundary of the town, is an attempt to maintain the last of a once-extensive area of vineyards just outside the gates of the former free imperial city of Frankfurt. *Spritzig* Riesling wines from grapes grown on heavy loam soil are a specialty of Frankfurt.

Label: It features an old etching of Hochheim with the vineyards. It also shows the coat of arms of the free imperial city of Frankfurt: a white eagle with a crown, on a red background.

Marketing: Direct from the estate and from the sales room in the Frankfurt town hall (Römer). There is only one list. A discount is granted to wholesalers.

Visits and tastings: By appointment, the buildings, cellar, and vineyards can be visited. Tastings may also be arranged.

From my notebook: There is a magnificent view of the vineyards and countryside toward the Main River, Mainz, the Odenwald, and the Hunsrück. A modern tasting room is suitable for large groups. The administrator, Mr. Dietrich, an agronomist, is an excellent interpreter of his well-made wines.

HOCHHEIM

Weingut Königin Victoria Berg

Address: 6203 Hochheim, Mainweg 2
Telephone: (06146) 5389

Location: In Hochheim-Süd
How to get there: Take the Wiesbaden-Darmstadt autobahn, turn off at Hochheim and continue 2 km.
Points of interest: The Queen Victoria memorial on the Königin Victoria Berg vineyard, 3 km east of Hochheim.
History: In 1846, the wine estate owner acquired the uncultivated land near the so-called "Dechantenruhe" and turned it into a vineyard. He succeeded in persuading Queen Victoria of England to visit this vineyard in 1850, and she granted him permission to bestow her name on it. In 1854, he erected a splendid memorial furnished with English Gothic turrets and an inscription commemorating the event. Rhine wines are often called "hock" in England—the word supposedly originating from Queen Victoria's preference for Hochheim wines. In 1918, the estate proprietor, Josef Neus, of Ingelheim, acquired the vineyard. Today it is managed by his son-in-law, Arndt-Richard Hupfeld.
Terrain and soils: The 15-acre vineyard is on gently sloping terrain and has loess and loess-loam soils.
Vineyard names: Königin Victoria Berg (entire vineyard)
Grape varieties: 100% Riesling.
The wines: Robust, racy, traditional Riesling wines that are mellow and well-balanced with little residual sugar.
Estate specialties: The Königin Victoria Berg Riesling.
Label: It has an original oval shape and features the Queen Victoria memorial in a wreath of grapes and vine leaves.
Marketing: Through the Neus Company in Ingelheim, and through

the wine estate Hupfeld Erben in Oestrich-Winkel. A large proportion is exported to England.

Visits and tastings: By appointment, the vineyards and the monument can be visited, and wine tastings can be held in the vaulted cellar of the estate or even on the Königin Victoria Berg itself. English-speaking personnel available.

From my notebook: Arranging for Queen Victoria to visit the vineyard was a clever idea that succeeded admirably. Even today this small estate is given great preference in English wine literature. J. Neus has additional vineyards in Ingelheim, where the main winery is, and also manages the Fürstlich Isenburg-Birstein'sche Weingut in Hochheim.

Rheinhessen

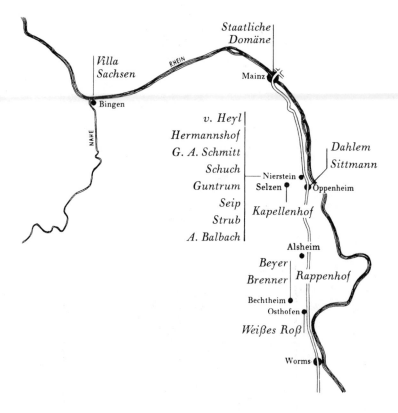

Staatliche
Domäne

Villa
Sachsen

RHEIN

Mainz

Bingen

NAHE

v. Heyl
Hermannshof
G. A. Schmitt
Schuch
Guntrum
Seip
Strub
A. Balbach

Nierstein
Selzen

Dahlem
Sittmann

Oppenheim

Kapellenhof

Alsheim

Beyer
Brenner

Rappenhof

Bechtheim

Osthofen

Weißes Roß

Worms

Weingut Villa Sachsen

Address: 6530 Bingen, Mainzer Strasse 184
Telephone: (06721) 5266

Location: The buildings and winery are in a charming country setting on a slope overlooking the Rhine River below the Rochus Chapel.

How to get there: Drive from Bingen toward Mainz as far as the Saint Ursula winery. A large wrought iron gate bears the words "Villa Sachsen."

Points of interest: The well-tended park with the administration buildings, resembling a forest manor; the magnificent view of the Binger Loch, Rüdesheim Hill, and the Rheingau; the old vaulted cellar with its rows of barrels.

History: The manor house, built by a Heilbronn nobleman in 1843, changed owners several times. It is the locale of an early novel, *The Country House on the Rhine,* published in 1869. In 1879, it was purchased as a country estate by Prince Friedrich Wilhelm von Hessen. About the turn of the century it was acquired by a Leipzig manufacturer, Dr. Berger, who developed it into a model wine estate, where some early wine auctions were held. Dr. Berger was the person who gave the estate the name Villa Sachsen. In 1963, it was acquired by the St. Ursula Weingut and Weinkellerei GmbH.

Terrain and soils: The 74 acres of vineyards are on steep slopes. The soils include quartzite (of which picturesque Rochus Hill is formed), loess, and loess-loam.

Vineyard names: Binger Scharlachberg (24.7 a.), Binger Kirchberg (19.8 a.), Binger Schlossberg-Schwätzerchen (12.4 a.), Binger Osterberg, Binger Kapellenberg, Binger Rosengarten.

Grape varieties: 55% Riesling, 20% Sylvaner, 15% Müller-Thurgau, 10% miscellaneous.

The wines: The individually barrel-aged Riesling wines are vigorous and almost tannic. The Sylvaner wines are appealing and charming; the Müller-Thurgaus are fruity and mild with a delicate acidity.

Estate specialties: Wines for diabetics.

Label: It features a picture of the estate buildings with the Rochus Hill. Up to and including Kabinett wines the basic color of the label is ivory, and from Spätlese upward the label is white with a gold edge.

Marketing: Mainly sold to the trade and restaurants. Exports have become more important during the last few years.

Visits and tastings: The cellars can be visited and wines tasted only by prior appointment.

From my notebook: For those who like to walk, a stroll to the neighboring Rochus Chapel and the Goethe-Ruhe memorial (commemorating Goethe's amusing description of the Rochus festival) is interesting. Well-trained personnel are available for tastings, when their duties in the St. Ursula winery (Goldener Oktober) attached to the estate permit.

MAINZ

Verwaltung der Staatlichen Weinbaudomänen Mainz

Address: 6500 Mainz, Ernst-Ludwig-Strasse 9
Telephone: (06131) 24680

Location: The offices and winery are in the center of the city.
How to get there: Drive through Kaiserstrasse and turn off at the Christuskirche (a church).

Point of interest: The well-tended vineyards with their extensive experimental program.

History: Founded in 1900 by the former grand duchy of Hesse to serve as a model vineyard. Today the estate is owned by the Rhineland-Palatinate state government.

Terrain and soils: The domain has five separate estates located in Bingen (37 a.), Bodenheim (32.1 a.), Nackenheim (34.6 a.), Nierstein (42 a.), and Oppenheim (44.5 a.). Of the total 190.2 acres of vineyards, 55% are on steeply sloping terrain and 45% are suitable for mechanical cultivation. The soils include quartzite, schist, sandstone, loamy sand, clay, and marl.

Vineyard names: Binger Scharlachberg, Binger Schlossberg-Schwätzerchen, Binger Kirchberg, Binger Osterberg, Bodenheimer Reichsritterstift (entire vineyard), Bodenheimer Hoch, Bodenheimer Silberberg, Bodenheimer Heitersbrünnchen, Bodenheimer Leidhecke, Nackenheimer Rothenberg, Nackenheimer Engelsberg, Niersteiner Ölberg, Niersteiner Glöck (entire vineyard), Oppenheimer Herrenberg, Oppenheimer Sackträger, Dienheimer Herrenberg, Dienheimer Kreuz, Dienheimer Paterhof, Dienheimer Siliusbrunnen, Dienheimer Tafelstein.

The Grosslage names are Niersteiner Auflangen and Niersteiner Rehbach.

Grape varieties: 39% Riesling, 32% Sylvaner, 13% Müller-Thurgau, 2.5% Scheurebe, 2% Ruländer, 2% Weissburgunder, 1.5% Gewürztraminer, 0.5% Morio-Muskat, 7.5% experimental varieties.

The wines: The good vineyards and soil conditions produce full-bodied, mellow wines with a mild, typically Rheinhessen character.

Estate specialties: A high proportion of fine wines.

Label: It is a vertically oriented rhombus that features the coat of arms of the Rhineland-Palatinate.

Marketing: The estate is a member of the Zentralkellerei Rheinischer Winzergenossenschaften Gau-Bickelheim (the Central Winery of the Rhine Vintners Cooperative). Sales are exclusively through this organization to dealers. The administration in Mainz sells to consumers on a small scale.

Visits and tastings: By appointment, the vineyards may be visited
and tastings can be arranged.

From my notebook: Under its director, Dr. Kern, this state wine
domain has set an example in the planting of new varieties and
experimenting with new methods of cultivation. Visits and wine
tastings are highly recommended for persons interested in new
grape varieties.

NIERSTEIN

Weingut Bürgermeister Anton Balbach Erben

Address: 6505 Nierstein 1, Mainzer Strasse 64
Telephone: (06133) 5585

Location: The estate buildings, winery, and offices are directly on
the Rhine River.

How to get there: Take route B-9 south from Mainz or north from
Worms.

Points of interest: Old sculptured casks hanging on the walls of the
large, vaulted cellar; the magnificent view of the Rhine River
and St. Kilian Church near the Niersteiner Kranzberg vineyard.

History: According to records, members of the Balbach family
have been active in viticulture for 14 generations (since 1650).
They created the excellent Im Pettenthal vineyard from a slope
that was still wooded in the nineteenth century. Today the estate is run by the Bohn family.

Terrain and soils: Of 44.5 acres of vineyards, 30% are on steeply
sloping, 20% on gently sloping, and 50% on flat terrain. The
soil is red schist.

Vineyard names: Niersteiner Pettenthal, Niersteiner Hipping, Niersteiner Ölberg, Niersteiner Kranzberg, Niersteiner Rosenberg,
Niersteiner Klostergarten, Niersteiner Bildstock.

The Grosslage names are Niersteiner Rehbach, Niersteiner Auflangen, Niersteiner Spiegelberg.

Grape varieties: 70% Riesling, 15% Sylvaner, 10% Müller-Thurgau, 5% Gewürztraminer and Ruländer.

The wines: Very well-balanced, with a ripe sweetness. Vigorous rather than mild.

Estate specialties: The estate attempts to produce typical Riesling wines. The proportion of Prädikat wines, mainly Ausleses, is very high.

Label: It features the family coat of arms: three palm branches over a stream.

Marketing: Sold to the trade, brokers, and a limited number of private customers. Large export business.

Visits and tastings: By appointment, visitors are welcomed in small groups of up to 20 persons. English-speaking personnel available.

From my notebook: A well-managed family business operated by Mr. and Mrs. Friedrich Bohn and their son, who studied viticulture at the Geisenheim Institute. Persons speaking only French or English will have no communication problem while visiting this estate.

NIERSTEIN

Weingut Freiherr Heyl zu Herrnsheim Mathildenhof

Address: 6505 Nierstein, Langgasse 3
Telephone: (06133) 5120

Location: The estate buildings, with the offices and winery, are in the center of the village. The buildings and the surrounding 5 acres of parks, gardens, and vineyards are enclosed by an old wall.

How to get there: Drive 16 km south from Mainz on route B-9 toward Worms. In the village itself take route B-420 to Wilhelm Strasse and follow Wilhelm Strasse to Langgasse.

Points of interest: The manor, the oldest part of which dates from the sixteenth century; the Landsknecht cellar, serving as the tasting room and bar; the experimental vine plantings in the estate gardens.

History: Acquired at the beginning of this century by Baron von Heyl, and extended to its present size in the course of time. The property was inherited in 1964 by Isa von Weymarn (nee Von Meding). Today Peter von Weymarn manages the estate.

Terrain and soils: Of the 49.5 acres of vineyards, 50% are on steeply sloping, 30% on gently sloping, and 20% on flat terrain. The soils are red schist, sandstone, loess, and loess-loam.

Vineyard names: Niersteiner Brudersberg (entire vineyard), Niersteiner Pettenthal, Niersteiner Hipping, Niersteiner Ölberg, Niersteiner Heiligenbaum, Niersteiner Orbel, Niersteiner Schloss Schwabsburg, Niersteiner Rosenberg, Niersteiner Findling, Niersteiner Bildstock, Niersteiner Kranzberg.

The Grosslage names are Niersteiner Rehbach, Niersteiner Auflangen, and Niersteiner Spiegelberg.

Grape varieties: 60% Riesling, 20% Müller-Thurgau, 15% Sylvaner, 5% Ruländer, Weissburgunder, Traminer, and test plots for new varieties, such as Scheurebe, Kerner, and Faber.

The wines: Individual barrel aging is still practiced here, and great efforts are made to produce wines typical of the district. They are clean and fruity, and have subtle nuances because of their well-balanced residual sugar.

Estate specialties: Rieslings that are typical of Rheinhessen, from simple Qualitätsweins to fine wines of the best qualities. A particular specialty is Mathildenhöfer Schoppen, a robust carafe wine in liter bottles, and Mathildenhöfer Sekt, a sparkling wine made from the estate wines. Single bottles of older vintages are still available. The price list includes a high proportion of award-winning wines.

Label: It was designed in 1893 by J. Sattler, a well-known commercial artist and book illustrator in his day, and has remained unaltered to the present time. It shows a cellar-master in a cowl-

like robe bearing the insignia of the Heylschen family. Fine
wines from Auslese upward are distinguished by a heraldic label
carrying the combined coats of arms of the Heyl and Ysenburg
families.

Marketing: Well represented in high-class restaurants and hotels.
two lists are issued, one for the trade and one for consumers.
The estate offers wines at fine-wine auctions.

Visits and tastings: By appointment, the cellars and experimental
vine plantings in the estate garden can be visited. Wine tastings
standing in the cellar, sitting in the tasting room (8–10 persons), and in the tasting hall (up to 40 persons) can be held
by arrangement. English-speaking personnel available.

From my notebook: The well-tended estate complex and cellars
have a dignified appearance. The estate promotes customer relations, and wines are introduced with informative background
details during the tastings. As an example, the estate holds a
large tasting on one Saturday in September, and all the wines on
the list are sampled. All customers of the estate are invited.

NIERSTEIN

Weingut Franz Karl Schmitt Hermannshof

Address: 6505 Nierstein, Mainzer Strasse 48
Telephone: (06133) 5525

Location: The offices and buildings, surrounded by a large garden,
are situated on the Rhine River.

How to get there: Drive 20 km from Mainz on route B-9 toward
Worms.

Points of interest: The cellar vaulting; the collection of old drinking vessels and old pictures of Nierstein.

History: In 1549, Jost Schmitt purchased his first vineyard in
Nierstein. Since then the establishment has been the property

of the Schmitt family. The villa was built by the energetic Mathilde Schmitt in 1924–25.

Terrain and soils: Of the 74.1 acres of vineyards, 50% are on flat, 30% on gently sloping, and 20% on steeply sloping terrain. The soils are mainly red schist, loess, and loess-loam. The red schist soil has given Nierstein a worldwide reputation.

Vineyard names: Niersteiner Hipping, Niersteiner Pettenthal, Niersteiner Orbel, Niersteiner Kranzberg, Niersteiner Ölberg, Niersteiner Zehnmorgen (entire vineyard).

Grape varieties: 65% Riesling, 20% Sylvaner, 7% Müller-Thurgau, 4% Ruländer, 2% Gewürztraminer, 2% miscellaneous.

The wines: The wines are mellow and well made. They have an attractive fruitiness, and their pleasant acidity makes them harmonious and elegant.

Estate specialties: In the *Kabinett* cellar of the estate is a small wine museum containing a few bottles of great vintages back to 1889. The Riesling wines are treated as a specialty in every quality category up to and including Trockenbeerenauslese.

Label: It features the family coat of arms, the dove in a nest being the old family symbol, which is also branded on the corks.

Marketing: Principally through the trade and brokers. A few direct sales. This is purely an estate business, and only wines produced from the estate's grapes are stocked.

Visits and tastings: By previous appointment, the buildings, cellar, and vineyards can be visited and wine tastings arranged.

From my notebook: A model estate, both viticulturally and vini-culturally. As it is a family business, the visitors are greeted by the proprietor, Hermann Franz Schmitt, and his sons, Franz Karl and Dr. Hans Rudolf Schmitt, lending the visit a personal touch. If at all possible, one should visit the estate's well-tended vineyards.

NIERSTEIN

Gustav Adolf Schmitt'sche Weingut

Address: 6505 Nierstein, Wilhelmstrasse 2
Telephone: (06133) 5151

How to get there: Drive from Mainz toward Worms for 16 km on route B-9.

Points of interest: The carved barrels; the modern bottle storage; the old, wooden cellar; the special old-wine cellar.

History: The estate has been family property since 1618. In 1919, a wine wholesale and export business was added.

Terrain and soils: The 123.5 acres of vineyards are mainly on flat and gently sloping terrain. The soils include red schist, loess, and loess-loam.

Vineyard names: Niersteiner Pettenthal, Niersteiner Heiligenbaum, Niersteiner Ölberg, Niersteiner Hipping, Niersteiner Bildstock, Niersteiner Paterberg, Oppenheimer Herrenberg, Dienheimer Tafelstein.

The Grosslage names are Oppenheimer Krötenbrunnen, Niersteiner Rehbach, and Niersteiner Auflangen.

Grape varieties: 50% Sylvaner, 25% Riesling, 20% Müller-Thurgau, 5% experimental varieties and miscellaneous types.

The wines: Pleasing, well-balanced Rheinhessen wines with a great deal of substance and character, but full and long lasting in the mouth.

Estate specialties: Single bottles of older vintages are still available. The price list contains a high proportion of fine wines, with vintages extending back to the 1953 Trockenbeerenauslese. The old vintages and great wines are also offered in half bottles. A number of wines have gained awards at home and abroad.

Label: The label for estate wines features the family coat of arms with the words "Weinbau seit 1618" (wine production since 1618) and "Erzeugerabfüllung" (estate bottled). The hammer, horseshoe, and horses indicate the original ancestral trade. The imperial eagle refers to the Nierstein coat of arms. The family ancestors were formerly electoral tax collectors, who collected and looked after the wines to be supplied to the emperor.

Marketing: Sold in Germany and in other countries by the estate's own representatives.

Visits and tastings: By appointment, the buildings, vineyards, and cellars can be visited. Wine tastings are given only by appointment.

From my notebook: This large estate, with its affiliated shipping firm, is of interest mainly to groups of persons already involved in the wine business. A staff of well-trained experts is available to give advice.

NIERSTEIN

Weingut Geschwister Schuch

Address: 6505 Nierstein, Oberdorfstrasse 22
Telephone: (06133) 5652

Location: In the center of the town near the Sankt-Martins-Kirche (a church).

How to get there: Take route B-9 from Mainz toward Worms, and in Nierstein take the main road through the marketplace toward Schwabsburg.

1973er **Rheinheſſen**

Amtl. Prüf.-Nr. 4 382 093 21 74

Nierſteiner Brudersberg
Riesling Spätlese
QUALITÄTSWEIN MIT PRÄDIKAT · ERZEUGERABFÜLLUNG
Weingut Freiherr Heyl zu Herrnsheim · Nierſtein a. Rh.

Weingut Geſchwiſter Schuch
Nierſtein am Rhein

Qualitätswein mit Prädikat
1971er
Nierſteiner Hipping
Riesling Spätlese
A. P. Nr. 4 382 331 373
Erzeugerabfüllung

Weinbergsbeſitz in Nierſtein Oppenheim und Dienheim

GUNTRUM

FAMILIENWAPPEN VERLIEHEN
ANNO 1545

DURCH KAISERLICHEN WAPPENBRIEF
DEN 31. MAI

Oppenheimer Sackträger
Riesling Auslese
Qualitätswein mit Prädikat
A. P. Nr. 4 907 187 81 72

ERZEUGER-ABFÜLLUNG **G** RHEINHESSEN
WEINGUT LOUIS GUNTRUM NIERSTEIN AM RHEIN

Points of interest: The tasting cellar, with old drinking vessels; the pleasant tasting room.

History: The estate was founded by Friedrich Schuch in 1817, and it has been in the family since then. The current proprietor's mother, Elisabeth Günther (nee Schuch), was the last of the Schuch family. With Diether Günther as owner, the estate is today in the possession of the sixth generation of the Schuch-Günther family.

Terrain and soils: Of the 39.5 acres of vineyards, 60% are on flat, 20% on gently sloping, and 20% on steeply sloping terrain. The soils are red schist, sandstone, loess, and loess-loam.

Vineyard names: Niersteiner Hipping, Niersteiner Ölberg, Niersteiner Spiegelberg, Niersteiner Orbel, Oppenheimer Sackträger, Dienheimer Falkenberg.

The Grosslage names are Niersteiner Rehbach and Niersteiner Auflangen.

Grape varieties: 35% Riesling, 25% Sylvaner, 10% Scheurebe, 8% Müller-Thurgau, 4% Ruländer, 18% miscellaneous varieties including Freisamer, Kerner, Huxel, Morio-Muskat, and others.

The wines: Mellow wines, characteristic of Rheinhessen, that are both well balanced and clean.

Estate specialties: The estate attempts to individually develop and age each wine according to the variety of grape used in the wine. Many fine and award-winning wines. Individual bottles of older vintages, as well as St. Nicholas Day and Eiswein rarities, are available.

Label: It features the seal of the village of Nierstein and has remained unaltered since the end of the nineteenth century.

Marketing: Sold to restaurants, the trade, and directly to private customers.

Visits and tastings: By appointment, the vineyards and cellar can be visited and wine tastings arranged.

From my notebook: A well-managed family business, which is prepared to accommodate visitors. The explanations given during the tastings are instructive, and Mr. Günther gives regular wine seminars if requested. The wines, with their vigorous character, are interesting and worthy of note.

NIERSTEIN

Weingut Louis Guntrum

Address: 6505 Nierstein, Rheinallee 57
Telephone: (06133) 5101

Location: The offices, buildings, and cellars are at the southern end
of Nierstein, directly on the Rhine, between the sloping vineyards and the river. There are also wine presses and a fermenting cellar in Oppenheim (located at Rathofstrasse 25).

How to get there: Drive from Mainz toward Worms for 16 km on
route B-9.

Points of interest: The large modern cellars; the impressive view
over the Rhine River which passes close to the building; the
charming Niersteiner Hölle vineyard, on the hill.

History: The business was founded in 1824 by Louis Philipp Guntrum, a cooper from Bensheim, as an inn and post station
called Zur Sonne. After the turn of the century the business was
centered in Rheinhessen, and the properties in Nierstein and
Oppenheim were developed. In the wine business the fourth
generation is today represented by Hermann and Lorenz, and
the fifth generation is represented by Hans-Joachim and Peter
Louis.

Terrain and soils: The estate controls a total of 148.3 acres. Of
the 128.5 acres of vineyards, 35% are on steeply sloping terrain, and the rest are on flat and gently sloping terrain. The
soils are red schist, sandstone, loess, and loess-loam.

Vineyard names: Niersteiner Findling, Niersteiner Ölberg, Nier-
steiner Pettenthal, Niersteiner Hipping, Niersteiner Klostergarten, Niersteiner Heiligenbaum, Niersteiner Orbel, Niersteiner
Paterberg, Niersteiner Hölle, Niersteiner Rosenberg, Oppenheimer Schützenhütte, Oppenheimer Schloss, Oppenheimer
Sackträger, Oppenheimer Herrenberg, Oppenheimer Kreuz,
Oppenheimer Herrengarten, Dienheimer Falkenberg, Dien-

heimer Tafelstein, Dienheimer Paterhof, Nackenheimer Rothenberg.

The Grosslage names are Niersteiner Rehbach, Niersteiner
Auflangen, Niersteiner Spiegelberg, and Oppenheimer Güldenmorgen.

Grape varieties: 30% Riesling, 25% Sylvaner, 25% Müller-
Thurgau, 9% Ruländer, 11% Scheurebe, Kerner, Gewürz-
traminer, Rieslaner, Perle, Morio-Muskat, Weissburgunder,
Siegerrebe, Bacchus, and Huxelrebe.

The wines: Individual processing guarantees typical representation
of grape varieties from each vineyard. The combination of
traditional and modern cellar technology produces clear and
well-balanced wines.

Estate specialties: Fine wines.

Label: The label features the family coat of arms, which was
granted in 1545. The word "Guntrum" is in large letters at the
very top of the label.

Marketing: Sold mainly to the wholesale trade. Considerable exports. A special event at the estate is the traditional May tasting,
at which the wines of the previous year are introduced.

Visits and tastings: By appointment, groups of up to 25 persons
can visit the winery during business hours. Wine tastings, individually compiled within reasonable cost limits, can be held
by arrangement. English-speaking personnel available.

From my notebook: The tours and tastings are very informative.
The friendly owners give careful attention to their establishment and its highly developed export business.

NIERSTEIN

Weingut Winzermeister Heinrich Seip, Kurfürstenhof

Address: 6505 Nierstein
Telephone: (06133) 5550

Location: In the middle of the town, near the Martinskirche (a church) on the Fronhof square.

Points of interest: The old manor, preserved as a national monument; the garden in front, with its parklike trees; the cellar with the impressive cruciform vaulting; the old press-house, which is suitable for wine tastings up to 100 persons; the wine-tasting hall (the Rittersaal) and the small wine tasting room; the original office furniture made of barrels.

History: The origin of the Kurfürstenhof is said to go back to a Roman estate that later became a Franconian royal residence and entered the possession of the Palatinate electors in 1375. In 1817, it became private property, and it was acquired in 1950 by the father of Heinrich Seip, the present proprietor. The Seip family is an old Nierstein vintner family.

Terrain and soils: Of the 74.1 acres of vineyards, 70% are on flat and gently sloping terrain, and the rest are on steeply sloping terrain. The soils include red schist, sandstone, limestone, marl, loess, and loess-loam.

Vineyard names: Niersteiner Paterberg, Niersteiner Bildstock, Niersteiner Kirchplatte, Niersteiner Findling, Niersteiner Klostergarten, Niersteiner Rosenberg, Niersteiner Pettenthal, Niersteiner Hipping, Niersteiner Kranzberg, Niersteiner Ölberg, Niersteiner Heiligenbaum, Niersteiner Schloss Schwabsburg, Niersteiner Orbel, Niersteiner Goldene Luft (entire vineyard), Oppenheimer Schloss, Dienheimer Tafelstein, Dienheimer Kreuz, Dienheimer Falkenberg, Nachenheimer Engelsberg.

The Grosslage names are Niersteiner Gutes Domtal, Niersteiner

Spiegelberg, Niersteiner Rehbach, Niersteiner Auflangen, Oppenheimer Krötenbrunnen, Dienheimer Güldenmorgen, and Nackenheimer Spiegelberg.

Grape varieties: 30% Sylvaner, 20% Müller-Thurgau, 15% Riesling, 25% Scheurebe, Kerner, Gewürztraminer, Weissburgunder, Freisamer, Ehrenfelser, Ruländer, Huxelrebe, Faber, Kanzler, Veltliner, and 10% experimental varieties such as Optima, Ortega, Bacchus, Reichensteiner, Az-4612, Az-4701.

The wines: The many types of grapes produce interesting wines. Some of the new varieties are used for increasing the bouquet of the estate's wines through blending. The character of the wine is harmoniously complemented by moderate residual sweetness.

Estate specialties: New and little-known varieties are a specialty of this estate. Heinrich Seip also succeeds in producing Eisweins almost every year. The estate has won many national and international awards.

Label: It features the coat of arms of the elector Karl Philipp, who rebuilt the Kurfürstenhof in 1722, and the family coat of arms of the present proprietor.

Marketing: Two price lists are issued: one for the trade and one for consumers. All direct consumer sales are transacted at the estate. A portion of the wine is sold at the auction of the Nierstein Wine Estate Owners Association. Heinrich Seip is particularly proud that the wines from the Niersteiner Goldene Luft vineyard are bought by the White House, in Washington, D.C.

Visits and tastings: By appointment, instructive tours of the buildings, cellar, and vineyard are conducted. Wine tastings are given in an original and amusing way, including an occasional program of folklore, and can be arranged for groups of up to 100 persons. English-speaking personnel available.

From my notebook: "The Kurfürstenhof is a national monument. The owner has yet to become one," say the people in Nierstein. Heinrich Seip informs and entertains his visitors with inventiveness and originality. The performance of the "Niersteiner Weinnasen" adds an almost carnival character to the wine tastings, and is a humorous warmly recommended evening's entertainment at a reasonable price. Try to visit this estate before Mr. Seip actually *is* declared a national monument.

NIERSTEIN

Weingut J. u. H. A. Strub

Address: 6505 Nierstein, Rheinstrasse 42, Postfach 11
Telephone: (06133) 5649

Location: In the middle of the town, near the marketplace.

How to get there: Take route B-9 from Mainz toward Worms.

Points of interest: The old half-timbered house; the "generation" barrel in the wine cellar.

History: For generations the family, which settled in Nierstein in the seventeenth century, has been in viticulture. The owner today is Rheinhart Strub.

Terrain and soils: The Erbhof Ulfenhof and Erbhof Chattenhof vineyards have more than 42 acres of vines on steeply sloping, gently sloping, and flat terrain. The soils are red schist, sandstone, loess, and loess-loam.

Vineyard names: Niersteiner Hipping, Niersteiner Ölberg, Niersteiner Heiligenbaum, Niersteiner Orbel, Niersteiner Brückchen, Niersteiner Paterberg, Niersteiner Bildstock, Dienheimer Falkenberg.

The Grosslage names are Niersteiner Rehbach, Niersteiner Auflangen, and Niersteiner Spiegelberg.

Grape varieties: 30% Riesling, 30% Sylvaner, 30% Müller-Thurgau, 10% Ruländer, Scheurebe, Gewürztraminer, and other varieties.

The wines: A wide selection is offered. The wines are well balanced and have a mild, pleasant character.

Estate specialties: Many Auslese and award-winning wines. The estate also produces a very dry wine with the seal of wine suitable for diabetics.

Label: It features the family coat of arms (three cornucopias), which is illustrated in the Siebmacher coat-of-arms book.

Marketing: Established regular clientele, primarily private customers. Presentation packages.

Visits and tastings: By appointment, the winery can be visited. Standing tastings in the cellar or seated tastings for small groups are possible.

From my notebook: A wine estate with a friendly atmosphere, where the proprietor and members of the family are actively involved.

SELZEN

Ökonomierat Schätzel Erben, Weingut Kapellenhof

Address: 6501 Selzen, Kapellenhof, Kapellenstrasse 18
Telephone: (06737) 204

Location: The estate buildings enclose a large court and are surrounded by a park, gardens, vineyards, and paddocks.

How to get there: From the north, take the autobahn south from Mainz, turning off at Mainz-Hechtsheim, and continue south through Harxheim and Mommenheim. From the south, take route B-9 to Nierstein, then continue west on route B-420 to Köngerheim and drive 2 km north. The estate is reached from the center of the village via a side road marked with a signpost.

Points of interest: The old winepress in front of the buildings; the park; the rustic tasting room, decorated with medallions and old wine-making tools.

History: In 1889, Emil Schätzel of Schlossgut Guntersblum, who later became an economic counselor, married into the former Kessel family. This was a typical Hessian multipurpose estate, and Schätzel emphasized wine production by extending the cellar, adding buildings, and constructing the manor house. His grandson, Volker Schätzel, is the current proprietor.

Terrain and soils: Of the 32.2 acres of vineyards in the Selz Valley, 40% are flat and 60% on southwest, gently sloping terrain. The soils are tertiary and alluvial, ranging from sandy loam to loamy clay.

Vineyard names: Selzener Rheinpforte (5 a.), Selzener Osterberg (5 a.), Selzener Gottesgarten (7.4 a.), Hahnheimer Knopf (11.1 a.), Hahnheimer Moosberg (3.7 a.).

The Grosslage name is Niersteiner Gutes Domtal.

Grape varieties: 25% Sylvaner, 20% Riesling, 20% Müller-Thurgau, 10% Ruländer and Gewürztraminer, 4% Portugieser, 21% new varieties, such as Scheurebe, Kerner, Faber, Huxelrebe, Ehrenfelser, Morio-Muskat, and Ortega.

The wines: Elegant, rich, full-bodied wines with a slight residual sweetness. Strong carafe wines are offered in liter bottles under the name "Kapellenhof." The same name is also used for a full, red wine and a mild rosé.

Estate specialties: The wine list shows five vintages. The special "Weinprobe-Privat" presentation (containing wines of different vintages and grape varieties) includes explanations and is an extremely informative wine tasting. The wines from new grape varieties are developed to maintain the character of each variety. The very dry wines have a yellow seal indicating suitability for diabetics. The price list contains many award-winning wines, and top-quality wines are available in half bottles.

Label: It features the family coat of arms that, according to the Siebmacher coat-of-arms books, originated in 1666. The individual vineyards are additionally identified by the various label colors.

Marketing: Principally to private clients. The estate will arrange for shipping if the client does not wish to do so.

Visits and tastings: By appointment, the winery and vineyards can be visited. Standing tastings are held for large groups in the cellar or in the park, depending on the weather. Seated tastings for up to 25 persons are possible in the tasting room.

From my notebook: A dignified, old wine estate that encourages personal contact with its customers. Wine lovers should con-

sider participating in Open-door Week (Woche der Offenen Tür), which takes place in September at the Kapellenhof. During this festive week the estate's wines can be casually tasted without commitment.

OPPENHEIM

Weingutsverwaltung Sanitätsrat Dr. Dahlem Erben KG

Address: 6504 Oppenheim, Wormser Strasse 50
Telephone: (06133) 3001

Location: The offices, estate buildings, and cellars are in the center of Oppenheim.

How to get there: Take route B-9 from Mainz for 20 km toward Worms.

Points of interest: The extensive cellars; the relics from the first century, excavated during the construction of a cellar; the old chapel, now arranged as a tasting room, which is said to have formerly belonged to Kloster Eberbach.

History: The wine estate has been in the family for generations, formerly as a typical multipurpose Hessian farm, and in its present form since 1923. The proprietors are Hans Wilhelm Dahlem and Klaus Dahlem.

Terrain and soils: Of the 66.7 acres of vineyards, 50% are on gently sloping, 9% on steeply sloping, and 41% on flat terrain. The soils are loess and loess-loam.

Vineyard names: Oppenheimer Sackträger (4 a.), Oppenheimer Herrenberg (8.4 a.), Oppenheimer Schloss (7.9 a.), Oppenheimer Kreuz (8.9 a.), Oppenheimer Herrengarten (18.3 a.), Oppenheimer Daubhaus (0.5 a.), Dienheimer Tafelstein (8.4 a.), Dienheimer Paterhof (3.5 a.), Dienheimer Falkenberg (5.4 a.), Guntersblumer Kreuzkapelle (1.5 a.).

Grape varieties: 30% Riesling, 25% Sylvaner, 23% Müller-Thurgau, 7% Ruländer, 2% Scheurebe, 2% Gewürztraminer, 11% experimental varieties.

The wines: Typical Rheinhessen wines that are well balanced, fruity, and flavorful. Individual barrel aging is still practiced.

Estate specialties: Many award-winning and fine wines. The assortment is surprisingly extensive and contains older vintages that are scarcely offered elsewhere.

Label: It features the family coat of arms, granted in 1702, and a section of a Merian etching of Oppenheim in 1643.

Marketing: Direct sales to regular clients. Active export business.

Visits and tastings: The winery and vineyards can be visited by appointment. Wine tastings are also possible for large groups. English-speaking personnel available.

From my notebook: The spacious cellarage on various floors is worth seeing and willingly shown. The wines are well made and exhibit the best characteristics of wines from this region.

OPPENHEIM

Weingut Carl Sittmann

Address: 6504 Oppenheim, Wormser Strasse 59
Telephone: (06133) 2222 *Telex:* 04187496

Location: The buildings and winery are at the southern side of Oppenheim at the edge of the Oppenheimer Sackträger vineyard.

How to get there: Take route B-9 from Mainz toward Worms.

Points of interest: The extensive large-scale winery; the former porter's lodge of the hospital, which was built in 1589 on the site of the Oppenheimer Gutleuthaus vineyard.

History: In 1879, Carl Sittmann, a trained cellar-master, founded the estate and soon developed it into a respected establishment. He was made an honorary citizen of the town of Oppenheim for his services and nominated commercial counselor. Today the owner is Mrs. Liselotte Itschner, M.D., a granddaughter of the founder. After the death of her brothers she took over the large concern and its affiliated wine-shipping firm.

Terrain and soils: Of the 185.3 acres of vineyards, 10% are on steeply sloping, 30% on gently sloping, and 60% on flat terrain. The soils include loess, loess-loam, and marl.

Vineyard names: Niersteiner Paterberg, Niersteiner Hipping, Niersteiner Heiligenbaum, Niersteiner Orbel, Niersteiner Ölberg, Niersteiner Rosenberg, Niersteiner Klostergarten, Niersteiner Findling, Niersteiner Kirchplatte, Oppenheimer Gutleuthaus, Oppenheimer Herrengarten, Oppenheimer Paterhof, Oppenheimer Schloss, Oppenheimer Kreuz, Oppenheimer Herrenberg, Oppenheimer Zuckerberg, Oppenheimer Sackträger, Oppenheimer Daubhaus, Dienheimer Schloss, Dienheimer Paterhof, Dienheimer Kreuz, Dienheimer Falkenberg, Dienheimer Tafelstein, Dienheimer Siliusbrunnen, Dienheimer Herrenberg, Alsheimer Frühmesse, Alsheimer Sonnenberg, Alsheimer Römerberg, Alsheimer Fischerpfad, Alsheimer Goldberg.

The Grosslage names are Niersteiner Spiegelberg, Niersteiner Auflangen, Niersteiner Rehbach, Oppenheimer Güldenmorgen, Oppenheimer Krötenbrunnen, Dienheimer Krötenbrunnen, Dienheimer Güldenmorgen, and Alsheimer Rheinblick.

Grape varieties: 37% Sylvaner, 18% Riesling, 15% Müller-Thurgau, 10% Ruländer, 10% Gewürztraminer, 6% Morio-Muskat, 2% Scheurebe, 2% new varieties.

The wines: This estate, the largest private vineyard proprietor in Rheinhessen, tries to preserve the individual characteristics of the grape varieties and vineyards. The wines are clean, well balanced, fruity, and mild.

Estate specialties: Interesting Auslese wines from various grape varieties. The rosé is considered a specialty.

Label: The estate wines are furnished with a white label bearing a green vine-leaf and grape design. It also incorporates the family coat of arms, dating from 1612. Wines marketed by the shipping firm have a different label.

Marketing: Wholesale only.

Visits and tastings: The buildings, cellar, and vineyards can be visited by appointment. Tastings must be arranged. English-speaking personnel available.

From my notebook: From small beginnings, this estate grew to its current large size and is still being extended. Walter Haury-Sittmann, a business graduate and the youngest member of the famly, conducts tours in an engaging manner and knows just how to relate the most interesting items of history. The atmosphere at this estate is reflected in its motto: Life is much too short to drink poor wine.

ALSHEIM

Weingut Rappenhof, Dr. Reinhard Muth

Address: 6526 Alsheim Bachstrasse 47
Telephone: (06249) 7115

Location: In the center of the village.
How to get there: Take route B-9 between Nierstein and Worms.
Points of interest: The vineyards, cellar, and winery.
History: The buildings date back to before the destruction of the village in 1689. The forebears of the present proprietor, Dr. Reinhard Muth, were well known in community and state politics. The grandfather of Mrs. Muth (nee Hirsch), loved to drive in a carriage drawn by a team of spirited black horses (*Rappen*). This is said to be the origin of the estate's name.
Terrain and soils: Of the 74.1 acres of vineyards, 50% are on gently sloping, 10% on steeply sloping, and 40% on flat terrain. The soils are light to medium-heavy loess with a certain amount of chalk and clay.
Vineyard names: Alsheimer Fischerpfad (8.9 a.), Alsheimer Frühmesse (11.6 a.), Alsheimer Sonnenberg (7.7 a.), Alsheimer Goldberg (16 a.), Guntersblumer Kreuzkapelle (4 a.), Guntersblumer Steinberg (6.9 a.), Guntersblumer Himmeltal (4 a.),

Guntersblumer Autental (1 a.), Guntersblumer Steig-Terrassen (1 a.), Guntersblumer Bornpfad (1.5 a.), Guntersblumer Eiserne Hand (7.4 a.).

Grosslage names, such as Alsheimer Rheinblick and Guntersblumer Vogelsgärten, are used only occasionally.

Grape varieties: 35% Riesling, 25% Müller-Thurgau, 12% Sylvaner, 8% Gewürztraminer, 5% Scheurebe, 3% Ruländer, 7% miscellaneous new varieties, 5% Portugieser and Pinot Noir.

The wines: Clean, typical Rheinhessen wines with moderate residual sweetness; the Riesling is the most important. The red wines and the rosé wines exhibit no residual sweetness.

Estate specialties: The latest seven vintages ripened well. Dry wines and wines suitable for diabetics are produced. A large number of awards have been won.

Label: It shows the coat of arms of the Hirsch family. Prädikatweins also carry the symbol of the Association of German Prädikatwein Producers.

Marketing: The wines are sold to consumers and to the trade; the wines from certain vineyards are reserved for the latter. The wine estate participates in auctions in Alsheim and Guntersblum, and in the Rheinhessen Wine Exchange (Rheinhessischen Weinbörse), which is a wine sales event of the Rheinhessen wine estates that was started in 1974 and is held every year in May in the electoral palace in Mainz.

Visits and tastings: By appointment, the cellar and vineyards can be visited. Cellar tastings are possible. A tasting room for up to 10 persons is available.

From my notebook: This estate is run as a family business. Dr. Muth, the son of a vintner and a trained economist, is president of the Rheinhessen Viticulture Association. Despite his many duties, he finds time to look after visitors himself, whenever possible. His knowledge of current problems in the wine industry makes a tasting conducted by him especially fascinating for people interested in the wine business.

BECHTHEIM

Weingut Richard Beyer

Address: 6521 Bechtheim, Pfandturmstrasse 12
Telephone: (06242) 804 and 873

Location: The buildings and cellar are in the center of the village.
How to get there: Bechtheim is 3 km west of route B-9, between Oppenheim and Worms. Follow route 409.
Points of interest: The old barrel cellar; the rustic tasting room, seating up to 50 persons.
History: According to records, the family has been active in viticulture since 1665. The current proprietor is Günter Beyer.
Terrain and soils: The 50 acres of vineyards can be mechanically cultivated and have loess and loess-loam soils.
Vineyard names: Bechtheimer Geyersberg, Bechtheimer Rosengarten, Bechtheimer Heiligkreuz, Bechtheimer Stein, Bechtheimer Hasensprung, Einselthumer Klosterstück, Zeller Klosterstück, Zeller Kreuzberg.
The Grosslage names are Bechtheimer Pilgerpfad and Bechtheimer Gotteshilfe.
Grape varieties: 20% Müller-Thurgau, 15% Riesling, 15% Scheurebe, 14% Sylvaner, 10% Gewürztraminer, 6% red-wine varieties, 20% new varieties, such as Kanzler, Kerner, Ehrenfelser, Reichensteiner, Optima, Huxelrebe, Schöburger, Würzer, Septimer, and Regner.
The wines: The Scheurebe, Riesling, and Müller-Thurgau wines are vigorous and fruity with subtle acidity, whereas the Sylvaners tend to be more flavorful.
Estate specialties: Fine wines and the fruity, new varieties, some being almost aromatic. The red wine is a Rheinhessen specialty.
Label: It shows the newly reconstructed winery.
Marketing: Sold directly to the consumer.
Visits and tastings: The vineyards and winery can be visited without an appointment, Monday through Friday, 9 A.M. to

11 A.M. and 1 P.M. to 4:30 P.M. Wines may also be tasted. English-speaking personnel available.

From my notebook: The young owner, Günter Beyer, a trained oenologist, is glad to show visitors his model, modernized winery. The tasting room is large and well designed.

BECHTHEIM

Brenner'sches Weingut

Address: 6521 Bechtheim, Pfandturmstrasse 20
Telephone: (06242) 894

Location: The buildings and winery are in the center of the village.

How to get there: Bechtheim is 3 km west of route B-9, between Oppenheim and Worms. Follow route 409.

Points of interest: The extensive cellars and pleasant tasting room.

History: The vineyard has been in the family since 1877. The viticultural tradition of Bechtheim dates back to a deed of gift to the Kloster Lorsch in 785, and unearthed relics indicate that it stems from as far back as the Roman period. The current owner of the estate is the mayor, Christian Brenner.

Terrain and soils: Of the 37 acres of vineyards, 80% are on gently sloping and 20% on flat terrain. The soils are loess and loess-loam.

Vineyard names: Bechtheimer Geyersberg (5 a.), Bechtheimer Rosengarten (5 a.), Bechtheimer Hasensprung (5 a.), Bechtheimer Heiligkreuz (6.2 a.), Bechtheimer Stein (2.5 a.).

The Grosslage names are Bechtheimer Pilgerpfad and Bechtheimer Gotteshilfe.

Grape varieties: 30% Sylvaner, 30% Müller-Thurgau, 20% Riesling, 6% Weissburgunder, 4% Ruländer, 4% Huxel, 2% Sieger, 2% Kanzler, 2% Spätburgunder.

The wines: The deep soil produces a robust, full Rheinhessen wine.

VERBAND DEUTSCHER
PRÄDIKATSWEINGÜTER
E.V.

Unsere Mitglieder besitzen
Lagen von Weltruf!

V
D P

Dieses Zeichen verbürgt
in Verbindung mit dem Kork-
brand einen Wein aus eigener
Erzeugung unseres Mitglieds.
Dieser Streifen darf nur ver-
wendet werden für amtlich
anerkannte
Qualitätsweine mit Prädikat.

VEREINIGUNG
RHEINHESSISCHER
RIESLINGGÜTER E.V.

Weingut Rappenhof

Dr. Reinhard Muth
Alsheim. Rhh.

RHEINHESSEN

ALSHEIMER FRÜHMESSE

Riesling Auslese

Erzeugerabfüllung

Rheinhessen

Qualitätswein mit Prädikat A.P.Nr. 4 252 175 08 72

Brenner'sches Weingut

WEINKELLEREIEN BECHTHEIM BEI WORMS AM RHEIN

RHEINHESSEN

1971   QUALITÄTSWEIN MIT PRÄDIKAT   1971

AMTLICHE PRÜFUNGSNUMMER 4 257 034 672

Bechtheimer Heilig Kreuz

RULÄNDER BEERENAUSLESE

ERZEUGERABFÜLLUNG

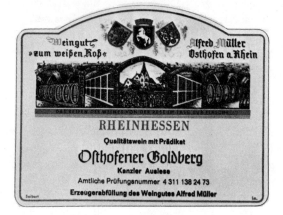

Weingut
»zum weißen Roß«

Alfred Müller
Osthofen a. Rhein

DAS REIFEN DES WEINES VON DER REBE IM FASS ZUR FLASCHE

RHEINHESSEN

Qualitätswein mit Prädikat

Osthofener Goldberg

Kanzler Auslese

Amtliche Prüfungsnummer 4 311 138 24 73

Erzeugerabfüllung des Weingutes Alfred Müller

The wines are individually aged, clean, and well balanced. The new varieties produce spicy and fruity wines.

Estate specialties: Many fine and award-winning wines. There is also a sparkling wine made from estate wines, and wine in liter bottles. The red wines, more delicate than dry, are also a specialty of the estate.

Label: It features the family coat of arms and the words "Seit 1877" (since 1877). It was designed by Professor Franz Müller, of Mainz.

Marketing: Sold to the trade, restaurants, and directly to consumers. Favorably priced pre-packed assortments and presentation packages are available.

Visits and tastings: Monday through Friday, 8 A.M. to 11 A.M. and 1 P.M. to 5 P.M. Wine tastings by appointment. English-speaking personnel available.

From my notebook: The estate goes out of its way to encourage individual customers and offers various pre-packed assortments of wine. The young owner, who is also the mayor of Bechtheim, and his wife devote much time to the development of their attractive estate and discuss their interesting wines in a charming and expert manner.

OSTHOFEN

Weingut Weisses Ross, Alfred Müller

Address: 6522 Osthofen, Friedrich-Ebert-Strasse 50
Telephone: (06242) 419

Location: In the center of the community.
How to get there: Drive 9 km north from Worms on route B-9.
Points of interest: The large estate buildings; the extensive cellars, with original and unusual features; the neighboring Bergkirche (a church), with the Osthofener Goldberg vineyard.
History: The estate was first mentioned in 1573 in connection with the tavern Zum Weissen Ross, a Thurn and Taxis post station.

The keeper of the post inn is said to have preferred harnessing white horses to coaches, and thus, the estate got its name. The wine estate itself was developed by the Muth family. It passed into the possession of the Müller family in 1912.

Terrain and soils: Of the 79 acres of vineyards, 15% are on steeply sloping, 40% on gently sloping, and 45% on flat terrain. The soils are mainly loess and loess-loam.

Vineyard names: Osthofener Goldberg (7.4 a.), Osthofener Kirchberg (2.5 a.), Osthofener Klosterberg (7.4 a.), Osthofener Liebenberg (7.4 a.), Osthofener Hasenbiss (12.4 a.), Bechtheimer Geyersberg (1.2 a.), Mettenheimer Michelsberg (14.8 a.), Mettenheimer Schlossberg (9.9 a.), Mettenheimer Goldberg (9.9 a.), Alsheimer Frühmesse (1.8 a.).

The Grosslage names are Gotteshilfe, Pilgerpfad, Krötenbrunnen, and Rheinblick.

Grape varieties: 30% Sylvaner, 20% Müller-Thurgau, 10% Riesling, 7% Ruländer, 6% Huxel, 5% Morio-Muskat, 4% Kanzler, 3% Traminer, 3% Kerner, 2% Bacchusrebe, 2% Optima, 2% Ortega, 2% Auxerrois, 4% red-wine varieties, such as Portugieser, Spätburgunder, and Heroldrebe.

The wines: The range of wines is large because of the many grape varieties grown. The wines are mild, as well as full-bodied. The special grape varieties yield very fragrant and spicy wines.

Estate specialties: The many new varieties. Single bottles of vintages back to 1959 are kept for special occasions, and estate sparkling wine is also produced.

Label: It features a white horse in the estate coat of arms, as well as the Bergkirche, an Osthofen landmark.

Marketing: Various methods of marketing are used; regular customers are supplied direct.

Visits and tastings: By appointment, the experimental plantings and the cellars are willingly shown. Wine tastings are held in the lovely tasting room. English-speaking personnel available.

From my notebook: As can be seen from the many types of grapes grown, the owner, Alfred Müller, has pioneered in the planting of new varieties. He operates the business along with his son and daughter and their families. With this family's sense of humor and practical thinking, the wine tastings are well organized and lively.

Rheinpfalz

Grünstadt

Kirchheim — *Hammel*

Weingut Pfeffingen
Annaberg
Bad Dürkheim — *Fitz-Ritter*

Wachenheim — *Dr. Bürklin-Wolf*
Forst — *Spindler*
Deidesheim — *v. Buhl*
DEUTSCHE — *v. Bassermann-Jordan*
WEINSTRASSE *Hahnhof*
Hoch
Haardt
Müller-Catoir Neustadt

Maikammer

Edenkoben

Siebeldingen — *Rebholz*

Emil Hammel u.Cie.

KIRCHHEIM AN DER WEINSTRASSE

Weingut und Weinkellerei

1723   I.D.H.

R H E I N P F A L Z

1973er

RIESLING KABINETT

Kirchheimer Schwarzerde

AUS EIGENEM LESEGUT

A. P. Nr. 5125037 6374 // 3552

R H E I N   P F A L Z

Karl Fuhrmann   vorm. Fritz Schnell

Weingut   Pfeffingen

bei Ungstein   16   22   Post Bad Dürkheim

1971er UNGSTEINER HERRENBERG

SCHEUREBE AUSLESE

QUALITÄTSWEIN MIT PRÄDIKAT A.P.NR. 5 141 045 5 72

ERZEUGERABFÜLLUNG

R H E I N -   P F A L Z

Qualitätswein mit Prädikat

AP Nr. 5 160 087 / 7 / 72

DÜRKHEIMER

ABTSFROHNHOF

RIESLING

BEERENAUSLESE

ERZEUGERABFÜLLUNG

K · FITZ · RITTER · BAD DÜRKHEIM

Emil Hammel u. Cie., Weingut und Weinkellerei

Address: 6719 Kirchheim, Weinstrasse Süd 4
Telephone: (06359) 3206

Location: The offices and winery are at the south side of the village.

How to get there: Take the Mannheim-Kaiserslautern autobahn, turning off at Grünstadt, and continue 2 km south.

Points of interest: The roomy cellars.

History: Since the time of Johann David Hammel, whose initials JDH and the date 1723 are still found on the vineyard boundary stones, the estate has been in the hands of the family. In the course of years it was extended to its present size, and a large winery was built. The current owner is Rudolf Hammel.

Terrain and soils: The 52 acres of vineyards are on flat and gently sloping terrain. There are various types of soil.

Vineyard names: Neuleininger Sonnenberg, Kleinkarlbacher Herrenberg, Kirchheimer Geisskopf, Kirchheimer Römerstrasse, Kirchheimer Steinacker, Kirchheimer Kreuz, Bissersheimer Goldberg, Dirmsteiner Mandelpfad.
The Grosslage names are Schwarzerde and Höllenpfad.

Grape varieties: 30% Riesling, 17% Müller-Thurgau, 12% Scheurebe, 10% Sylvaner, 8% Ruländer, 6% Gewürztraminer, 5% Siegerrebe, and 12% miscellaneous, mostly experimental varieties.

The wines: Robust country wines of high quality.

Estate specialties: The Scheurebe and Gewürztraminer grapes, growing in rich, limy soil, yield wines with a strong bouquet.

Label: It features the emblem of the founder carved on the vineyard boundary stones: a shooting vine in the shape of a bishop's staff.

Marketing: Sold mainly through the trade; some direct sales to regular clients.

Visits and tastings: By appointment, visits and wine tastings in the cellar may be arranged for groups.

From my notebook: "These are real carafe wines that will treat you kindly even if you drink a little extra," says a company brochure. The rapid growth of the winery demonstrates that the customers agree. Wines made and developed from grapes purchased from other estates are offered at unusually low prices under the trade name "Grafschaft Leiningen."

BAD DÜRKHEIM

Weingut Pfeffingen

Address: 6702 Bad Dürkheim, Weinstrasse
Telephone: (06322) 8607

Location: The estate is located on the German Wine Road and consists of a distinctive group of buildings surrounded by vineyards.

How to get there: Take route B-271 (the German Wine Road) from Bad Dürkheim toward Ungstein.

Points of interest: the attractive estate buildings; the Roman stone coffins found in the garden during excavation; the well-tended vineyards; the original tasting room.

History: According to indications, the estate area was inhabited before Roman times. Portions of the current estate buildings were part of a church complex. However, the church and the cemetery were swept away in the nineteenth century. Recently the old estate buildings were beautifully renovated by the present proprietor, Karl Fuhrmann.

Terrain and soils: Of the 19.8 acres of mostly consolidated vine-yards, 50% are on gently sloping and 50% on flat terrain. The soil is mainly marl.

Vineyard names: Ungsteiner Herrenberg and Ungsteiner Nussriegel. The Grosslage name is Ungsteiner Honigsäckel.

Grape varieties: 30% Riesling, 20% Müller-Thurgau, 12% Sylvaner, 15% Scheurebe, 10% Gewürztraminer and Morio-Muskat, 13% Ruländer, Ortega, and Optima.

The wines: Juicy, ripe wines that are faithful to the grape varieties and are rich in nuances. Analysis figures are given in the price list for the dry wines. The latest five vintages are available.

Estate specialties: A high proportion of Prädikat wines and fine wines are made from Riesling and Scheurebe grapes. All wines carry the German wine seal, and nearly all have won awards, including many national and state awards.

Label: It features the coat of arms of the Schnells (the in-laws of the present proprietor), which was granted in 1622 and bears a rampant unicorn.

Marketing: Almost exclusively by direct sale to regular customers. A 5% discount is given when the purchaser makes his own shipping arrangements.

Visits and tastings: Visits and tastings are possible during business hours, but an appointment must be made for groups. Interesting tasting room.

From my notebook: The estate promotes close customer relations. It is worthwhile to see this clean, modern establishment because the entire operation from vine to consumer can be observed. Karl Fuhrmann, president of the Rheinpfalz Vintners Association, operates this model estate.

BAD DÜRKHEIM

Weingut K. Fitz-Ritter

Address: 6702 Bad Dürkheim, Weinstrasse Nord 51
Telephone: (06322) 5389

Location: The estate buildings, winery, and immediate vineyards
are at the edge of the town, opposite the Dürkheim barrel.

How to get there: Take route B-37 or route B-271 (German Wine
Road).

Points of interest: The classic house, dated 1785; the picturesque
half-timbered inner courtyard; the 250-year-old standstone
sentry box; the park, with its rare trees.

History: The family, which originally immigated from Scotland,
has been active in viticulture in Bad Dürkheim since the eighteenth century. Four houses were built, one of which is the
town hall today. As a sideline in 1828, Johann Fitz constructed
a winery for sparkling wines, which is now one of the oldest in
Germany. He also carried the black protest flag and made a
speech at the Maxburg festival of the first German democracy
in 1832.

Terrain and soils: Of the 50 acres of vineyards, 50% are on gently
sloping and 50% on flat terrain. The soils range from loamy
sand to clay and loam.

Vineyard names: Dürkheimer Michelsberg (1.7 a.), Dürkheimer
Spielberg (2.5 a.), Dürkheimer Abtsfronhof (entire vineyard,
7.9 a.), Dürkheimer Rittergarten (5 a.), Dürkheimer Hochbenn, (5 a.), Dürkheimer Steinberg, (1.5 a.), Ungsteiner
Herrenberg (3.7 a.), Wachenheimer Mandelgarten (3.7 a.).

The Grosslage names are Dürkheimer Schenkenböhl, Dürkheimer
Feuerberg, and Deidesheimer Hofstück.

Grape varieties: 65% Riesling, 5% Ruländer, 4% Sylvaner, 1%
Spätburgunder, 25% miscellaneous, mostly experimental varieties.

The wines: The fruity, flowery wines are vigorous and robust. The estate's various soils provide interesting nuances in the wines, which are further emphasized by individual barrel aging.

Estate specialties: A high proportion of fine wines. The estate offers a selection of pre-packed assortments and presentation cartons, some containing a combined assortment of sparkling and still wines.

Label: It features the trademark of the estate (a knight on horseback jumping over vine) in a black circle.

Marketing: Mostly direct to consumers.

Visits and tastings: By appointment, the buildings, cellars, and vineyards can be visited. Wine tastings are given in the old-style German tasting room holding up to 60 persons. English-speaking personnel available.

From my notebook: Visitors, individually or in groups, are graciously received by Mr. Konrad Fitz, the junior manager of the estate, who conducts the tours. Visitors in a hurry can select a pre-packed assortment to take with them for later tasting. The estate started producing sparkling wine in 1828 to make use of the small, acidic wines. Together with the sparkling wineries of Kessler, in Esslingen, and Grempler, in Grünberg (Schlesien), both of which were founded in 1826, this estate is one of the pioneers of German sparkling wine.

BAD DÜRKHEIM

Stumpf-Fitz'sches Weingut Annaberg

Address: 6702 Bad Dürkheim-Leistadt
Telephone: (06322) 2202

Location: In a broad valley basin open to the south, lying between Bad Dürkheim and Leistadt.

How to get there: Take route B-37 or route B-271 to Bad Dürkheim, and then drive 2 km from Bad Dürkheim toward Leistadt.

Points of interest: The estate buildings, beautifully situated among the vineyards at the edge of the Pfälzer Woods; the view to the south over the Rhine plain; the old cellar hewn out of shell limestone, with its barrel vaults coated with black cellar mold (Cladosporium Cellare).

History: Judging from the numerous relics, the vineyards were cultivated by the Celts and the Romans. In 1545, the counts of Leiningen were recorded as having been the owners. Louis Fitz acquired the estate in 1870 and developed it into a model establishment. Under his successors, Eugen Stumpf-Fitz and navy surgeon-general Dr. O. Nenninger, the estate gained a reputation that reaches far beyond the immediate region. The present owners are Dr. E. Meder and his wife.

Terrain and soils: The 32.1 acres of vineyards are on gently sloping terrain and the soils are mainly loess and loess-loam.

Vineyard names: Annaberg (entire vineyard, 18.3 a.), Dürkheimer Hochbenn (5.9 a.), Kallstadter Kreidkeller (7.9 a.).

The Grosslage names are Dürkheimer Feuerberg and Dürkheimer Hochmess.

Grape varieties: 53% Riesling, 11% Ruländer, 10% Sylvaner, 7% Weissburgunder, 7% Scheurebe, 5% Müller-Thurgau, 4% Gewürztraminer, 3% Morio-Muskat.

The wines: They are clean, elegant, and fruity. The delicate acidity, paired with a subtle sweetness, creates excellent balance. The low yield per acre, the extremely late harvests, and the careful treatment in the cellars are the factors credited for the excellent quality of the wines.

Estate specialties: A high proportion of Spätlese and Auslese wines. Well represented at the national and state wine judgings, where several high awards have been won.

Label: It features the coat of arms of the Nenningers, originally a noble family in Württemberg of which Mrs. Meder is a member. The left side of the label shows the estate trademark: a black "A" on a golden hill.

Marketing: Direct to regular customers and to the trade.

Visits and tastings: By appointment, the estate can be visited and tastings can be held for people interested in purchasing wine. English-speaking personnel available.

From my notebook: This is a wine estate set in an idyllic landscape with ideal microclimatic and cellar conditions. The high-quality wines are a result of well-tended vineyards and careful aging, both in barrel and bottle. Dr. Meder and his wife personally manage the estate with loving care.

WACHENHEIM

Weingut Dr. Bürklin-Wolf

Address: 6706 Wachenheim, Weinstrasse 65
Telephone: (06322) 8956

Location: The offices and the winery are in the middle of the village.

How to get there: Wachenheim is on route B-271 (German Wine Road) between Bad Dürkheim and Deidesheim.

Points of interest: The old cellar, with its modern extension in the Kolb'schen Hof (named after the former owner, Count Kolb von Wartenberg); the historical wine room; the well-tended park in the Unteren Hof, with its view of the vineyards; the Rhine Valley and the wooded heights of the Mittelhaardt.

History: As early as 1579 the name Bürklin (Schultheiss in Wachenheim) is recorded in the town's land register in connection with vineyard properties. In 1759, Johann Peter Wolf, who came from an old Palatinate vintner family, became administrator of the electoral winery. His son, Johann Ludwig Wolf, developed the property in Wachenheim into one of the largest high quality-wine estates in Germany from 1777 to 1846. In 1875, his granddaughter married a confidential counselor, Dr. Albert Bürklin, vice-president of the imperial parliament. Under his management the Bürklin-Wolfe name became established.

Terrain and soils: The 222.4 acres of vineyards are on gently

RHEIN · PFALZ

WEINGUT ANNABERG
BEI BAD DÜRKHEIM/WEINSTRASSE

1973er *Kallstadter Annaberg*
Scheurebe Spätlese   (71803)

Erzeugerabfüllung   A. P. Nr. 5 123 155 1 74

QUALITÄTSWEIN MIT PRÄDIKAT

RHEIN · PFALZ

Weingut Dr.Bürklin-Wolf
WACHENHEIM/WEINSTRASSE

Wachenheimer Gerümpel
Riesling Auslese

Erzeugerabfüllung · A. P. Nr. 5 142 043 25 72

QUALITÄTSWEIN MIT PRÄDIKAT

Weingut   Deidesheim
Reichsrat v. Buhl   Rheinpfalz

Forster Ungeheuer
Riesling Spätlese
Qualitätswein mit Prädikat   A. P. Nr. 5 106 044/18/72
ERZEUGERABFÜLLUNG

sloping and flat terrain, and all may be mechanically cultivated. The soils are gravel, loamy sand, clay, marl, loess, and loess-loam.

Vineyard names: Wachenheimer Gerümpel, Wachenheimer Goldbächel, Wachenheimer Rechbächel (entire vineyard), Wachenheimer Schlossberg, Wachenheimer Böhlig, Wachenheimer Altenburg, Wachenheimer Luginsland, Wachenheimer Königswingert, Wachenheimer Mandelgarten, Forster Kirchenstück, Forster Jesuitengarten, Forster Ungeheuer, Forster Pechstein, Forster Bischofsgarten, Deidesheimer Leinhöhle, Deidesheimer Kalkofen, Deidesheimer Hohenmorgen, Deidesheimer Langenmorgen, Ruppertsberger Hoheburg, Ruppertsberger Gaisböhl (entire vineyard), Ruppertsberger Nussbien, Ruppertsberger Linsenbusch.

The Grosslage names are Wachenheimer Schenkenböhl, Forster Schnepfenflug, and Deidesheimer Hofstück.

Grape varieties: 88% Riesling, 12% experimental varieties.

The wines: The wines are individually barrel aged, and the most prominent wines are the elegant, fruity Rieslings. In the price list the wines are accurately and clearly characterized as ranging from dry, light, wine suitable for diabetics to noble, sweet, full wines.

Estate specialties: A high proportion of fine wines. Half bottles of expensive Beerenauslese and Trockenbeerenauslese wines are offered. The estate has won an impressive number of high awards. Single bottles of good older vintages are preserved for special occasions.

Label: The label carries the combined Bürklin-Wolf coat of arms and has been in use for almost 100 years in different variations.

Marketing: The wines are sold through various channels. The trade is granted discounts for large quantities.

Visits and tastings: By appointment, the estate buildings, the first-class vineyards, and the winery can be visited. Wine tastings will be held for potential clients by arrangement. English-speaking personnel available.

From my notebook: This model establishment is one of the most famous wine estates in Germany. The current proprietor, Dr. Albert Bürklin, has been the vice-president of the German

Vintners Association since its founding and is a passionate advocate of quality wine production. The separate sales room, where wines can be tasted during business hours, is a great advantage to the visitor in a hurry.

FORST

Eugen Spindler—Weingut Lindenhof

Address: 6701 Forst, Weinstrasse 55
Telephone: (06326) 338

Location: The estate buildings, with a long facade, gated twin entrances, and a stone relief showing a stylized linden tree, are in the center of the village.

How to get there: Follow the German Wine Road north from Neustadt or south from Bad Dürkheim.

Points of interest: The village, situated in charming countryside at the foot of the Haardt Mountains; the spaciously arranged estate buildings; the extensive, vaulted sandstone cellars with wooden barrels.

History: The family has been in viticulture since 1620. Three generations ago the large vineyard property was divided into three estates: "Eugen Spindler" (now Lindenhof), "Heinrich Spindler," and "Wilhelm Spindler." The present proprietor, Peter Spindler, a councillor for the Deidesheim rural district, is following in the footsteps of his ancestors, who were also important public officials: representatives in the state and imperial parliaments, mayors, and councillors.

Terrain and soils: The estate has a total of 33.4 acres under cultivation. There are warm southern slopes, southeastern slopes, and flat terrain. The soils include red sandstone, rich loess, heavy clay, and magmatite.

Vineyard Names: Forster Jesuitengarten, Forster Ungeheuer, Forster Pechstein, Deidesheimer Grainhübel, Deidesheimer Leinhöhle, Deidesheimer Kieselberg, Deidesheimer Herrgottsacker, Ruppertsberger Hoheburg, Ruppertsberger Reiterpfad, Ruppertsberger Nussbein, Ruppertsberger Linsenbusch.

The Grosslage names are Forster Mariengarten and Forster Schnepfenflug.

Grape varieties: 65% Riesling, 15% Müller-Thurgau, 3% Scheurebe, 8% Ruländer, 4% Gewürztraminer, 5% new varieties.

The wines: Extract-rich, full wines with well-balanced residual sweetness and a delicate fruitiness. In processing all of its wines, the estate uses individual barrel aging, early bottling, and bottle aging under ideal storage conditions. The estate wines in liter bottles are an excellent value.

Estate specialties: Elegant, fruity Rieslings that reach their peak after two to four years in the bottle.

Label: The data required by law is shown simply and clearly in gold print on a white background.

Marketing: Mainly direct to regular customers. Three price lists are issued each year.

Visits and tastings: By appointment, potential customers are received in the house or in the cellar. Small groups are preferred.

From my notebook: Lindenhof is a well-organized family business and is typical of small businesses in this area, where the family does most of the work and hires little outside help. As a practical man, Peter Spindler provides factual, down-to-earth information to visitors.

DEIDESHEIM

Weingut Reichsrat von Buhl

Address: 6705 Deidesheim
Telephone: (06326) 210

Location: The offices and winery are in the center of the village, situated in the vineyards of the most important area of the Mittelhaardt.

How to get there: Take route B-271 (German Wine Road).

Points of interest: The vaulted cellar, wiith its long rows of barrels; the carved barrels.

History: In 1849, Franz Peter Buhl owned the Peter Heinrich Jordan Erben estate, which he inherited from his uncle, and he entered it in the land register under his own name. Franz Eberhardt Buhl, who died in 1921, was an imperial counselor to the Bavarian throne and was also made a nobleman by a Bavarian king. His widow continued to manage the estate until her death in 1952, and Baron Theodor von und zu Guttenberg inherited the estate. Since his death in October 1972 his son, Baron Georg Enoch von und zu Guttenberg, has been the proprietor.

Terrain and soils: The 222.4 acres of vineyards are 90% on flat terrain. The soils are gravel, loamy sand, clay, marl, loess, and loess-loam.

Vineyard names: Deidesheimer Grainhübel, Deidesheimer Hergottsacker (11.5 a.), Deidesheimer Kieselberg (11.4 a.), Deidesheimer Paradiesgarten, Deidesheimer Leinhöhle, Deidesheimer Mäushöhle, Deidesheimer Nonnenstück (7.7 a.), Deidesheimer Letten (3.6 a.), Forster Elster, Forster Süsskopf (6.2 a.), Forster Freundstück (5.4 a.), Forster Bischofsgarten (34.6 a.), Forster Musenhang (5.2 a.), Forster Pechstein (13.8 a.), Forster Ungeheuer (20.3 a.), Forster Stift (3.6 a.), Ruppertsberger Reiterpfad (7.9 a.), Ruppertsberger Hoheburg, Ruppertsberger Linsenbusch (10.8 a.), Wachenheimer Luginsland (4.5 a.).

The Grosslage names are Gimmeldinger Meerspinne, Forster Schnepfenflug an der Weinstrasse, and Deidesheimer Hofstück.

Grape varieties: 85% Riesling, 10% Sylvaner, 5% Müller-Thurgau.

The wines: Individual barrel aging is practiced here, and importance is placed on maintaining the characteristic of the grape variety. The extensive list contains the most recent five vintages and includes a wide range of wines, from simple, robust carafe wines to full, sweet, fine wines.

Estate specialties: The estate specializes in the highest-quality Rheinpfalz wines. Even in the middle of the nineteenth century wines from the estate won high awards internationally in Paris, Brussels, Chicago, and other cities.

Label: The label features the coat of arms of the Von Buhl family.

Marketing: Mainly through the trade. The estate wines are regularly found in high-class restaurants and hotels.

Visits and tastings: By appointment, the cellars can be visited and standing tastings held for groups. English-speaking personnel available.

From my notebook: Because of its size and historical tradition, this is one of the most important wine estates in the Rheinpfalz. The estate hotels, Reichsrat von Buhl and Haardt Hotel, located next to the offices, have tasting rooms where wine tastings are given by arrangement and typical Palatinate food is served. The estate wines are particularly good when served with Palatinate specialties, such as liver sausage and blood sausage.

DEIDESHEIM

Weingut Geheimer Rat Dr. von Bassermann-Jordan

Address: 6705 Deidesheim, Postfach 20
Telephone: (06326) 206

Location: In the center of Deidesheim.

How to get there: Take route B-271 (German Wine Road) to Deidesheim. The old Kirchgasse, starting directly at the market-place, leads to the gate of the estate.

Points of interest: Above all, the extensive barrel cellar dating from the Middle Ages, with later additions forming one unique unit. The estate also has an extensive wine museum with some very old exhibits. The oldest item is a Roman wine with an approximate date of 100 A.D.—250 years older than the oldest wine in the Speyer Wine Museum.

History: The Ketschauer Hof, a fief of the Prince-Bishop of Speyer, has been in the hands of various families since about 1250. In 1816, it became the possession of the Jordan family, which owned vineyards in Rheinpfalz as early as 1718. Andreas Jordan (1775–1848) is considered to be the founder of quality viniculture in this area. His son, Ludwig Andreas-Jordan, a member of the state parliament and the German imperial parliament, was the last male member of the Jordan family. When he died in 1883 the estate was taken over by his son-in-law and subsequent descendants.

Dr. H. C. Friedrich von Basserman-Jordan, an internationally recognized wine historian, is the author of a work on the history of viniculture (1907–23) that is still considered to be a standard reference. For decades he held the most important offices in his profession and for a long time had tremendous influence on

German viniculture. In recognition of his achievements as a scientist and pioneer in viniculture, the German Agricultural Society established the Friedrich von Bassermann-Jordan medal in 1957. This medal can only be presented to a maximum of 10 living persons, who must have rendered outstanding service to German viniculture.

Terrain and soils: The 98.8 acres of vineyards are mostly on gently sloping terrain. The soils are gravel, loamy sand, clay, marl, loess, and loess-loam.

Vineyard names: Deidesheimer Grainhübel, Deidesheimer Hohenmorgen, Deidesheimer Kieselberg, Deidesheimer Leinhöhle, Deidesheimer Kalkofen, Deidesheimer Herrgottsacker, Deidesheimer Mäushöhle, Deidesheimer Langenmorgen, Forster Jesuitengarten, Forster Kirchenstück, Forster Ungeheuer, Forster Pechstein, Forster Freundstück, Forster Elster, Forster Stift, Forster Musenhang, Ruppertsberger Reiterpfad, Ruppertsberger Spiess, Ruppertsberger Nussbien, Ruppertsberger Hoheburg, Ruppertsberger Linsenbusch, Dürkheimer Michelsberg, Dürkheimer Spielberg, Ungsteiner Herrenberg.

The Grosslage names are Deidesheimer Hofstück, Forster Mariengarten, Forster Schnepfenflug, Dürkheimer Hochmess, and Ungsteiner Honigsäckel.

Grape varieties: 95% Riesling, 2% Gewürztraminer, 3% experimental varieties.

The wines: All wines are still individually aged in oak barrels. They range from agreeable and elegant to vigorous and racy. All have a delicate floweriness.

Estate specialties: The Rheinpfalz Riesling at its most noble. The estate has samples of wines from every vintage back to 1880. Numerous national and international awards have been won, some from the middle of the nineteenth century.

Label: Designed by Professor Otto Hupp. It features the family coat of arms.

Marketing: Sold to wholesalers, restaurants, and directly to private customers. Some export business.

Visits and tastings: By appointment, visits can be made and wine tastings arranged. English-speaking personnel available.

From my notebook: The estate, located in the center of the old wine community of Deidesheim, has a leading position among the centers of German wine culture. A visit can be a unique experience for a wine lover interested in history, particularly when Dr. L. von Bassermann-Jordan, an art historian, conducts the tour.

DEIDESHEIM

Weingut Hahnhof

Address: 6705 Deidesheim, Weinstrasse 1
Telephone: (06326) 296 and 555

Location: The offices and winery are at the northeast side of the town, directly at the edge of the vineyards.

How to get there: Take route B-271 (German Wine Road).

Points of interest: The beautiful view from the estate buildings toward the Mittelhaardt and the Rhine plain; the extensive cellars.

History: The estate was founded in 1929 by Hanns Hahn. In opening the first Pfalzweinstuben (wine pubs) in Berlin and other cities he made an important contribution to the popularity of Rheinpfalz wines.

Terrain and soil: Of the 66.5 acres of vineyards, 13% are on steeply sloping, 28% on gently sloping, and 59% on flat terrain. The soils are gravel, loamy sand, clay, marl, loess, and loess-loam.

Vineyard names: Deidesheimer Herrgottsacker (6.2 a.), Deidesheimer Mäushöhle (2 a.), Deidesheimer Kalkofen (1.2 a.), Deidesheimer Grainhübel (3.7 a.), Deidesheimer Leinhöhle (1.2 a.), Deidesheimer Paradiesgarten (3 a.), Forster Freundstück (5 a.), Forster Jesuitengarten (3.7 a.), Forster Ungeheuer (6.9 a.), Forster Elster (3 a.), Forster Musenhang (2 a.), Forster Pechstein (3 a.), Ruppertsberger Mandelgarten (2 a.), Ruppertsberger Nussbien (1.5 a.), Ruppertsberger Königsbacherweg (3.7 a.).

The Grosslage names are Deidesheimer Hofstück, Forster Mariengarten, Forster Schnepfenflug.

Grape varieties: 57% Riesling, 25% Müller-Thurgau, 12% Sylvaner, 4% Ruländer, 2% Traminer.

The wines: The wines are fresh, fruity, and full, with a well-balanced, ripe sweetness—particularly in the 1971 wines. The list is very extensive (four vintages) extending from very dry, diabetic-quality wines to Trockenbeerenauslese and sparkling wines, all produced in the same winery.

Estate specialties: Emphasis is placed on the Rheinpfalz Riesling. The proportion of award-winning and fine wines is unusually high.

Label: It features two roosters (taken from the family coat of arms), which hold a coat of arms bearing the Palatinate lion.

Marketing: Most of the wines are sold in the estate's 19 restaurants. The restaurants, which serve Palatinate specialties, are located in Munich, Augsburg, Heidelberg, Mannheim, Ludwigshafen, Frankfurt, Hamburg, and Deidesheim. The wines are also offered for direct sale.

Visits and tastings: By appointment, the estate winery, meat-packing operation, and bakery can be visited. In the winery and in the tasting rooms of various sizes in the Deidesheimer Hof hotel, which also belongs to the estate, individually organized wine tastings can be held and a simple snack served. English-speaking personnel available.

From my notebook: The manor, set in idyllic countryside, has become a modern winery, administration headquarters, and supply house for the estate's 19 restaurants. The co-owner and director, Arthur Hahn, Jr., a trained oenologist, takes time from his many business engagements to personally introduce his wines to interested wine lovers. The estate handles large groups well.

DEIDESHEIM

Carl Josef Hoch'sche Güterverwaltung

Address: 6705 Deidesheim, Weinstrasse 10
Telephone: (06326) 221

Location: At the edge of Deidesheim on the road to Forst.
How to get there: Take route B-271 (German Wine Road).
History: In 1828, Carl Josef Hoch founded a company of the same name in Neustadt, which today owns three wine estates: Weingut Landesökonomierat Louis Hoch Erben, located in Neustadt; Weingut Dr. Feinhard, located in Deidesheim; and Weingut Josef Reinhardt II, located in Deidesheim.
Terrain and soils: The 140.8 acres of vineyards are on gently sloping and flat terrain. The soils are gravel, loamy sand, clay, marl, loess, and loess-loam.
Vineyard names: Hambacher Feuer, Hambacher Kaiserstuhl, Neustadter Mönchgarten, Neustadter Erkenbrecht, Haardter Bürgergarten, Haardter Mandelring, Haardter Herzog, Mussbacher Mandelring, Mussbacher Eselshaut, Mussbacher Schlössel, Gimmeldinger Biengarten, Gimmeldinger Kappellenberg, Gimmeldinger Mandelgarten, Gimmeldinger Schlössel, Deidesheimer Grainhübel, Deidesheimer Herrgottsacker, Deidesheimer Kalkofen, Deidesheimer Kieselberg, Deidesheimer Leinhöhle, Deidesheimer Mäushöhle, Deidesheimer Paradiesgarten, Deides-

heimer Nonnenstück, Forster Elster, Forster Jesuitengarten, Forster Kirchenstück, Forster Ungeheuer, Ruppertsberger Hoheburg, Ruppertsberger Linsenbusch, Ruppertsberger Nussbien,
Ruppertsberger Reiterpfad.

The Grosslage names are Meerspinne, Rebstöckel, Mariengarten,
and Hofstück.

Grape varieties: 65% Riesling, 25% Sylvaner, 4% Müller-
Thurgau, 3% Weissburgunder, 1% Ruländer, 2% miscellaneous.

The wines: Full, typical Mittelhaardt wines ranging from very
dry, wines suitable for diabetics to the finest Auslese.

Estate specialties: Rieslings from the best vineyards in the area.

Label: Each of the three estates has its own label.

Marketing: Exclusively through wholesalers.

Visits: Only possible in special cases. English-speaking personnel
available.

From my notebook: This estate, with its large winery, sells only to
wholesale buyers. The wines come from the finer sites in the
Mittelhaardt area of Rheinpfalz.

HAARDT

Weingut Müller-Catoir

Address: 6730 Neustadt 13
Telephone: (06321) 2815

Location: The estate buildings are in Haardt, a little above Neustadt, at the foot of the Haardt Mountains, with a wide view
over the Rhine plain.

How to get there: Drive 1 km west from Neustadt.

Points of interest: The beautiful view of the Rhine plain; the
vaulted barrel cellar; the eighteenth-century tasting room.

History: A family property since 1744. The wine estate was managed by women from 1897 to 1968 (the great-grandmother, grandmother, and mother of the present proprietor) and was featured in a German television program, "Wine and the Intelligent Women."

Terrain and soils: Of the 43.5 acres of vineyards, 70% are on flat terrain and 30% are on gently sloping terrain. The soils are gravel, loamy sand, clay, marl, loess, and loess-loam.

Vineyard names: Haardter Bürgergarten (5.7 a.), Haardter Herrenletten (3 a.), Haardter Herzog (0.5 a.), Haardter Mandelring (6.2 a.), Neustadter Mönchgarten (5 a.), Neustadter Grain (2.2 a.), Mussbacher Eselshaut (13.8 a.), Gimmeldinger Mandelgarten (1 a.), Gimmeldinger Schlössel (0.5 a.), Hambacher Römerbrunnen (5.7 a.).

The Grosslage name is Gimmeldinger Meerspinne.

Grape varieties: 25% Riesling, 13% Ruländer, 12% Müller-Thurgau, 12% Scheurebe, 10% Sylvaner, 8% Kerner, 7% Gewürztraminer, 4% Morio-Muskat, 4% Portugieser, 2% Weissburgunder, 2% Huxel, 1% Rieslaner.

The wines: Full wines with much fruitiness and spice. Delicate acidity and subtle sweetness provide elegance and balance.

Estate specialties: Based on the awards won by its wines, this estate is one of the most successful in Rheinpfalz. The favorite grape is the Scheurebe. A 1964 Scheurebe Trockenbeerenauslese with 237.3 degrees Öchsle won the Rheinpfalz Outstanding Wine award in 1969 and also other awards.

Label: It features the coat of arms of the Catoir family. Shown are the tools and emblem of the tanners who immigrated from France about 1600.

Marketing: 98% sold directly to private customers.

Visits and tastings: Monday through Friday, from 8 A.M. to 12 noon and 1 P.M. to 5 P.M. Wine tastings are held free of charge for small groups.

From my notebook: A charmingly landscaped estate, where people interested in wine are graciously welcomed by the young proprietor, Heinrich Catoir. The high quality of this estate's wine is due to careful vine pruning, extremely late harvesting, and highly conservative cellar techniques (no fining agents of any type are used).

SIEBELDINGEN

Weingut Ökonomierat Rebholz

Address: 6741 Siebeldingen, Weinstrasse 56
Telephone: (06345) 439

Location: In the center of the village. The estate buildings can be recognized by the half-timbered gables above the entrance and a symbol composed of the letter "R" in a cluster of grapes.

How to get there: From Landau take route B-10 toward Pirmasens/ Saarbrücken, or coming from the north, take the German Wine Road.

Points of interest: The courtyard; the numerous awards in the tasting room; the terraced vineyards in the beautiful country-side.

History: The Rebholz family has been in viticulture in Siebeldingen for about 300 years. Counselor Eduard Rebholz, the father of the present proprietor, was famous in the original carafe-wine area of the Oberhaardt as a pioneer of new methods of training vines. He also produced fine wines not considered possible there.

The Müller-Thurgau variety attained its reputation as a quality grape through Eduard Rebholz when he made a Trockenbeer-enauslese from it for the first time in 1949. Today Hans Rebholz and his wife manage the estate.

Terrain and soils: Of the 22.2 acres of vineyards, one third are on steeply sloping terrain and the rest are on gently sloping terrain. The geological fault that forms the Rhine plain has left various types of soils here including red sandstone, rubble, red schist, limestone, and loess-clay.

Vineyard names: Siebeldinger im Sonnenschein, Siebeldinger Rosenberg, Birkweiler Kastanienbusch.

The Grosslage name is Siebeldinger Königsgarten.

Grape varieties: 30% Riesling, 30% Müller-Thurgau, 10%

Gewürztraminer, 10% Ruländer, 10% Spätburgunder, 10% Muskat-Ottonel, Muskateller, and experimental plantings of new varieties.

The wines: Dry wines are favorites here. The wines have a hearty freshness and racy character. The Prädikat wines are vigorous and elegant. Special efforts are made to maintain the character of the grape variety.

Estate specialties: The estate is unique in German viticulture because there are no chaptalized wines produced here. QbA (Qualitätswein bestimmter Anbaugebiete) wines are not represented in the list, which jumps from Tafelweins to Prädikat wines. The Tafelweins (Hans Rebholz maintains that the term "Landwein" or "country wine" would be more appropriate) and Kabinett wines are dry, and the higher class Prädikat wines are fermented to be as dry as possible. The proportion of award-winning wines is very high.

Label: It features the company symbol: an "R" in a grape cluster, created in a very plain style by the owner's brother. A further feature is the cursive typography used on the label.

Marketing: Almost exclusively to the individual consumer, with shipping service available. The brief explanations on the price list are very informative.

Visits and tastings: Contact with clients is considered important here. Small groups up to 15 persons are gladly welcomed. An appointment is necessary.

From my notebook: This establishment has unusual production methods and taste concepts. These are emphasized by the proprietor, who expresses his ideas clearly and convincingly. Very much recommended for the wine lover who is interested in production processes.

Baden

Hornberg

Neckarzimmern

Karlsruhe

RHEIN

Durbach

NECKAR

Offen
burg

v. Neveu

v. Metternich

Staufenberg

Ihringen

Freiburg

Blankenhornsberg

*Markgraf
von Baden*

Salem

Meersburg

Staatsweingut

1971 er **Burg Hornberger Wallmauer**
Muskateller Auslese

A.P. Nr. 6060672

Qualitätswein
mit Prädikat

FREIHERRL. VON GEMMINGEN-HORNBERG'SCHES WEINGUT BURG HORNBERG AM NECKAR

*Gräflich
Wolff Metternich'sches
Weingut*

*vorm. Freiherr
Zorn von Bulach
Durbach / Baden*

Baden

Durbacher Schloßberg

CLEVNER TRAMINER SPATLESE
A.P. Nr.: 501/22/73

QUALITÄTSWEIN MIT PRÄDIKAT

Freiherrlich von Gemmingen-Hornberg'sches Weingut, Burg Hornberg

Address: 6951 Neckarzimmern, Burg Hornberg
Telephone: (06261) 2348

Location: The castle of Burg Hornberg is situated high above the vineyards in the Neckar Valley in Baden.

How to get there: Coming from Heidelberg, take route B-37 along the Neckar River to Neckarzimmern. Branch off in the center of the village at the signpost "Burg Hornberg." Drive up the steep hill for 2 km and park in the castle courtyard.

Points of interest: The castle; the castle museum, with weapons, armor, Roman relics, and medieval equipment; the uniquely furnished castle restaurant.

History: Burg Hornberg was first recorded in 1184, but in legend is of earlier date. In 1517, Götz von Berlichingen acquired the castle, selected it as his permanent residence, wrote his memoirs, and died in it. At the beginning of the seventeenth century the castle was acquired by the Gemmingen family, which still owns it today. Since the time of the Roman-Limes wall, viticulture has been practiced here, and during the medieval period it was greatly developed.

Terrains and soils: Of the 50.7 acres of vineyards, 14.8 acres are in Michelfeld, about 30 km from the main operation in Neckarzimmern. Most of the vineyards are on terraced, steeply sloping terrain. In Neckarzimmern the soil is mainly limestone, and in Michelfeld the soil is marl.

Vineyard names: Burg Hornberger Wallmauer (14.8 a.), Burg Hornberger Götzhalde (21 a.), Schloss Michelfelder Himmelberg (14.8 a.).

Grape varieties: 30% Riesling, 20% Müller-Thurgau, 15% Sylvaner, 10% Spätburgunder, 5% Samtrot, 20% Muskateller, Traminer, Ruländer, and Weissburgunder.

The wines: Similar to wines of the southern Bergstrasse. They are robust, with aftertaste, full of fruitiness and spice, and exhibit the ripeness made possible by steep slopes. Individual barrel aging maintains the different characters of the grape varieties. Blends are stated on the labels.

Estate specialties: Numerous high awards have been won at the state and national wine judgings. The Muskateller and Traminer Auslese are full bodied and have a fine, noble spiciness.

Label: It features a view of the Burg Hornberg with the vineyards, and at the bottom left, the family coat of arms. At the top right there is a portrait of the former castle owner, Götz von Berlichingen.

Marketing: Direct sale to restaurants, hotels, and private customers.

Visits and tastings: During regular visiting hours, the castle can be viewed without an appointment. The castle restaurant, Im alten Marstall, is open all day and serves the estate wines. Tastings in the cellar are only possible in special cases.

From my notebook: The Burg Hornberg, with the castle restaurant and the small hotel, situated high above the vineyards, is most warmly recommended to wine lovers. The well-made, elegant, full wines indicate the devotion of the owner, Baron Hans-Wolf von Gemmingen-Hornberg, who is a trained oenologist and manages this unique estate.

DURBACH

Gutsverwaltung Freiherr von Neveu

Address: 7601 Durbach
Telephone: (0781) 73182

Location: The estate lies in Hespengrund, a tributary valley of the Durbach Valley, halfway up the hill opposite Schloss Staufenberg.

How to get there: Take the Karlsruhe-Basel autobahn. When coming from Karlsruhe, turn off at Appenweier, traveling through Windschläg to Durbach (8 km). Coming from Basel, turn off at Offenburg and drive through Rammersweier to Durbach (12 km). The estate is 2 km northeast from the center of Durbach.

Points of interest: The picturesque tributary valley in which the estate is situated; the carved barrels; the racks of barrels in the cellar.

History: In 1660, the estate was in the possession of a Strasbourg doctor. In 1832, it was bought by Prince-Bishop Franz Xaver von Neveu for his nephew. The family of Baron von Neveu manages the estate today.

Terrain and soils: The 29.6 acres of vineyards are on steeply sloping terrain, and the danger of erosion of the magmatite soil is high.

Vineyard names: Durbacher Josephsberg (21 a.), Durbacher Ölberg (2.5 a.), Ortenberger Freudental (1.2 a.), Ortenberger Schlossberg (5 a.).

Grape varieties: 40% Riesling, 30% Traminer, 15% Müller-Thurgau, 15% Spätburgunder.

The wines: Full, fruity wines that exhibit the character of the grape variety.

Estate specialties: Awards have been won at state and national wine judgings. In 1962, 1965, and 1966 Eisweins were produced.

Label: It features the family coat of arms (two crossed silver anchors on a green background). On some of the labels the name of the present proprietor is featured.

Marketing: Formerly by direct sales. Since 1961 the central winery of the Baden Vintners Cooperative in Breisach has taken the entire output of the estate after the wine has been made in the estate cellars. The cooperative then bottles the wine and sells it through its own sales organization.

Visits: The cellar and vineyards can be visited by appointment.

From my notebook: The wines from the Neveu estate have a special place in the sales program of the Baden cooperative and are the only wines which are sold under an estate name. Wines are no longer offered for sale by the estate itself.

DURBACH

Gräflich Wolff Metternich'sches Weingut, vorm. Freiherr Zorn von Bulach

Address: 7601 Durbach, Grohl 117
Telephone: (0781) 5779

Location: The estate buildings are in the middle of the village. Picturesquely surrounded by woods, the steep vineyards climb to a height of 300 meters (330 yd).

How to get there: Take the Karlsruhe-Basel autobahn. Coming from Karlsruhe, turn off at Appenweier and drive 8 km through Windschläg to Durbach. Coming from Basel, turn off at Offenburg and drive 12 km through Rammersweier to Durbach.

Points of interest: The former *Schloss* cellar; the wonderful view from the vineyards to the community of Durbach and the surrounding valleys.

History: Since 1420 the Durbach estate has been in the hands of the family of Zorn von Bulach, which has its ancestral seat in Osthausen (Alsace). About 1840, the estate was entailed by Baron Ernst Maximilian Zorn von Bulach, and entailment was not broken until 1918. During this period more land was purchased, and the establishment was brought up to modern standards. In 1936, the estate was inherited by Countess M. C. Wolff Metternich (see Baroness von Bulach), who died in 1967. The proprietor today is Count Paul Joseph Wolff Metternich.

Terrain and soils: Of the 74.1 acres of vineyards, 80% are on steeply sloping terrain and 20% are on gently sloping terrain. The steep slopes have acid magmatite soil; the gentle slopes have loess and loess-loam soils.

Vineyard names: Durbacher Schloss Grohl (14.8 a.), Durbacher Schlossberg (39.5 a.), Durbacher Plauelrain (5 a.), Lahrer Herrentisch (14.8 a.).

Grape varieties: 25% Traminer and Gewürztraminer, 20% Riesling, 18% Müller-Thurgau, 16% Spätburgunder, 10% Ruländer, 5% Scheurebe, 3% Weissburgunder, 2% Muskat-Ottonel, 1% miscellaneous.

The wines: The estate tries to emphasize the individual characters of the different grape varieties. Late harvests increase the proportion of fine wines. Particular importance is placed on retaining the natural acidity, which is rounded off with a slight residual sweetness.

Estate specialties: Some fine wines are maintained in a special bottle cellar to provide wines 10 years old and older for special occasions. Specialties of the establishment are a dry sparkling wine fermented in the bottle, and a matured brandy. Many award-winning wines.

Label: It features the proprietor's coat of arms. The individual qualities are also indicated by colors: Qualitätswein = blue edge; Kabinett = green edge; Spätlese = red edge; Auslese and above = gold edge.

Marketing: To the trade, hotels, and restaurants, as well as to private customers. Only one price list is issued, which contains about 30 wines and appears two or three times a year, depending on the sales situation and wine stocks. The estate is represented at the Durbach wine festival (spring), the Offenburg wine festival (fall), and the Offenburg wine market.

Visits and tastings: Visits can be made during working hours. Wine tastings are held for prospective purchasers, and large wine tastings can be arranged by appointment. A newly furnished tasting room holding up to 30 persons is available.

From my notebook: The estate buildings and vineyards are in lovely surroundings. The interesting assortment of well-made wines makes a visit to this wine estate a special event, especially when the manager, Mr. Schilli, conducts the tour and comments on the wines.

DURBACH

Markgräflich Badisches Weingut Schloss Staufenberg

Address: 7601 Durbach, Schloss Staufenberg
Telephone: (0781) 2778

Location: The manor, with the offices and winery, is in the middle
of the vineyards, 380 m (415 yd) above sea level, at the top of
a hill on the edge of the upper Rhine plain.

How to get there: Take the Karlsruhe-Basel autobahn. Coming
from Karlsruhe, turn off at Appenweier and drive 8 km through
Windschläg to Durbach. Coming from Basel, turn off at Offenburg and drive 12 km through Rammersweier to Durbach. From
there to the manor it is 3 km.

Points of interest: The magnificent panoramic view from the
Schloss to the heights of the Black Forest, the Rhine plain, the
Kaiserstuhl, and the Vosges in Alsace; the extensive cellar; the
tree wine press; the carved barrels; the picturesque vineyards.

History: Schloss Staufenberg was built in the eleventh century as
a castle by the Duke of Zähringen. The viticulture is also said
to date from this period. The margraves of Baden held Staufenberg as a fief for 600 years and finally purchased it in 1832.

Formerly mixed agriculture was practiced, but only vines have been grown since 1956. The proprietor is Margrave Max von Baden. He resides in Salem on the Lake of Constance.

Terrain and soils: The 64.2 acres of vineyards are mainly on steeply sloping terrain in the immediate vicinity of the *Schloss.* The soil is acid magmatite.

Vineyard names: All wines are called Durbacher Schloss Staufenberg, which the wine law considers a section of the village.

Grape varieties: 35% Riesling, 25% Müller-Thurgau, 20% Traminer and Gewürztraminer, 10% Pinot Noir, 7% Ruländer, 3% experimental varieties.

The wines: The different varieties of grapes produce many types of wines. Well-made, full, mild wines with a delicate acidity are offered from two or three vintages.

Estate specialties: A high proportion of award-winning wines. Two special awards from the ministry of agriculture have been won. High-quality wines up to Trockenbeerenauslese.

Label: The label formerly featured the coat of arms of Schloss Staufenberg. Because of coordination with the associate winery in Salem on the Lake of Constance, the coat of arms of the dukes of Zähringen appears on all the labels.

Marketing: Direct sales. There is only one price list, with discounts being granted for large purchases.

Visits and tastings: By appointment, the courtyard, cellar, and vineyards can be visited. Wine tastings are individually compiled by arrangement. People on outings should note that the estate also sells wine on Saturdays, Sundays, and holidays at slightly higher prices. Open 9 A.M. to 6 P.M.

From my notebook: An excursion to this wine estate, in its charming setting and with its wide selection of wines, is well worth while. The administrator, Nikolaus Dühr, is a well-versed wine expert, who is happy to give information on the estate, the cellar, and the wines. A red wine, known as Eberblut, and other wines grow on a wonderful south slope in the Murg Valley at the affiliated wine estate of Schloss Eberstein (about 24.7 acres). They are also processed and marketed at Schloss Staufenberg.

IHRINGEN AM KAISERSTUHL

Versuchs- und Lehrgut Für Weinbau Blankenhornsberg

Address: 7811 Ihringen
Telephone: (07668) 217

Location: The estate buildings and vineyards are on a hill at the southwest side of the Kaiserstuhl, in the community of Ihringen.

How to get there: Drive northeast from Breisach to Ihringen and then 3 km to the estate.

Points of interest: The wonderful view of the Rhein valley (with Breisach in the foreground), Alsace (with the south Vosges mountains in the background), and the Black Forest; the experimental vine plantings and the model vineyards; the old wine cellar, with the cruciform vaulting built of brick.

History: The wine estate of Blankenhornsberg was founded in 1842–44 by the Blankenhorn brothers from Müllheim (Baden). Professor Dr. Adolph Blankenhorn (1843–1906), lecturer for viticulture and viniculture at the technical school in Karlsruhe, developed it into an experimental estate. In 1919, it was purchased by the Baden Chamber of Agriculture. Since 1954 it has been run by the Freiburg Viniculture Institute as an experimental and training facility.

Terrain and soils: Of the 61.8 acres of vineyards, 70% are on steeply sloping, 20% on gently sloping, and 10% on flat terrain. The soils are magmatite and loess.

Vineyard names: All the production areas of the estate are consolidated in the Doktorgarten vineyard and entered as such in the vineyard register. As Blankenhornsberg is an independent section of the community, all wines are offered for sale under the Blankenhornsberger name.

Grape varieties: 20% Müller-Thurgau, 16% Ruländer, 13%

Riesling, 11% Spätburgunder, 9% Weissburgunder, 22% miscellaneous, mainly experimental varieties.

The wines: A wide assortment of different types, including little-known experimental varieties. The careful production methods used here are typical for this area.

Estate specialties: A large number of awards has been won at state and national wine judgings. Single bottles of older vintages are still available. Many Auslese and Beerenauslese wines are also available.

Label: A vertically oriented rhombus featuring the coat of arms of the Blankenhorn family (three horns).

Marketing: Direct sales to private customers, hotels, restaurants, and dealers.

Visits and tastings: Visits can be made upon application, but wine tastings are only held in special cases. Sample bottles can be purchased during regular business hours.

From my notebook: A tour through the experimental plantings conducted by the manager, Erich Meinke, is very informative. The many types of wines offer an excellent opportunity for comparisons.

MEERSBURG

Staatsweingut Meersburg

Address: 7738 Meersburg, Seminarstrasse 8
Telephone: (07532) 6085

Location: The offices and cellars are in the riding school of the Neue Schloss (formerly the residence of the prince-bishops) in the upper part of Meersburg. The estate buildings are on the Wetterkreuz, a hill on the Lake of Constance, offering an excellent view.

Points of interest: The modern winery in the riding school of the

Schloss; the beautifully situated vineyards along the shore of the lake; the wine museum, containing an old press and the Meersburg Turkish barrel, an item of particular interest.

History: Vineyards on Meersburg Hill were first recorded in 1210. In 1802, the vineyard properties of the prince-bishops, first recorded in 1346, were acquired by the Baden crown. In 1812, a domain administration was established. After severe frost damage in the winter of 1956–57 additional vineyards were purchased and consolidated with the existing acreage. In 1969, a further 14.8 acres at Hohentwiel, near Singen, were acquired by the Meersburg administration. The estate is subordinate to the finance minister of the state of Baden-Württemberg.

Terrain and soils: Of the 153.2 acres of vineyards, 113.7 acres are on the Lake of Constance, 14.8 acres at Hohentwiel, and 24.7 acres in Gailingen on the upper Rhine. The Meersburg vineyards are on gently and steeply sloping terrain with moraine soils. At Hohentwiel, which is 193 feet above sea level and probably the highest vineyard in Germany, the terrain is steeply sloping and the soils are magmatite, marl, and loam.

Vineyard names: Meersburger Chorherrnhalde, Meersburger Rieschen, Meersburger Bengel, Meersburger Jungfernstieg, Meersburger Lerchenberg, Meersburger Fohrenberg, Meersburger Sängerhalde, Hohentwieler Olgaberg, Gailinger Ritterhalde.

The Grosslage name is Meersburger Sonnenufer.

Grape varieties: 50% Pinot Noir, 30% Müller-Thurgau, 10% Ruländer, 10% Riesling, Traminer, and other varietas.

The wines: The Meersburg wines are very clean, racy, and elegant. The majority of the Pinot Noir grapes are processed into full bodied, spritzig rosé wines. The wines offered are limited almost exclusively to the latest vintage.

Estate specialties: Fine wines up to Trockenbeerenauslese are offered. The Pinot Noir rosé wines are a great specialty.

Label: It shows the Baden coat of arms in red and gold.

Marketing: Direct sales, with many private customers. A regular supplier to hotels and restaurants on the Lake of Constance.

Visits and tastings: By appointment wine tasting visits can be made. A fee is charged.

From my notebook: Both the wine and countryside make this an interesting estate. The view from the offices out to the Lake is beautiful. One should allow plenty of time to visit this estate, its vineyards, the winery, and the wine museum. The director, Mr. Adams, is well-versed on the history, viticulture, and wines of the estate.

SALEM

Weingüter Max Markgraf von Baden

Address: 7777 Salem, Schloss
Telephone: (07553) 81271

Location: The offices and winery are in Schloss Salem.
Points of interest: The extensive former monastery of Salem, in idyllic surroundings; Birnau and Schloss Kirchberg on the shore of the Lake of Constance.
History: Founded in 1137 by Cistercian monks; rebuilt and converted in 1697. In 1803, the gigantic monastery complex with its agricultural estates passed into the hands of the margraves of Baden during secularization. The proprietor today is Margrave Max von Baden.
Terrain and soils: The 190.3 acres of vineyards are on three estates: Weingut Birnau (98.9 a.), Weingut Schloss Kirchberg (42 a.), and Weingut Bermatingen (49.4 a.).
Vineyard names: Bermatinger Leopoldsberg, Birnauer Kirchhalde, Schloss Kirchberger Schlossberg, Meersburger Chorherrnhalde.
Grape varieties: 64% Müller-Thurgau, 30% Spätburgunder, 3% Ruländer, 3% experimental varieties.
The wines: The Lake of Constance wines distinguish themselves by a pleasant, fruity character and racy acidity.

Estate specialties: The rosé wines have always been considered a specialty. In the last few years the Müller-Thurgau wines have gained in importance because of their fruity acidity.

Label: It bears the Zähringer coat of arms.

Marketing: Sales direct from the estate.

Visits and tastings: The *Schloss* and museum are open from 9 A.M. to 6 P.M. during the summer. In the winter, by appointment only. Wine tastings and visits to the winery must be arranged in advance.

From my notebook: The countryside around Schloss Salem and the wine estate is charming. For those interested in culture and history, illustrated brochures about the former monastery, the basilica, and Birnau are available.

Württemberg

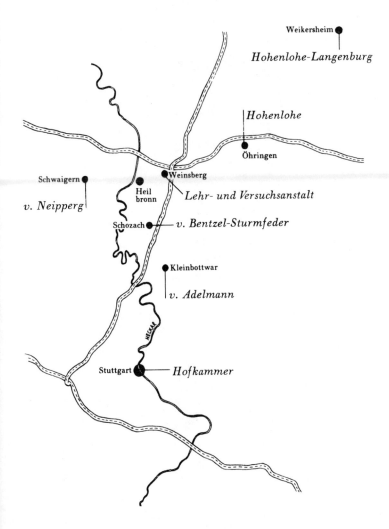

Weikersheim

Hohenlohe-Langenburg

Hohenlohe

Öhringen

Schwaigern

v. Neipperg

Weinsberg

Heil
bronn

Lehr- und Versuchsanstalt

Schozach

v. Bentzel-Sturmfeder

Kleinbottwar

v. Adelmann

NECKAR

Stuttgart

Hofkammer

WÜRTT. HOFKAMMER-KELLEREI STUTTGART

1973 er

Untertürkheimer Mönchberg

Riesling Spätlese

QUALITÄTSWEIN MIT PRÄDIKAT · WÜRTTEMBERG

Amtl. Prüf.- Nr. 233 052 74

A.P.Nr.
217 002 73

KLEINBOTTWARER

Brüsseler Spitze

Eßmund Riesling

SPÄTLESE

Qualitätswein mit Prädikat

SCHLOSSKELLEREI

GRAF v. ADELMANN

WÜRTTEMBERG

Goldene
Preismünze der Landesweinprämiierung 1973

Schloßkellerei   Graf v. Neipperg
Weingut   Schwaigern

Württemberg

Neipperger Schloßberg

1971 er Lemberger Auslese

Qualitätswein mit Prädikat

A.P.Nr. 226 024 73

Württembergische Hofkammer-Kellerei

Address: 7000 Stuttgart, Hölderlinstrasse 32
Telephone: (0711) 294587

Location: The offices are located in Hölderlinstrasse. The winery is in the old *Schloss* in the center of Stuttgart with vineyards at Maulbronn, Mundelsheim, Untertürkheim, Stetten, and Hohenhaslach.

How to get there: To visit the historic cellar in the old *Schloss,* park on the Karlsplatz, directly in front of the entrance to the winery.

Points of interest: The *Schloss* cellar, which dates from the fourteenth century; impressive rows of barrels.

History: The vineyard properties of the house of Württemberg date back to the Middle Ages. Later, monastery property (Eilfingerberg near Maulbronn) was acquired. The construction of the *Schloss* cellar was started in 1320. Today the proprietor of the wine estate is Duke Philipp Albrecht von Württemberg, who resides at Schloss Altshausen near Ravensburg.

Terrain and soils: Of the total estate area of 79 acres, 58 acres are devoted to vines, the terrain being mostly steeply and gently sloping. The soil is mainly marl, with some limestone in Mundelsheim. Grapes are pressed at Eilfingerberg, Untertürkheim, and Mundelsheim, and the grape-must is taken to the winery in Stuttgart.

Vineyard names: Maulbronner Eilfingerberg, Klosterstück (both Maulbronner vineyards are entirely owned by the estate and together account for 42 acres), Hohenhaslacher Kirchberg (6.2 a.), Mundelsheimer Käsberg (5 a.), Untertürkheimer Mönchberg (17.3 a.), Untertürkheimer Altenberg (1.2 a.), Stettener Brotwasser (entire vineyard, 7.4 a.).

The Grosslage names are Stromberg, Weinsteige, and Wartbühl.

Grape varieties: 55.4% Riesling, 19.6% Trollinger, 6.9% Limberger, 6.4% Sylvaner, 3.9% Spätburgunder, 3.4% Traminer, 2.9% Müller-Thurgau, 1.5% Portugieser.

The wines: The special characteristics of the vineyards, vintages, and grape varieties are emphasized by leaving little residual sugar and by individual barrel aging. The red wines are almost dry, but are still soft, the 1971 being particularly rich in extract. The wines grown on red marl are very fruity.

Estate specialties: Single bottles of older vintages (1953, 1959) are still available. Many award-winning wines. Eilfingerberg Traminer and Limberger are especially full-bodied and are considered to be a specialty.

Label: The label is very simple and features the stylized coat of arms of the house of Württemberg (deer horns in a yellow field).

Marketing: Only one list is issued and discounts are granted to the trade. The wines are well represented in high-class restaurants and hotels. For sale in small quantities on certain afternoons in the *Schloss* winery.

Visits and tastings: The winery can be visited by appointment. Wine tastings are given in the tasting room (up to 30 persons) or in the cellar.

From my notebook: A visit to this historic and impressive cellar, in one of the oldest buildings in Stuttgart, can be easily combined with a visit to the center of the city. The Hofkammer wines are from the finest vineyards in Württemberg. Arrangements should be made with the financial counselor, Mr. Schaal, in the administrative offices.

KLEINBOTTWAR

Weingut Brüssele, Schlosskellerei Graf Adelmann

Address: 7141 Steinheim-Kleinbottwar, Burg Schaubeck
Telephone: (07148) 331

Location: The castle of Burg Schaubeck is situated on the southeast side of Kleinbottwar in the idyllic Bottwar Valley, with its castles and vineyards. The offices, the bottle cellar, and the residence of the family of Count Adelmann are in the castle, while the winery is in the center of the village.

How to get there: Take the Stuttgart-Heilbronn autobahn, turning off at Grossbottwar/Mundelsheim, and then travel 7 km to Grossbottwar, and a further 4 km to Kleinbottwar.

History: Viticulture was first recorded in the Bottwar Valley in 950. From the very beginning Burg Schaubeck, which was built by a family of the same name in the thirteenth century, included vineyards. In 1853, the castle and wine estate were inherited by the Von Brusselle family. Wines from the estate have ever since then been termed "Brüssele," which is a Swabian variation of the family name. In 1914, the wine estate was inherited by Countess Adelmann, the last of the Brusselle family, through marriage. The present owner, Count Raban Adelmann, a diplomat and politician, manages the estate in an exemplary fashion.

Terrain and soils: Of the total 125.5 acres of vineyards, 31.4 acres in almost one piece is near Kleinbottwar on marl soil, and 76.6 acres are in the area of Hoheneck-Ludwigsburg where the soil is limestone. The terrain is mostly steep or gently sloping.

Vineyard names: All wines carry the name Brüssele. The wines from the Trollinger grape are occasionally called Kleinbottwarer Oberer Berg, and the Rieslings, Kleinbottwarer Süssmund.

Grape varieties: 53% red-wine varieties, 47% white-wine varieties.

20% Riesling, 20% Trollinger, 8.2% Limberger, 7% Müller-
Thurgau, 8.2% Muskateller, 5.2% Traminer, 3.8% Kerner,
3.2% Sylvaner, 2.3% Ruländer, 1.7% Urban, 20.4% various
Burgundy types, such as Samtrot, Clevner, and Müllerrebe.

The wines: Well-made, elegant wines which are delicately fruity
and well balanced. With their delicate and flowery character,
they differ from the usual robust wines of Württemberg. The
red wines are soft and velvety. Little residual sugar.

Estate specialties: A high proportion of fine wines, which also have
very little residual sugar. The estate has actively participated in
wine competitions for more than 100 years. The Muskat-
Trollinger is a great specialty of the estate. The best Rieslings
are named Brüssele'r Spitze Süssmund Riesling. Single bottles
of older wines from 1959 are still available.

Label: It shows the castle of Burg Schaubeck, the family coat of
arms, and the word "Brüssele." Special bottlings (Brüssele'r
Spitze) carry a special label with a lace pattern as background.

Marketing: Only one price list, many regular customers, considerable export business. The new vintage is always offered for sale
the following autumn.

Visits and tastings: The castle and vineyards can be visited by
appointment. Small tastings are held in the castle tasting room
during business hours. Larger tastings, together with a visit to
the castle, can be arranged only by previous appointment as
they are held in the private apartment of the owner. English-
speaking personnel available.

From my notebook: The wines are of the highest quality. The
many types of wine and individual barrel aging encourages one
to try the entire assortment. The countryside surrounding the
vineyards and the castle is beautiful. The proprietor, Count
Adelmann, is well versed in history and viniculture, and speaks
five languages. For those who have the good fortune to have
him as guide, a visit to Burg Schaubeck will be a memorable
occasion. Advance arrangements are necessary.

SCHOZACH

Gräflich von Bentzel-Sturmfeder'sches Weingut

Address: 7129 Schozach
Telephone: (07133) 7829

Location: The estate buildings are in the middle of the village; the vineyards are in the immediate vicinity of the village.

How to get there: Take the Stuttgart-Heilbronn autobahn, turn off at the Ilsfeld road, and drive 3 km in the direction of Ilsfeld. From there, drive 2 km in the direction of Heilbronn to Schozach.

Points of interest: The cellar, built in 1711; the well-tended vineyards, on beautiful slopes.

History: In 1396, Baron Friedrich von Sturmfeder was granted the estate as a fief by Count Eberhard von Württemberg, and it passed down to his successors. The present proprietor, Count Hanfried von Bentzel-Sturmfeder-Horneck zu Sternau-Hohenau, lives in Schloss Thurn in upper Franconia.

Terrain and soils: Two thirds of the 49.5 acres of vineyards are on gently sloping and steeply sloping terrain. The soils vary from loam to clay with loam. The air circulates freely in this open countryside thus favoring the growth of healthy grapes, which are rarely affected by noble rot (Botrytis cinerea).

Vineyard names: Schozacher Roter Berg (49.4 a.). The Grosslage name is Kirchenweinberg. The subregion name is Württembergisch Unterland.

Grape varieties: 25% Riesling, 18% Pinot Noir, 14% Samtrot, 11% Müller-Thurgau, 10% Müllerrebe, 6% Portugieser, 5% Limberger, 4% Ruländer, 4% Clevner, 2% Kerner, 1% Traminer.

The wines: The heavy soil contributes to give the wines a rich bouquet and body. All are comparatively dry. The red wines

are full bodied and soft, with little acidity. The young wines
become drinkable comparatively late in spite of barrel aging.

Estate specialties: As the wines are rapidly sold out, they are not
regularly entered for awards. Despite this, awards for outstanding wines were won by the estate at state judgings in 1964 and
1970. Samtrot, Clevner, and Müller-Thurgau wines are very
flowery. Because noble rot seldom appears, Beerenauslese and
Trockenbeerenauslese wines are rarely made.

Label: It features the coat of arms of the Sturmfeder family.

Marketing: Sold principally to regular clients. Only two vintages
are on the list and almost 60% are in liter bottles. The restaurant in Schloss Thurn (upper Franconia) carries the estate
wines.

Visits and tastings: The cellar and vineyards can be visited by appointment only. Standing tastings in the cellar are held for large
groups; for less than 20 people, seated tastings can be held in
the tasting room.

From my notebook: The half-hour tour through the vineyards and
beautiful countryside, under the expert guidance of the administrator, Mr. Blankenhorn, is highly recommended. The rich
assortment of wines, individually barrel aged, makes enlighten-
ing comparative tastings possible. The estate buildings and surroundings have a genuine, warm, village atmosphere.

SCHWAIGERN

Gräflich von Neipperg'sches Weingut und Schlosskellerei

Address: 7103 Schwaigern, Schloss

Telephone: (07138) 312

Location: The *Schloss* is situated next to the Gothic town church
in the middle of the community.

How to get there: The community is directly on route B-293. Take the Stuttgart-Heilbronn autobahn, and when coming from Stuttgart, turn off at Heilbronn and drive 15 km to Schwaigern. Coming from Frankfurt-Mannheim-Heidelberg, turn off at Bonfeld and drive 10 km to Schwaigern.

Points of interest: The old bottle and cask cellar below the *Schloss;* the park, with the town wall; the town church (formerly the family's private chapel); the village of Neipperg, with the Burg Neipperg castle 5 km away in the charming landscape of the Zabergäu, on the slopes of the Heuchelberg.

History: The majority of the vineyards have been in the possession of the house of Neipperg since about 1200. Until the Thirty Years' War the family's influence was restricted to Swabia and Franconia. After the seventeenth century, however, the family played an important role in the politics of the old empire and the Austro-Hungarian monarchy. The present head of the family is Count Josef-Hubert von Neipperg.

Terrain and soils: Of the 61.8 acres of vineyards, 40% are on steeply sloping, 30% on flat terrain. The soils are limestone and marl. The estate uses a unique method of terracing the steep slopes.

Vineyard names: Schwaigerner Ruthe (entire vineyard, 16 a.), Neipperger Schlossberg (entire vineyard, 39.5 a.), Klingenberger Schlossberg (entire vineyard, 6.2 a.).

Grape varieties: 24% Müllerrebe, 20% Riesling, 18% Limberger, 18% Burgunder, 12% Traminer, 8% Muskateller and Müller-Thurgau.

The wines: Individual barrel aging is still practiced. The latest vintage is first offered for sale when the next is ripening on the vine. The Riesling is robust and rather dry; the Traminer is subtly fragrant; the red wines are deep in color and full.

Estate specialties: The estate is traditionally known for its red-wine. The Limberger, colloquially called Lemberger, is said to have been introduced by the family after the Thirty Years' War and has been accorded special attention ever since. Among the white wines, the Traminer is a specialty and is said to have established the reputation of the estate as a white-wine producer in the eighteenth century. The wine list also includes Eisweins.

Samples of fine, older vintages are reserved for special tastings. The estate participates regularly in wine judgings.

Label: The label features the coat of arms of the house of Neipperg: three silver rings on a silver background.

Marketing: The wines are principally sold to private customers and restaurants. Special terms of sale are offered to the trade.

Visits and tastings: Wine tastings and visits are possible if application is made well in advance. Count Neipperg is well known for his clever and entertaining commentaries at wine tastings. English-speaking personnel available.

From my notebook: A wine estate in the old Württemberg tradition. Amusing comments are given for the wines in the price list. For example, "1969 Müller-Thurgau (to the bottle, darling)," "1970 Riesling Kabinett (although a cabinet member, it's not without quality)," "Traminer Spätlese (from grapes with an aristocratic quality—noble rot)," "1970 Schwarzriesling (rope wine: Open bottle and attach a rope to it. You can then haul in the bottle and rescue it if your spouse tries to drink it.)" Who can resist trying one of these?

WEINSBERG

Staatliche Lehr- und Versuchsanstalt für Wein und Obstbau

Address: 7102 Weinsberg, Hallerstrasse 6
Telephone: (07134) 6121

Location: In the middle of the village.
How to get there: Take the Stuttgart-Heidelberg autobahn, turning off at Weinsberg, and drive 2 km to the village.
Points of interest: The modern experimental winery; the viticultural college and experimental stations in the wonderful coun-

tryside near Weinsberg, Gundelsheim, and Burg Wildeck; the old terraced vineyards dating from the twelfth century, near Gundelsheim.

History: The oldest German training and experimental facility for viticulture and cellar technology. Established by King Karl of Württemberg in 1868 because of the poor economic situation in viticulture at the time. At the beginning there were six students and 22 acres of vines. After World War II the cellar-technology department was enlarged by Mr. Klenk, the director. In 1970, Dr. Goetz became the director. Today the establishment has 125 staff members and a worldwide reputation.

Terrain and soils: The total area controlled is 158.6 acres. Of the 36.5 acres of vineyards, 70% are on steeply sloping, 20% on gently sloping, and 10% on flat terrain. The soils are limestone, marl, loess, loam, and gravel.

Vineyard names: Weinsberger Schemelsberg (32.1 a.), Weinsberger Ranzenberg (6.2 a.), Abstatter Burg Wildeck (29.6 a.), Gundelsheimer Himmelreich (19.8 a.), Talheimer Schlossberg (5.7 a.).

The wines from the vine-breeding areas are not for sale. The Grosslage name for wines from smaller plots is Lauffener Kirchenweinberg.

Grape varieties: 15.6% Müller-Thurgau, 14.6% Riesling, 13.7% Ruländer, 10.5% Pinot Noir, 8.8% Müllerrebe, 6.6% Limberger, 5.1% Traminer, 5% Samtrot, 4.4% Trollinger, 3% Portugieser, 2.4% Kerner, 1.8% Sylvaner, 1.3% Weissburgunder, 0.6% Heroldrebe, 0.5% Helfensteiner, 4.8% experimental white-wine varieties, and 1.4% experimental red-wine varieties. Kerner, Herold, Samtrot, and Helfensteiner are Weinsberg crossings.

The wines: The wines are carefully made to be faithful to the area and vintage. Particular attention is given to fruit and aroma. Weinsberg encourages using as little sulfur as possible, a practice followed in the production of its own wines. In order to maintain their natural characteristics, only enough residual sugar is allowed to round off the wines. The latest vintage is offered for sale when the new vintage is ripening on the vine.

Estate specialties: All wines offered for sale are entered in the

Württemberg state wine judging. In 1970, 90% of all wines submitted received first prizes, and 6% received second prizes. A rare-wine library is maintained for instructional and consultation purposes. A high proportion of Beerenauslese and Trockenbeerenauslese wines are produced. The Limberger is considered a specialty of the establishment and exceeds the Spätburgunder in fullness and fruitiness.

Label: It features the small state coat of arms (three lions).

Marketing: Only one list, which is supplemented when required. Discounts are granted to the trade.

Visits and tastings: By appointment, the cellar, vineyards, and the vine-breeding station can be visited. Wine tastings can be given in the tasting room (up to 40 persons), in a lecture room (up to 80 persons), or standing in the cellar.

From my notebook: A visit to this establishment is informative for both experts and novices. Experienced personnel conduct the wine tastings, which because of the wide assortment of wines, are very instructive. One should have plenty of time to visit the interesting and beautiful outlying areas, too.

ÖHRINGEN

Fürst zu Hohenlohe-Öhringen'sche Schlosskellerei

Address: 7110 Öhringen Marktplatz
Telephone: (07941) 7081

Location: The office and winery are in the *Schloss* at the market place in Öhringen. The vineyards and press-house are at the foot of the Verrenberg hill about 5 km west of Öhringen.

How to get there: Take the Stuttgart-Heidelberg autobahn for 15 km beyond the Weinsberg cloverleaf toward Schwabach-Öhringen.

Points of interest: The *Schloss* cellar, built 1610–16, with wooden barrels; a 5500-gallon cask dated 1702 that serves as a tasting room for up to 12 persons; a poem by Nikolaus Lenau on a wooden panel that is a souvenir of his visit to the *Schloss* cellar in 1856.

History: The house of Hohenlohe was recorded as early as the twelfth century. The two leopards in the family coat of arms are indicative of the Hohenlohes' participation in the Crusades in the Hohenstaufen train. The wine estate on the Verrenberg has been in the possession of the family for centuries. The current proprietor is Prince Kraft zu Hohenlohe-Öhringen.

Terrain and soils: The 44.5 acres of vines are in one vineyard on the south slope of the Verrnberg hill. The soils are loam, clay, and marl.

Vineyard names: Verrenberger Verrenberg (entire vineyard).

The Grosslage name is Lindelberg. The subregion name is Württembergisch Unterland.

Grape varieties: 25% Müller-Thurgau, 25% Riesling, 12% Limberger, 10% Sylvaner, 8% Kerner, 3% Portugieser, 4% Ruländer, 5% Traminer, 5% Pinot Noir, 3% Muskateller.

The wines: Individual processing and barrel aging accentuate grape-variety characteristics. The Verrenberg is one single vineyard with consistent soils, and therefore, interesting comparisons can be made among the many grape varieties. The wines are also bottle aged. Prädikat wines are offered for sale in the summer of the year following the harvest. The wines have little residual sweetness.

Estate specialties: Although the Hohenlohe land produces very little red wine, the red wines of this estate are of surprisingly high quality. Almost all the wines in the price lists have won awards at the state wine judgings.

Label: The label features the Hohenlohe coat of arms. The white wines have a white label and the red wines have a black label.

Marketing: The wines are well represented in high-class restaurants and hotels. Sales in small quantities from the *Schloss* sales room at the market place in Öhringen during normal business hours.

Visits and tastings: The cellar can be visited by appointment only.

The sales manager, Karl Schmitt, arranges individual wine tastings for prospective purchasers.

From my notebook: The Hohenlohe land between the Tauber, Jagst, and Kocher rivers, with its former residences, small villages, vineyards, and woods, is set in charming countryside and is easily reached from the autobahn. The small town of Öhringen is especially pretty. The wide assortment and individual barrel aging are characteristic of this estate, and the sales room in the *Schloss* is pleasant for the tourist in a hurry. The complete assortment is also offered at the Waldhotel Friedrichsruhe, located about 6 km north of Öhringen. The hotel, also property of the Hohenlohe family, is notable for its antique furniture. It was built as a hunting lodge in 1712.

WEIKERSHEIM

Fürstlich Hohenlohe Langenburg'sche Weingüter

Address: 6992 Weikersheim, Schloss
Telephone: (07934) 298

Location: The vineyards are located on the "Romantic Road." The cellar and sales room are located in Schloss Weikersheim.
How to get there: Take the Stuttgart-Heilbronn autobahn, driving beyond Weinsberg, and turn off at Schwabbach. Take route B-19 for about 40 km. On the Würzburg autobahn, turn off at Würzburg-Heidingsfeld and drive about 40 km on route B-19.
Points of interest: Schloss Weikersheim, with its famous knights' hall; the garden, with the orangerie; the modern cellar.
History: Viticulture has been practiced in Weikersheim for many centuries. Today the proprietor is Prince Kraft zu Hohenlohe Langenburg. The winery and vineyards are rented to Hermann

Lidy, the former manager of the Württemberg central cooperative.

Terrain and soils: The vineyards cover about 57 acres and are mainly on gently sloping and steeply sloping terrain.

Vineyard names: Weikersheimer Karlsberg, Weikersheimer Schmecker.

Grape varieties: Riesling, Sylvaner, Müller-Thurgau, Ruländer, Traminer, Pinot Noir, and some experimental varieties.

The wines: Mild, well-balanced, clean wines that appeal to modern tastes and demonstrate the transition from Württemberg to Franconian wines. They are extremely fresh and flowery. Hermann Lidy is an advocate of modern cellar technology, and his cellar uses only tanks.

Estate specialties: An exceptionally high proportion of award-winning wines. Of the 32 wines on the 1972 price list, only six did not win awards. According to Mr. Lidy, 80 to 90 per cent of all wines are submitted to be judged, and a wine has never returned without an award. Wines of older vintages are no longer available.

Label: The label features the coat of arms of the owner, and has been unaltered for many years. It was used as early as 1900.

Marketing: A regular clientele rapidly exhausts supplies. The price list appears once a year.

Visits and tastings: By previous application, the cellar and vineyards can be visited. The tasting room, where sales are also made, can accommodate up to 12 persons.

From my notebook: The vineyards and winery are very modern. About 45 acres of vines have sprinkler systems, and no wooden barrels are used in the cellar. As a result, the wines have their own fresh, flowery character. A visit is interesting even for experts.

Franconia
(Franken)

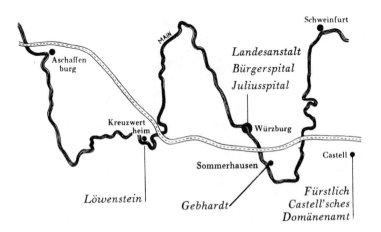

Schweinfurt

Aschaffen
burg

MAIN

Landesanstalt
Bürgerspital
Juliusspital

Kreuzwert
heim

Würzburg

Castell

Sommerhausen

Löwenstein

Gebhardt

Fürstlich
Castell'sches
Domänenamt

CASTELL

Fürstlich Castell'sches Domänenamt

Address: 8711 Castell
Telephone: (09325) 212

Location: The village of Castell lies on the west slope of the Steiger
Forest. The offices, winery, and wine store are in the village
center.

How to get there: Take the Würzburg-Nürnberg autobahn, turning
off at Schweinfurt-Süd/Wiesentheid, and drive 4 km south on
route B-286.

Points of interest: The footpaths in the country, running along the
vineyards to the heights of the Steiger Forest; the *Schloss* park,
with paddocks and riding hall, where the annual Castell wine
festival takes place; the vaulted cask and bottle cellar; the
"Weinstall," once a horse stable and now a uniquely furnished
wine pub that serves the estate wines.

History: The first recorded member of the family was Rupert de
Castello, who was mentioned in 1057. In 1205, the head of the
family was elevated to a count. Viticulture was first recorded in
1258, and the records of wine harvests in Prince zu Castell's
archives date back to the fifteenth century. The oldest map of
the area shows that the acreage of vineyards in 1497 was con-
siderably larger than it is today. The proprietor, Prince zu
Castell-Castell, lives with his family in the *Schloss* in the middle
of the village. The Castell Bank, founded in 1774, also has its
seat in Castell.

Terrain and soils: Of the 111.2 acres of vineyards located around
the village, 85% are on gently sloping and 15% on steeply
sloping terrain. The soils are mainly loam, clay, and marl.

Vineyard names: Casteller Schlossberg (17.3 a.), Casteller Reit-

steig (2.5 a.), Casteller Bausch (29.6 a.), Casteller Trautberg
(5 a.), Casteller Hohnart (13.6 a.), Casteller Kirchberg (3.7
a.), Casteller Kugelspiel (37 a.), Casteller Feuerbach (2.5 a.).
The Grosslage name is Casteller Herrenberg, but it is rarely used.

Grape varieties: 40% Müller-Thurgau, 30% Sylvaner, 30% Perle,
Rieslaner, Scheurebe, Traminer, Auxerrois, Ortega, Siegerrebe,
Morio-Muskat, Kerner, Albalonga, Bacchus, Mariensteiner,
Pinot Noir, and experimental red-wine varieties.

The wine: The rich, deep marl soil gives the wine a particular
taste: fruity, earthy, spicy and lively, vigorous acidity. They are
typical representatives of the Steiger Forest area and the Franconian wine country. The attempts to preserve the characteristics of the grape varieties in the wine are noteworthy.

Estate specialties: A high proportion of award-winning wines. New
varieties are handled with an emphasis on maintaining individual characterstics.

Label: Clear and not elaborate, it features the simple family coat
of arms, which has remained the same since it was first recorded. Oval labels for *Bocksbeutel* bottles; rectangular labels for
liter and Bordeaux-type bottles. Depending on the vineyard
name, different color capsules are used: Schlossberg = white,

Hohnart = red, Bausch = black, Kirchberg = yellow, Trautberg = green, Kugelspiel = orange, Reitsteig (red wines only = red. The award-winning wines have capsules with one or two rings in white, red, and gold.

Marketing: Sold almost exclusively in *Bocksbeutel* bottles to the trade, restaurants, and private clients. Only one price list is issued, which appears up to five times a year. Trade discounts up to 20% are given. Wines are sold at the original list prices in the wine store.

Visits and tastings: By appointment, the church, archives, and *Schloss* cellar can be visited. Wine tastings are also given. English-speaking personnel available.

From my notebook: The charmingly situated wine village of Castell is worth an excursion. The *Schloss* park is very inviting. The wine tastings in the vaults of the cellar offer, especially when they are conducted by the domain counselor, Adolf Steinmann, an hour's course in Franconian wines that is a memorable experience. The bottle-fermented sparkling wine, "Castler Herrenberg," is a specialty of the estate. The uniquely furnished Weinstall (telephone: 09325-463), situated next to the winery, is open from 11 A.M. (closed on Mondays), and besides serving the estate wines, also serves good food.

SOMMERHAUSEN

Weingut Ernst Gebhardt

Address: 8701 Sommerhausen, Hauptstrasse 5
Telephone: (09333) 287   *Telex:* 068695

Location: In the center of Sommerhausen.
How to get there: Take the Frankfurt-Nürnberg autobahn, turning off at Würzberg-Randersacker, and proceed 5 km south on route B-13.

Points of interest: The market village surrounded by walls and towers; old presses in the courtyard of the estate; old sculptured barrels; the Bacchus fountain designed by Richard Rother winner of the wine culture prize. (Bacchus has the features of Dr. Ado Kraemer, the author of various books on Franconian wine).

History: The wine estate was first mentioned under the name of Adelmann in 1723. In 1761, Jakob Gebhardt married into the family and his grandson, Ernst, bestowed his name on the company in 1850. The estate has been in the family of the present proprietors, Karl and Ernst Hügelschäffer, since 1888.

Terrain and soils: The 34.6 acres of vineyards are all on steeply sloping terrain, at an angle of 60 degrees in some cases. All the vineyards were replotted during the consolidation and can now be better cultivated.

Vineyard names: Randersackerer Sonnenstuhl (3 a.), Randerackerer Teufelskeller (2.5 a.), Marktbreiter Sonnenberg (3 a.), Eibelstadter Kappellenberg (2.5 a.), Sommerhäuser Reifenstein (2.7 a.), Sommerhäuser Steinbach (21 a.).

The Grosslage name is Sommerhäuser Ölspiel.

Grape varieties: 50% Sylvaner, 25% Müller-Thurgau, 10% Scheurebe, 15% miscellaneous.

The wines: They are well developed and appealing, exhibiting a typical Franconian character, but they are fuller than the conservative type of wine from this area because of a well-balanced residual sweetness. They all bear the German wine seal. The latest four vintages are offered on the wine list; some fine wines from other vintages are also available.

Estate specialties: Much attention is given to the Sylvaner and Scheurebe varieties, from which wines are produced in qualities up to Trockenbeerenauslese. The proportion of fine wines and award-winning wines in the list is impressively high.

Label: It features the Franconian coat of arms and the new Sommerhausen insignia. The symbol of the Gebhardt estate is also shown.

Marketing: Sales mainly to hotels, restaurants, and wholesalers. Direct sales to consumers every day, including holidays, in the "Bocksbeutelstation" directly opposite the winery.

Visits and tastings: The vineyards and winery can be visited by appointment and seated tastings for up to 60 persons can be handled.

From my notebook: Tours of the estate and wine tastings are conducted in an expert and impressive manner. The estate also functions as a wine shipper, but the proprietors take a great personal interest in the estate wines.

WÜRZBURG

Bayerische Landesanstalt für Wein- und Gartenbau

Address: 8700 Würzburg, Residenzplatz 3
Telephone: (0931) 52431 and 52484

Location: The offices, main winery, sales department, and shipping department are in the Rosenbachpalais, the former residence of prince-bishops and kings. The training winery is in Veitshöchheim, and the *Schloss* winery is located in the Aschaffenburger Schloss. The vineyards are distributed in thirteen villages from Schweinfurt-Bamberg to Aschaffenburg.

How to get there: Travel from the main train station via Kaiserstrasse and Theaterstrasse to the Residenzplatz square. When looking toward the Residenz, the Rosenbachpalais is on the left.

Points of interest: The court cellar below the Residenz was built in 1719, and architecturally, is one of the most beautiful wine cellars in the world (against the wall there are wooden barrels, the oldest dated 1684). Three wine barrels dated 1784, one holding 13,000 gallons and two holding 5,200 gallons, and the 1784 baroque wine press with a wooden spindle are exceptionally impressive. There is a beautiful view of Würzburg from the vineyards Würzburger Leisten, Würzburger Schlossberg, and Würzburger Stein.

History: the prince-bishops and dukes of Franconia who resided in Würzburg acquired in the course of centuries large vineyard holdings, which have belonged to Bavaria since 1814. In 1952, the offices and sales department of the state estate of Würzburg, the Veitshöchheim Training and Experimental Institute, and the vine breeding station at Würzburg all became the Bavarian State Institute for Viticulture, Orchard Husbandry, and Horticulture, under Dr. Breider who retired in 1973. His successor is Dr. Georg Scheuerpflug.

Terrain and soils: The total area controlled by the domain is 459.6 acres. Of the 274 acres of vineyards, 60% are on steeply sloping and 40% on gently sloping terrain. The vineyards are scattered over various villages and have different soils, including limestone, loam, clay, marl, red sandstone, and magmatite.

Vineyard names: Hörsteiner Abtsberg (30.9 a.), Grossheubacher Bischofsberg (7.9 a.), Dorfprozeltener Predigstuhl (29.9 a.), Kreuzwertheimer Kaffelstein (14.3 a.), Erlenbacher Krähenschnabel (12.4 a.), Hammelburger Trautlestal (30.9 a.), Thüngersheimer Scharlachberg (55.6 a.), Veitshöchheimer Wöflein (11.1 a.), Würzburger Stein (76.6 a.), Würzburger Innere Leiste (15.8 a.), Würzburger Schlossberg (7.7 a.), Würzburger Abtsleite (4.2 a.), Würzburger Pfaffenberg (18.5 a.), Randersackerer Teufelskeller (8.1 a.), Randersackerer Pfülben (5.4 a.), Randersackerer Marsberg (17.3 a.), Randersackerer Sonnenstuhl (2.5 a.), Ippesheimer Herrschaftsberg (25.9 a.), Abtswinder Altenberg (14.8 a.), Handthaler Stollberg (14.8 a.).

The Grosslage names are Hörsteiner Reuschberg, Hammelburger Burg, Thüngersheimer Ravensburg, Würzburger Himmelspforte, Randersackerer Ewig Leben, Frankenberger Schlosstück, Abtswinder Schild.

Grape varieties: 18% Sylvaner, 16% Müller-Thurgau, 13% Rieslaner, 13% Riesling, 12% Perle, 7% Ortega, 3% Mariensteiner, 18% Scheurebe, Ruländer, Traminer and experimental varieties.

The wines: The wines are aged in barrels to bring out characteristics typical of their type and grape variety. The fruity Franconian Rieslings and the many other varieties are interesting. The wines made from the newly bred varieties are a special feature of the domain.

Estate specialties: Many award-winning wines. The proportion of Auslese, Beerenauslese, and Trockenbeerenauslese wines is high.

Label: There are two types of labels. An oval label features the Bavarian coat of arms and the words "Bayer. Landesanstalt für Wein- und Gartenbau." Red wines, also supplied in *Bocksbeutel* bottles, have a red label; white wines have a beige label. A rectangular label with the Bavarian coat of arms is reserved for liter bottles.

Marketing: White wines, red wines and rosé wines are usually sold in *Bocksbeutel* bottles. A quantity discount is given to the trade. The consumer list contains an especially large selection. The institute's wines are sold by the glass in the Hofkellerei wine restaurant in Würzburg, in the wine restaurant in the Aschaffenburg Schloss, in the "Ratsstube" in Veitschöchheim, and in the estate restaurant at Stollberg near Handthal (Steigerwald).

Visits and tastings: By appointment, the Hofkellerei in Würzburg and the Schlosskellerei in Aschaffenburg can be visited. The wine tastings, which are also held for larger groups up to 250 persons, are very impressive. The price of the tasting is from $8 to $13 per person, depending on the scope and quality of the wines. Its duration is about 2 or 3 hours.

From my notebook: A richly illustrated brochure, sent on request or given to visitors, has detailed information about the Bavarian State Institute, its wineries, and its outlying facilities. This historic center of Franconian viticulture and viniculture should be visited at least once by every wine lover.

WÜRZBURG

Bürgerspital zum Heiligen Geist

Address: 8700 Würzburg, Theaterstrasse 19
Telephone: (0931) 50363

Location: The offices and winery are in the center of the city next to the hospice. The vineyards are tended from four outlying facilities.

How to get there: Drive from the railway station via Kaiserstrasse to Theaterstrasse. Use the gate at number 19, and park in the courtyard.

Points of interest: The Gothic hospital church (built in 1731) and cellars; the extensive Würzburger Stein vineyard at the edge of the city, with a wonderful view of Würzburg.

History: The foundation was created in 1319 by Johann von Steren. The income from the foundation, especially from the wine estate, has maintained the old age home for centuries to this day. The average age of the 120 pensioners in the home is 82, and this high average is attributed to the medieval custom of providing every pensioner with a daily carafe of wine from the hospital cellars at mealtime. The Bürgerspital is also said to be the first Würzburg winery to bottle wine in *Bocksbeutel* bottles. Today it is a corporate body and is subordinate to the Würzburg city council. The director of the foundation is Heinz Zeller, who is extremely well versed in viticulture and history, and enjoys presenting interesting information from the rich archives of the foundation.

Terrain and soils: The estate has a total of 271.8 acres of land in various villages. Of the 185.3 acres of vineyards currently in production, 70% are on steeply sloping and 30% on gently sloping terrain. The soils around Würzburg are limestone, loam, and clay; in the Steigerwald area the soil is marl.

Vineyard names: Würzburger Abtsleite (46.9 a.), Würzburger

Stein (79 a.), Würzburger Pfaffenberg (91.4 a.), Würzburger Innere Leiste (6.2 a.), Randersackerer Teufelskeller (14.8 a.), Randersackerer Pfülben (6.2 a.), Randersackerer Marsberg (2.5 a.), Thüngersheimer Scharlachberg (5 a.), Michelauer Vollburg (7.4 a.), Himmelstadter Kelter (2.5 a.).

Grape varieties: 28% Sylvaner, 23% Müller-Thurgau, 18% Riesling, 7% Ruländer, 5% Traminer, 3% Spätburgunder, 4% Scheurebe, Rieslaner, Weissburgunder, Kerner, Perle, and experimental varieties.

The wines: The well-made wines are elegant and well balanced. They are somewhat fuller than the usual Franconian wines; the 1971 vintage was especially full. The cellar technology is exemplary. Two vintages are generally offered, but older vintages of Auslese quality are also available.

Estate specialties: Many of the highest awards have been won. Some wines carry the diabetic wine seal. Older Auslese and Beerenauslese vintages are still listed.

Label: "A. Do. 1319" and the coat of arms on the label refer to the creator of the foundation, Johann von Steren. An oval label is used for white wines and a rectangular label for red wines, which are in Burgundy-type bottles.

Marketing: White wines are sold only in *Bocksbeutel* bottles. One list for consumers and one list with quantity discounts for the trade. The overall assortment, including rare wines, is offered in the famous Bürgerspital-Weinstuben restaurant (Theaterstrasse 19), along with hot and cold food. The Bürgersaal is available for private parties of up to 80 persons.

Visits and tastings: By appointment, the winery and vineyards can be visited. Standing tastings can be held in the cellar; seated tastings in the Kellerstube up to 50 persons). The individually compiled wine tastings are very instructive and highly recommended.

From my notebook: Do not miss the famous Würzburger Stein vineyard when you are in the area. Tours and wine tastings at the Bürgerspital are carefully conducted. The director of the foundation, Mr. Zeller, the manager of the wine estate, Mr. Friese, and the cellar-master, Mr. Braungardt, conduct the tastings and tours personally.

WÜRZBURG

Juliusspital-Weingut

Address: 8700 Würzburg, Juliuspromenade 19
Telephone: (0931) 51610 and 50067

Location: The offices and winery are situated next to the Fürstenbau building in the Juliusspital park in the center of the city.
The vineyards are in various villages in lower Franconia.

How to get there: Drive from the main railway station via Kaiserstrasse, turn into the Juliuspromenade, and continue to the east
wing of the Juliusspital on Klinikstrasse. The Juliusspital wine
restaurant is on the ground floor of this wing. The winery and
the wine estate offices are located at Klinikstrasse 7.

Points of interest: The Fürstenbau building; the Spitalkirche (a
church); the rococo apothecary; the old anatomical department;
the old, 250-meter-long wine cellar, with sculptured casks and
rows of barrels.

History: The Juliusspital wine estate is the most important of the
commercial establishments belonging to the Juliusspital charitable foundation. Founded by Prince-Bishop Julius Echter von
Mespelbrunn, the foundation maintains a hospital with 500 beds
and an old age home with 220 beds. The cornerstone of the
extensive foundation buildings was laid in 1576.

Terrain and soils: One of the largest wine estates in Germany. Of
the 296.5 acres of vineyards, 60% are on steeply sloping and
40% on gently sloping terrain. The soils are limestone in Würzburg and Randersack; Limestone, loam, and clay in Eschendorf
and Volkach; marl in Iphofen and Rödelsee; and red sandstone
in Bürgstadt.

Vineyard names: Würzburger Stein (49.4 a.), Würzburger Innere
Leiste (9.9 a.), Würzburger Pfaffenberg (39.5 a.), Würzburger
Abtsleite (39.5 a.), Randersackerer Pfülben (12.4 a.), Rander-

sackerer Teufelskeller (9.9 a.), Randersackerer Marsberg (7.4 a.), Iphöfer Julius-Echter-Berg (27.5 a.), Iphöfer Kronsberg (19.8 a.), Rödelseer Küchenmeister (17.3 a.), Rödelseer Schwanleite (2.5 a.), Escherndorfer Lump (5 a.), Bürgstädter Mainhölle (19.8 a.), Dettelbacher Berg-Rondell (19.8 a.), Vollkacher Karthäuser (17.3 a.).

Grape varieties: 42.3% Sylvaner, 23.5% Müller-Thurgau, 12.5% Riesling, 4.4% Scheurebe, 3.7% Traminer, 3.4% Ruländer, 3% Spätburgunder, 7.2% miscellaneous and experimental varieties.

The wines: Well-made wines of the classical Franconian type. The Riesling wines are vigorous and robust. Residual sugar is kept low, and barrel aging is considered important.

Estate specialties: Many wines have won awards at the state and national wine judgings. The proportion of fine wines is high, and the Scheurebe, Morio-Muskat, and Traminer wines are particularly distinctive.

Label: It features the founder's coat of arms: a shield with three rings, crossed swords and croziers; the sword being the symbol of the temporal authority of the Duke of East Franconia, and the crozier being the symbol of the ecclesiastical authority of the bishops. The label colors indicate the type of wine: green = Qualitätswein bestimmter Anbaugebiete, black = Qualitätswein mit Prädikat, red = red wines of all qualities. The red wines are sold in *Bocksbeutel* bottles.

Marketing: Almost exclusively in *Bocksbeutel* bottles, with the remainder in liter bottles sold as carafe wines to restaurants.

Price lists for the trade and individual consumers are sent on request.

Visits and tastings: By appointment, the winery below the Fürstenbau building can be visited during normal business hours. The tours are conducted by the estate's wine expert. If an appropriate number of persons take part (maximum 60), wine tastings can be held in one of the two comfortable tasting rooms or as a standing tasting in the cellar by candlelight. Application must be made 14 days in advance for wine tastings.

From my notebook: One of the most venerable wine estates in Germany. The gigantic complex of the foundation, park, and cellar in the center of Würzburg impresses every visitor. The Juliusspital Weinstube, one of the most famous Würzburg wine restaurants, is in the east wing of the Juliusspital. In its pleasant atmosphere visitors experience Franconian hospitality along with good wines from the Juliusspital estate. The Frankenstube (45 persons) and the Iphöfer Kammer (40 persons) are available for private parties. Telephone number for the wine restaurants: (0931) 54080.

KREUZWERTHEIM

Fürstlich Löwenstein-Wertheim-Rosenberg'sches Weingut

Address: 6983 Kreuzwertheim, Rathausgasse 5
Telephone: (09342) 6505

Location: The offices and cellars are in the center of the village, next to the Protestant church.
How to get there: Take the Frankfurt-Würzburg autobahn and turn off at Marktheidenfeld toward Wertheim (5 km).

Points of interest: The vaulted cellar, some of which dates from the sixteenth century; the old terraced Homburger Kallmuth vineyard on the Main River between Lengfurt and Homburg.

History: The Satzenberg and Kemelrain vineyards passed into the hands of the Löwensteins when the Cistercian abbey of Bronnbach (founded in 1151) was secularized. These vineyards are some of the oldest in the Tauber Valley. The proprietors of the wine estate and the terraced vineyards of Kallmuth are the Princes zu Löwenstein-Wertheim-Rosenberg.

Terrain and soils: The 69.4 acres of vineyards are mainly on terraced, steeply sloping terrain. The soils are shell limestone, loam, clay, and red sandstone.

Vineyard names: Homburger Kallmuth (29.6 a.), Lengfurter Alter Berg (9.9 a.), Lengfurter Oberrot (2 a.), Kreuzwertheimer Kaffelstein (1.5 a.), Reichholzheimer Satzenberg (14 a.), Bronnbacher Kemelrain (6.2 a.).

Grape varieties: 65% Sylvaner, 19.9% Müller-Thurgau, 3.6% Riesling, 2.9% Rieslaner, 2.4% Pinot Noir, 1.6% Scheurebe, 1.6% Perle, 1.2% Traminer, 0.8% Frühburgunder, 1% miscellaneous.

The wines: As is stated in the price list, "The wines offered are very dry and aged in wood." Of the 17 wines in the 1972 price list, at least 13 were dry enough to be suitable for diabetics. Wines are individually processed according to the grape variety involved, and it is the custom of the estate to place the German wine seal on all *Bocksbeutel* wines.

Estate specialties: All wines are of the classic Franconian type—a specialty of this estate. Fine wines up to a Trockenbeerenauslese with high awards are offered.

Label: It features the Löwenstein coat of arms. An oval label is used on *Bocksbeutel* bottles, and a rectangular label is used on red wines, which are in Burgundy bottles.

Marketing: Sold to the trade, restaurants, and direct to consumers. A very clean, mild schnapps is distilled and sold under the name Frankentrost. The estate is an approved supplier of altar wines. The estate wines are sold in the Löwenstein restaurant, Hotel Restaurant Sankt Hubertus "Wirtshaus im Spessart," located in Windheim near Hafenlohr. The wines are also served in the Goldener Adler and the Alten Schloss, both of which are located in Wertheim.

Visits and tastings: The cellars and vineyards can be visited by appointment. Wine tastings are individually compiled by arrangement. English-speaking personnel available.

From my notebook: An estate that consistently produces wines of the classical Franconian type. One should allow plenty of time for a visit to this attractive area. The terraced Homburger Kallmuth vineyard is impressive, and you should be sure to visit the well-preserved former Cistercian monastery of Bronnbach, the seat of the Löwenstein family. During the summer guided tours are given throughout the day.

Reference Section

How to Read a German Wine Label

The 1971 German wine law is so specific about bottle labels, that today's German wine labels are exceptionally reliable and probably the most precise in the world. Such exactness does not hamper the producer, for he can still produce any kind of wine he desires. But, once he has produced that wine, he'll find it is extremely difficult to misrepresent it as something better than it is. Therefore, the consumer who understands how to read a modern German wine label can be assured of knowing exactly what he's buying, and getting exactly what he wants.

Normally, a German wine label contains the following information:

Quality category

Region of origin

Subregion (*Bereich*) or collective site (Grosslage) or individual vineyard (*Einzellage*)

Vintage

Grape variety

Name of the producer or bottler

Certification number (for Qualitätsweins)

The grape variety and vintage may be omitted if the taste of the wine is not typical of them. Other terms or symbols allowed on the label are:

Trocken (dry)

Für Diabetiker geeignet (suitable for diabetics)

Quality designations and awards, such as the seal of the Deutsche Landwirtschafts-Gesellschaft (German Agricultural Association), awards presented at national wine judging, awards presented at state wine judgings, and quality designations for Baden wines.

Previous terms, such as *natur* (natural), *naturrein* (naturally pure), *Naturgewächs* (natural growth), *Wachstum* (growth), and *Originalabfüllung* (original filling, estate bottled) are no longer allowed on the label. They have been replaced by a simpler, clearer system.

The
Quality Categories

The 1971 German wine law provides for three quality categories; the two highest categories must be verified with a certification number. Precise standards exist for each quality category, thus allowing the consumer to get an immediate idea of the general quality of the wine by looking at the label.

Classification	Legal Minimum Requirements	Remarks
1. Tafelwein	Made only from suitable grape varieties growing in approved locations; the wine must contain at least 8.5% alcohol	Light, easily digestible for consumption in large quantities
2. Qualitätswein bestimmter Anbaugebiete (QbA)	The wine must be officially tested and furnished with a certificate number; its taste must be typical for the region of origin and it must be free of faults; minimum grape-must density 63° Öchsle.	Richer in extract; typical wines of the region, of approved quality for daily consumption
3. Qualitätswein mit Prädikat Kabinett class	Certification number required An official preharvest check, analysis, and tasting are required; chaptalization not allowed; minimum grape-must density 73° Öchsle	High quality to best possible quality Elegant, fully ripened wines of better class
Spätlese class	Grapes harvested late in fully ripened condition; minimum grape-must density 85° Öchsle	Rich, full taste
Auslese class	Selection and separate pressing of only completely ripe grapes; minimum grape-must density 95° Öchsle	Noble wines for special occasions
Beerenauslese class	Only selected grapes with noble rot; minimum grape-must density 125° Öchsle	Same as Auslese class
Trockenbeeren-auslese class	Only selected shrunken grapes with noble rot and highest extract concentration; minimum grape-must density 150° Öchsle	Same as Auslese class

Classification	Legal Minimum Requirements	Remarks
Eiswein	The grapes are harvested and pressed while they are frozen	A rarity in all Prädikat classes

The Öchsle rating indicates the natural ripeness and the grape-must density of the harvested grapes. The legal minimum requirements differ depending on the type of wine (red or white), the grape variety (early or late ripening), and the region. The figures in the above table are based on Rheingau Riesling.

Tafelwein

As the name implies, these are light, fresh carafe wines suitable for daily meals.

Deutscher (German) Tafelwein must:
- —be produced exclusively from grapes harvested in Germany
- —be made exclusively from recommended, approved, or provisionally approved grape varieties
- —contain a natural minimum alcohol content of 5% (44° Öchsle)—in Baden 6% (50° Öchsle)
- —with chaptalization, contain at least 8.5% alcohol

Deutscher Tafelwein may:
- —have a total alcohol content up to 15%
- —not bear *"bestimmte Anbaugebiete"* nor specific vineyard names.

An example of the least specific Tafelwein label:

> Deutscher Tafelwein
> Weisswein
> Sonniger Herbsttrunk
> Abgefüllt in der Weinkellerei X in Y-Stadt

A wine bearing the above label is a blend of grapes, which were harvested in various German table-wine regions. Because the geographic origin may be no more accurate than *Deutscher* (German), the label must also state whether the wine is red or white (*Weisswein*). *Abgefüllt* (bottled) indentifies who bottled the wine and where.

Example of the most specific label:

> Deutscher Tafelwein
> Rhein
> Südliche Weinstrasse
> 1972er
> Böchinger Silvaner
> Erzeugerabfüllung Winzer X in Y-Dorf

Tafelweins may not carry individual vineyard names on the label. These are exclusively retained for Qualitätsweins. All other geographical designations, however, may be used, such as the names of towns, communities, subregions, and Tafelwein regions. The term *Erzeugerabfüllung* (bottled by the producer) indicates that the wine was made by the producer from grapes harvested by him, and was also bottled by him.

Qualitätswein bestimmter Anbaugebiete

Wines of this quality category are richer in extract, typical of the region of origin, and appropriate for daily consumption.

A Qualitätswein bestimmter Anbaugebiete must:

—be officially tested and carry the certification number on the label. A certification number is given to a wine only when it has been judged to be typical of its origin and grape variety, and is faultless in appearance, odor, and taste.

—have a higher degree of ripeness (higher grape-must density) than Tafelwein

A Qualitätswein bestimmter Anbaugebiete may:

—originate in one of the designated Qualitätswein regions

—only be made from approved grape varieties grown in approved vineyards

Example of the least specific label allowed for a Qualitätswein bestimmter Anbaugebiete:

```
Qualitätswein Rheinhessen
Amtliche Prüfungsnummer 4 22 115 042 73
Rebenglut
Abfüller: Weinkellerei X in Y-Stadt
```

The name of the designated region, the term *Qualitätswein,* and the certification number must always appear. The example indicates that the wine is made from grapes from various parts of the designated region (Rheinhessen), but that none of them amount to 75%. Therefore, the label may carry a geographical designation no more specific than the name of the region. *Rebenglut* is a proprietary or trade name; such names are permitted in all wine groups. As data on the grape variety and vintage are not given, the wine is probably a blend of vintages and varieties.

Example of a label with the most specific information for a Qualitätswein bestimmter Anbaugebiete:

```
Mosel-Saar-Ruwer
Qualitätswein
Amtl. Pr. Nr. 3 125 012 030 73
Kaseler Hitzlay
Erzeugerabfüllung Weingut X in Y-Dorf
```

If a single vineyard is given as the geographic origin, 75% of the grapes used must have grown in that vineyard. The rest must come from the same designated region. Together with the vineyard designation the village or community may also be stated. In this case, the vineyard name is Hitzlay, and the village name is Kasel. Names of vineyards and subregions may only be used, however, when they have been officially registered. "Amtl. Pr. Nr." is the abbreviation for *Amtliche Prüfungsnummer*—for an explanation of this and *Erzeugerabfüllung*, see the wine-term dictionary in this reference section.

Qualitätswein mit Prädikat

The German fine wines are grouped in this quality category. The elegance, bouquet, and fullness of these wines have made them world famous. The requirements are much stricter than those for a Qualitätswein bestimmter Anbaugebiete.

A Qualitätswein mit Prädikat must:

—stem from one single subregion within one of the designated regions

—be submitted to the inspection commission with a certificate attesting the type of harvest and the grape variety

Five Prädikat classes are contained in this category and are more closely explained in the previous pages.

Example of a label with the least specific information for a Qualitätswein mit Prädikat:

> Württemberg
> Qualitätswein mit Prädikat
> Bereich Remstal-Stuttgart
> Spätlese
> A. P. Nr. 218 112 73
> Abfüllung Weinkellerei X in Y-Stadt

As in the case of the Qualitätswein bestimmter Anbaugebiete, the designated region, the designation of the quality category, and the certification number must be given for a Qualitätswein mit Prädikat. The Qualitätswein mit Prädikat must stem from one single subregion (*Bereich*). The example indicates that it is a blend of varying proportions coming from the subregion of Remstal-Stuttgart, but from various vinters (shown by the *Abfüllung* statement). In this case, no single wine amounts to 75%, and therefore, no narrower designation of origin can be given than the name of the subregion. All wines, however used in this blend must meet the requirements of the quality class stated (Spätlese, in this case).

Here is an example of a label with the most specific information for a Qualitätswein mit Prädikat:

> Nahe
> Qualitätswein mit Prädikat
> 1971er
> Langenlohnsheimer Rothenberg
> Riesling Auslese
> Erzeugerabfüllung, A.P. Nr. 1 13 020 025 72

The explanations for the previous example also apply here with the limitation that 75% of the grapes must have been grown on the vineyard stated and in the year stated. The term *Erzeugerabfüllung* is explained in the wine-term dictionary in this reference section. An association of producers (a cooperative, for example) may use the term *Erzeugerabfüllung* instead of giving grape variety and harvest details.

Certification Number

A certification number may be granted to a wine that fulfills the legal requirements for a Qualitätswein. In order for a wine lover to be able to decode a wine label, the meanings of the individual figures in the certification number are given here:

Example: 6 33 050 001 73

6 = the code of the inspection board (in this case, the Eltville Viticulture Office, which is responsible for Rheingau and Hessische Bergstrasse); because this is not uniform nationally, it is not always given

33 = location of the winery or wine estate

050 = code of the wine estate or bottler

001 = application number for this lot of wine. Each time a new lot of wine is bottled, sample bottles must be submitted for inspection and that particular lot is assigned a number. The numbers run in yearly sequence, starting with 000 at the beginning of each year. In this example, this is the first lot of the year submitted for inspection by this applicant.

73 = The year of application; *not* necessarily the vintage year.

German-English Dictonary of Wine-Appreciation Terms

In Germany, as in other countries, members of the wine trade describe wines with words that may not be familiar to the average person. These words occasionally appear on wine labels in German and are often found on German restaurant menus. The wine lover, therefore, will find the following list useful, as it contains explanations for the most common German wine-appreciation terms. The parentheses following the initial German term contain the equivalent wine term in English or the literal translation in cases where an appropriate term has not been established in English. For explanations of technical terms, see the separate list in this reference section.

Abgang (aftertaste)—The lingering of a wine's taste in the mouth. The longer the taste remains, the better.

Abgebaut (declined)—Reduced in quality because of excessive age.

Alkoholreich (high alcohol content)—Usually used to describe heavy wines. When a wine is unbalanced and negatively affected by high alcohol, the words *brandig, schnapsig,* and *spritzig* are used.

Arm (poor)—The term for a small, thin wine.

Aroma (aroma)—One of the scent elements of wine, often associated with the grape variety. See *Bukett.*

Ausdruck (character)—See *Charakter.*

Ausgebaut (fully matured)—Ready for drinking.

Blank (bright)—The opposite of dull. Not as bright as *glanzhell.*

Blass (pale)—Lacking in color. Such paleness is often the result of too much sulphur.

Blind (cloudy)—Slightly dull. Unclear.

Blindprobe (blind tasting)—A wine tasting in which the names of the wines are unknown to the tasters.

Blume (floweriness)—The agreeable natural scent of a wine. Commonly associated expressions are *edle Blume* (noble floweriness), *feine Blume* (fine floweriness), and *zarte Blume* (delicate floweriness). *Bukett* is a more complete scent element.

Böckser (bad eggs)—The odor of sulphur (bad eggs) due to faulty processing.

Bodengeschmack im Wein (earthy taste)—Also referred to as *Bodenton,* or adjectivally, *Erdig.* It can result from the grapes being fouled by earth.

Brandig (excessive alcohol)—See *alkoholreich.*

Breit (boring)—Full but without finesse. Usually not enough acidity.

Bukett (bouquet)—Rich floweriness of the wine. Contributors to bouquet included the grape variety, fermentation, aging, noble rot (Botrytis), and maderization.

Charakter (character)—The sum of all the scent and taste properties. "The wine has character" indicates a vigorous, robust wine.

Damenwein (ladies wine)—Usually a pleasing, elegant wine with little noticeable acidity.

Dünn (thin)—The same as *arm, leer.*

Duft (fragrance)—Similar to floweriness, but more delicate. The adjectival form is *duftig* (fragrant).

Edel (noble)—Highest compliment for fine wines. Used in such terms as *Edelfirne* (noble maderization), Edelsüsse (noble sweetness), and *Edelwein* (noble wine).

Elegant (elegant)—A term for optimally balanced wines with fine character.

Extrakt (extract)—The substance dissolved in wine, such as sugar, acids, salt, and glycerin, with the exception of alcohol. Full-bodied wines have high extract percentages.

Fassgeshmack (barrel flavor)—A musty, woody odor. Usually considered to be undesirable.

Fein (fine, subtle)—Delicate.

Fest (firm)—The term for wines with robust but not unpleasant acidity.

Feurig (fiery)—Often used to describe good red wines that are rich in alcohol. The proper amount of alcohol can give life, power, and fire to a wine.

Finesse (finesse)—The fine nuances in scent and taste found in fine wines.

Firne (maderization)—A condition found in old wines that have acquired an oxidation bouquet. If the resulting product is agreeable, it may be called *Edelfirne* (noble maderization) or *Sherryton* (sherry flavor), which is even more complimentary.

Flach (flat)—Without character or any special properties. Small.

Flüchtig (evasive)—A term for wines in which the scent elements are only noticeable for a short time and do not last. Small wines are usually *flüchtig.*

Flüchtige Säure (volatile acidity)—Acetic acid. Makes a wine taste vinegary when present in sufficient quantities.

Frucht (fruit)—The aroma of the grape variety; pleasantly refreshing in a clean wine. The adjectival form is *fruchtig.*

Fuchsgeschmack (foxy flavor)—The distinctive flavor of wines made from native American grapes and their crosses. Also called *Foxton*.

Fülle (fullness)—Body.

Gerbstoffreich (high in tannin)—Dry-tasting; much tannin.

Gestoppt (not completely fermented)—A term for wines with unbalanced sweetness caused by stopping the fermentation before all of the natural sugar has been converted.

Glanzhell (brilliant)—Completely clear.

Glatt (smooth)—Balanced, elegant, somewhat full with mild acidity.

Grasig (grassy, green)—A term for wines with the unripe taste of stems or grape skins caused by the grapes being too heavily pressed. Acidic wines of poor-ripening vintages may also be called *grasig*.

Grün (green)—A color tint of white wine. Also unripe acidity.

Harmonisch (well balanced)—All the taste components of the wine have been blended in an optimum way. Both ordinary and fine wines should be well balanced.

Herb (noticeably acidic)—The wine has pronounced acidity and little residual sugar.

Herzhaft (hearty)—Strong and full. Scent and taste substances, acids in particular, are pronounced but not unpleasant.

Hochfarbig (deeply colored)—Intensively or deeply colored. Usually seen as a yellow or yellow-brown color in white wines that have too little sulphur and have been exposed to air. Such wines usually lose freshness, too.

Holzig (woody)—Smelling of wood. Usually found in wines that have been stored in poorly prepared new barrels.

Jungwein (young wine)—A wine in which the main fermentation has been concluded, and the wine has started to clear.

Kahmig (yeasty)—Musty. Smelling of yeast.

Kernig (vigorous)—Robust, lively, full bodied.

Knochig (bone dry)—The term for wine with unpleasantly high acidity. Often used in the same sense as *harter Knochen* (hard bone).

Korkgeschmack (cork flavor)—A corklike odor caused by an imperfect cork. Sometimes confused with the flavor imparted by excess age.

Körper (body)—Fullness. Found in wines that are rich in extract, vigorous, and robust.

Körperarm (weak in body)—Light, thin, poor.

Kratzig (scratchy)—"Scratchy" tasting in the throat. Caused by an excess of acetic acid.

Kurz (short)—Without aftertaste.

Lebendig (lively)—A term for youthful wines with fruity acidity and a little carbon dioxide.

Leer (empty)—Thin.

Leicht (light)—Denotes small wines with little alcohol or extract.

Lieblich (pleasant)—A term for mild, low-acid wines that are well balanced and have a pleasant bouquet and taste.

Luftgeschmack (oxidation flavor)—A flavor appearing in wines that have remained open to the air for a long time or in wines that have been stored in partially full barrels. In the extreme positive sense, called *Sherryton* (sherry flavor).

Markant (prominent)—Robust, with a definite and typical character.

Matt (dull)—Tired, stale. A wine that no longer has freshness.

Mäuseln (mousy)—A term describing wines with a peculiar unpleasant taste and scent caused by incorrect vinification. Occurs more often in apple wines than in grape wines.

Nase (nose)—The floweriness, fragrance, and general scent of the wine.

Nerv (nerve)—Pronounced acidity and robustness. The adjectival form is *nervig*.

Nett (nice)—Small, clean, without special characteristics.

Pikant (piquant)—Elegant, with an especially fine, fruity acidity.

Plump (clumsy)—The wine is unbalanced, without character, and has high extract content.

Rassig (racy)—Hearty, lively. Robust but not unpleasant acidity. The substantive form is *Rasse*.

Rauh (rough)—Not as strong a term as *kratzig*. This taste is usually caused by too much tannin. It can also refer to an old wine with too much sulphur.

Reif (ripe)—Optimum stage of maturation in a wine. A young wine can also be *reif* when it stems from well-ripened grapes. Variations are *abstichreif* (ready for racking), schönungsreif (ready for fining), *abfüllreif* (ready for bottling), and *flaschenreif* (ready for bottling).

Rein, reintönig (clean)—Absolutely clean without ancillary tastes or scents.

Restsüsse (residual sugar)—The sugar left in wine after the fermentation is completed.

Rückgrat (backbone)—Used in the expression *"Der Wein hat Rückgrat"* (the wine has backbone), meaning the wine is vigorous, full, and has robust acidity.

Samtig (velvety)—A term for balanced, elegant red wines that balance their dryness with extract and alcohol, and leave a smooth impression on the tongue. Assmannshausen red wines are often called *samtig*.

Sauber (clean)—Scent and taste are flawless. Often the only praise for small wines that are not objectionable, but are not outstanding, either.

Schal (stale)—Without freshness, past prime, empty and dull.

Schimmelgeschmack (moldy flavor)—A musty odor usually caused by poorly tended, moldy barrels.

Schnapsig (excessive alcohol)—The term for a wine with so much alcohol that the taste is strongly affected.

Schwanz (aftertaste)—The aftertaste of a wine. The taste that lingers after swallowing. Also called *Abgang*.

Schweif (aftertaste)—Same as *Schwanz*.

Schwer (heavy)—Rich in alcohol, with much extract. Usually used for wine produced in southern Europe.

Sortenbukett (varietal bouquet)—The bouquet of the grape variety in a wine. For example, Riesling, Müller-Thurgau, or Traminer bouquet.

Spiel (interplay)—The interaction of rich nuances. Wines with piquant acidity usually have much *Spiel*.

Spritig (excessive alcohol)—Too much alcohol. See *alkoholreich*.

Spritzig (crackling)—A term for fresh, usually young wines with lively acidity. Such wines often contain carbon dioxide dissolved in the wine, but it is not always noticeable.

Stahlig (steely)—With wines high in acidity, this is a stronger term than *nervig* and *rassig*.

Stoffig (substantial)—A term for robust wines that are rich in extract. The substantive form is *Stoff* (substance).

Süffig (appealing)—A term for fresh, usually small, somewhat sweet carafe wines, which are easy to drink.

Trocken (dry)—Lacking in sweetness. A term usually used with sparkling wines and sherries.

Überschwefelt (too much sulphur)—Wines with this characteristic can be recognized by their pungent odor.

Umschlagen (turned)—The wine is unclear because of secondary fermentation or the precipitation of dissolved chemicals.

Unenwickelt (underdeveloped)—A term for unripe wines that are not yet completely matured.

Unharmonisch (unbalanced)—The taste components, such as acidity, alcohol, and sweetness, are not well balanced.

Unterschwefelt (lacking sulphur)—A wine with too little sulphur may taste oxidized, cannot be stored for long periods, and rapidly becomes old.

Verschlossen (closed)—The wine does not fully release its taste nuances. This can occur with underdeveloped wines that have been bottled shortly before being tasted or wines that have recently traveled a long distance.

Voll (full)—Same as *körperreich*.

Warm (warm)—A term for full, red wines with optimum alcohol.

Weich (weak)—Mild and low in acidity.

Weinig (vinous)—The term for full, fruity wine. The expression *viel Wein* (much wine) is also used. Somewhat less intense than *saftig*.

Wuchtig (heavy)—Heavy, full.

Würzig (spicy)—Stronger than *fruchtig*. The characteristic of the noble bouquet of a great wine.

Zart (delicate)—Fine, subtle.

German-English Dictonary of Technical Wine Terms

Some technical wine terms used in Germany have no equivalent in English. The following list contains many of those terms, as well as other technical terms that you may encounter when reading about German wines or discussing them with estate personnel. The parentheses following the initial German term contain the equivalent wine term in English or the literal translation in cases where an appropriate term has not been established in English. For explanations of wine-appreciation terms, see the separate list in this reference section.

Amtliche Prüfungsnummer; A. P. Nummer (certification number)—A number shown on the labels of all Qualitätsweins since July 1971. It guarantees that the wine meets the legal quality requirements, has been officially analyzed, and has had its taste checked by expert tasters.

Anbaugebiet (producing region)—A legally defined region of origin for Qualitätsweins. Used in the expression *Qualitätswein bestimmter Anbaugebiete*. In Germany there are 11 such regions authorized to produce higher-quality wines: Ahr, Mittelrhein, Moselle-Saar-Ruwer, Nahe, Rheingau, Hessische Bergstrasse, Rheinhessen, Rheinpfalz, Baden, Württemberg, and Franconia (Franken). The shorter word *Gebiet* is also used.

Anreichern (chaptalization)—The addition of sugar to the grape-must according to the provisions of the 1971 German wine law. This operation is only allowed in cases where natural conditions have prevented the grapes from developing enough sugar to ferment satisfactorily.

Arrondiert (consolidated)—Combined; formed as a large, single, homogeneous vineyard from many smaller vineyards. The 1971 German wine law consolidated 20,000 vineyards into 3,000. Parts of a large consolidated vineyard may still be owned by different individuals.

Auslese (selected harvest)—The third-highest Prädikat class. On labels of German wine produced after July 1971, the word *Auslese* may only be used when the phrase *Qualitätswein mit Prädikat* appears. Such a label, which must also display an *Amtliche Prüfungsnummer,* indicates that the wine is a high-quality wine made from selected, fully ripe grapes that may have been subjected to noble rot (Botrytis).

Beerenauslese (selected grape harvest)—The second-highest Prädikat class. On labels of German wines produced after July 1971, the word *Beerenauslese* may only be used when the phrase *Qualitätswein mit Prädikat* appears. Such a label, which must also display an *Amtliche Prüfungsnummer,* indicates that the wine is a high-quality wine made from individually selected, overripe grapes that have been subjected to noble rot (Botrytis).

Bereich (subregion)—The 11 Qualitätswein regions (*Anbaugebiete*) in Germany are divided into 32 subregions, each of which is called a *Bereich.* If a wine is produced from grapes grown in one of these subregions, the bottle label may show the subregion name, but may not also carry a Grosslage or vineyard name.

Bocksbeutel (flask)—A flat-shaped bottle. Only Qualitätsweins from the designated region of Franconia (Franken), the Tauber Valley in Baden and the Schüpfergrund, as well as from the communities of Neuweier, Steinbach, Umweg, and Varnhalt, may be sold in this special bottle.

Bodenart (soil type)—The type of soil according to its chemical and physical composition. The taste of a wine is strongly influenced by the type of soil where the grapes were grown.

Botrytis (Botrytis cinerea, noble rot)—A beneficial mold that attacks grapes, removing moisture while retaining the sugar and flavor elements, and preventing the grapes from spoiling. As a result, the grapes shrivel and are extremely rich. When the grapes are only moderately affected and are individually selected during the harvest, a Beerenauslese wine is produced. When the grapes are very shriveled and individually selected during the harvest, a Trockenbeerenauslese wine is produced. Botrytis only forms on grapes when certain humidity and temperature conditions exist—most notably in Germany and France, although recent rare occurances have yielded wines in the United States and other countries. Also called *Edelfäule* in German.

Bundesweinprämierung (national wine judging)—Considered to be the highest test of quality for a German wine, this wine judging is conducted annually by the German Agricultural Association (DLG). The following awards are given: *Grosser Preis der DLG* (highest award), *Silberner Preis der DLG* (second-highest award) *Bronzener Preis der DLG* (third-highest award), and *Ehrenpreis des Bundesministers für Ernährung, Landwirtschaft und Forsten* (medal of honor of the minister of agriculture).

Cabinet (cabinet)—See *Kabinett*.

Cabinetkeller (cabinet cellar)—A Gothic vaulted cellar in Kloster Eberbach, in Rheingau, from which the wine designation *Cabinet* (now *Kabinett*) stems.

Diabetikerwein (diabetic wine)—Formerly the general designation for light wines with little residual sugar. All such wines produced after July 1971 must bear the phrase *Für Diabetiker geeignet* (suitable for diabetics) and may not contain more than 4 grams per liter of unfermented sugar nor more than 12% alcohol. The analysis information must be given on the bottle. A *Diabetikerwein* may be furnished with a label on the back of the bottle showing data established by a DLG analysis confirming the wine's suitability for diabetics.

Diabetiker-Weinsiegel (diabetic wine seal)—A seal granted by the German Agricultural Association (DLG) to wines that have been re-examined for their quality and adherence to the limitations of wines suitable for diabetics. Points are given in the same manner as for the *DLG Weinsiegel*.

Deutsche Weinsiegel Trocken (German dry-wine seal)—A yellow wine seal introduced in March 1974 for wines having less than 4 grams per liter of residual sugar and subject to examination by the DLG. Points are awarded in the same manner as for the *DLG Weinsiegel*.

DLG (*Deutsche Landwirtschafts-Gesellschaft*)—The German Agricultural Association, an independent organization.

DLG-Weinsiegel (DLG wine seal)—A quality symbol for German wines that are voluntarily submitted to the German Agricultural Association and assessed on a point system by an independent group of experts. The seal is only given to wines that receive at least two points more than required by the government wine inspection for a Qualitätswein mit Prädikat, and three points more than the government mimimum for a Qualitätswein bestimmter Anbaugebiete.

Drahtrahmenerziehung (wire-trellis training)—A modern method of supporting vines in espalier-like rows to facilitate cultivation. Older methods include the single-stake method (*Pfahlerziehung*) and the single-stem method (*Einzelstockerziehung*).

Edelfäule (noble rot)—See *Botrytis.*

Einzellage (individual vineyard)—The smallest geographic unit recognized by the German wine law; a separate, unbroken plot with one name, as opposed to a group of vineyards (see *Grosslage*). About 3,000 individual vineyards now exist in Germany. An *Einzellage* may be divided among several owners, each of which might produce a different wine depending on his cultivation and processing methods.

Eiswein (ice wine)—A wine produced from grapes that were frozen on the vine when the air temperature remained below 21°F for several hours. The grapes are picked while still frozen and are rushed to the press-house. When pressed, the water in the grapes remains behind as ice, while a sugar-rich syrup forms a grape-must from which the wine is made. An Eiswein may be produced in all Prädikat classes; the word *Eiswein* is added to the Prädikat designation.

Elbling—A white-wine grape that is thought to have been introduced into Germany by the Romans. Grown mainly in the Moselle-Saar-Ruwer area. Accounts for less than 2% of the white-wine grapes grown in Germany.

Erziehung (training)—The way in which a vine is pruned and supported. Examples are head pruning (*Kopfschnitt*), single-stem training (*Einzelstockerziehung*), and wire-frame training (*Drahtrahmerziehung*).

Erzeugerabfüllung (producer-bottled)—This word on a bottle label indicates that the wine was bottled by the producer and was not sold to a shipper or middleman for bottling. About the same as "estate bottled." Prior to July 1971 other terms were also allowed; see *Originalabfüllung.*

Federweiser (new wine)—Grape-must in which the fermentation is declining and in which the sweetness has been drastically reduced.

Fermentation (nonalcoholic fermentation)—Enzymatic processes, mainly in sweet grape-musts, with differing effects, such as the grape-must turning brown or the pectin precipitating. In English and French, fermentation refers to the conversion of sugar to alcohol, a process called *Gärung* in German.

Flurbereinigung (government-controlled consolidation)—a government program to improve the efficiency of viticulture by creating single larger vineyard areas out of many smaller dispersed plots. The program involved terrain improvement, road construction, and general consolidation.

Füllreif (ready for bottling)—The condition of a wine when it is developed enough to be bottled. Also called *flaschenreif*.

Fungizid (fungicide)—A chemical for combating fungus diseases on vines.

Gärung (alcoholic fermentation)—The conversion of the sugar in grape-must into alcohol and carbon dioxide by the action of yeast.

Gebiet (region)—See *Anbaugebiet*.

Geschein (flower)—The flowering of the vine. The flowers are produced in panicles.

Gewürztraminer—A white-wine grape grown mainly in the Rheinhessen, Rheinpfalz, and Baden regions. Very similar to the Traminer, but spicier. Widely grown in the Alsace area of France, where it is known by the same name. Accounts for less than 1% of the white-wine grapes grown in Germany.

Grosslage (collective site)—All Qualitätsweins in Germany must come from registered vineyards and each vineyard (*Einzellage*) will usually be a member of a local group of vineyards called a Grosslage. The vineyards in each Grosslage are not selected according to their proximity to social or geographical features, but are vineyards that, in the opinion of German wine experts, have similar terrain, soils, and climatic conditions. A Grosslage, therefore, may include villages, hills, or areas of any size. The shapes of the many (about 150) Grosslages are irregular and vary in area from 125 to 3,700 acres; some contain dozens of vineyards, and others contain only a few.

A producer (or bottler) may choose to put a Grosslage name on his wine instead of an individual vineyard name for several reasons. He may feel that a particular vintage has not yielded wines characteristic of the vineyard; the Grosslage name may be better known than the vineyard name; or he may want to freely mix his wine with that of a neighboring vineyard to produce a blend. In any case, samples of every Grosslage wine must be submitted for official inspection, as is required for any Qualitätswein. The wine must be flawless and must have characteristics typical for the Grosslage before a certification number is awarded and the Grosslage name may be used.

A Grosslage name is the second-most specific geographical indication of a wine's character (the most specific is an individual vineyard name). Wines from the same Grosslage, of course, will vary somewhat because of the different production techniques and cultivation used by various producers, but there will still be a great deal of similarity (when the grape variety and vintage are matched).

The Grosslage idea is one of the most important concepts in German viniculture, and it is an ingenious method of establishing uniformity categories *within* quality categories. While it is true that few producers use Grosslage names for their very best wines, it is not true that Grosslage wines are substandard. Indeed, they may be superior to wines with vineyard names. The important thing to remember is that the producer gains more latitude in making a Grosslage wine because he is permitted to blend more freely. For the consumer who does not demand a detailed description of a wine's origin, the benefit is quality wine for less money.

Grosslage names may be used for any Qualitätswein, including all Prädikat classes. An individual vineyard name may not be used on the same label with a Grosslage name.

Hybride (cross)—A wine that is a cross between European and American varieties. Due to the unproven character of the wine produced from such crosses, they are not approved for use in making German wines.

Jungfernwein (virgin wine)—The first wine produced from a newly planted vineyard, usually in the third year.

Kabinett (cabinet)—The most basic Prädikat class. On labels of German wines produced after July 1971, the word *Kabinett* may only be used when the phrase *Qualitätswein mit Prädikat* appears. Such a label, which must also display an *Amtliche Prüfungsnummer,* indicates that the wine in question is a high-quality wine that has not been chaptalized (see *Anreichern*) and has an alcoholic content that exceeds a prescribed minimum. Prior to 1971, *Kabinett* was usually written *Cabinet.*

Lage (site, vineyard)—The general term for a site or location. For specific terms, see *Grosslage* and *Einzellage.*

Maische (pulp)—Crushed, broken grapes.

Messwein (sacramental wine)—Previously only unchaptalized wine acceptable as an altar wine in Germany. Today any Qualitätswein may be used. Foreign altar wines must meet the requirements of the Roman Catholic Church.

Morio-Muskat—A white-wine grape that is a cross between the Sylvaner and the Weissburgunder. Grown mainly in the Rheinhessen and Reinpfalz regions. Accounts for slightly more than 3% of the white-wine grapes grown in Germany.

Mostgewicht (grape-must density)—The sugar content of the grape-must, ascertained in terms of specific gravity and expressed in Öchsle degrees in Germany.

Müller-Thurgau—A white-wine grape that is a cross between the Sylvaner and the Riesling varieties. It has become popular in recent years because of its high yield and is now the most widely planted grape variety in Germany. Grown extensively in the Rheinhessen, Rheinpfalz, and Baden regions. Accounts for 30% of the white-wine grapes grown in Germany.

Naturrein (pure)—According to the old wine law this term was used for unchaptalized wines. Under the new German wine law this term is no longer allowed, as its meaning is inherent in the phrase *Qualitätswein mit Prädikat.*

Öchsle—The name of a method of determining sugar density in grape-must. Developed by Ferdinand Öchsle in the early nineteenth century, the Öchsle scale is important to German vintners in the production of wine. The German wine law prescribes minimum Öchsle ratings in the production of all high-quality wines.

Originalabfüllung (estate bottled)—Under the old wine law this term was used for wines made only from estate grapes. Since July 1971 the terms *Erzeugerabfüllung* or *Aus eigenem Lesegut* have been used.

Portugieser—A red-wine grape grown mainly in the Rheinhessen, Rheinpfalz, Württemberg, and Ahr regions. Accounts for 42% of the red-wine grapes grown in Germany.

Prädikat (attribute)—On labels of German wines produced after July 1971, the word *Prädikat* may only be used in the phrase *Qualitätswein mit Prädikat.* The five Prädikat classes are: Kabinett, Spätlese, Auslese, Beerenauslese, and Trockenbeerenauslese. In order to qualify for any of these five classes, a wine must meet strict requirements for such items as minimum alcohol content, ripeness of the grape, grape variety and date of harvest. Each wine is officially checked for conformity and must bear a certification number.

Prädikatswein (wine with special attribute)—See *Qualitätswein mit Prädikat.*

Qualitätsstufen (quality levels)—The basic wine qualities stipulated by the 1971 wine law. The qualities are, in ascending order: Tafelwein, Qualitätswein bestimmter Anbaugebiete (QbA), and Qualitätswein mit Prädikat. Within the Qualitätswein mit Prädikat category there are five classes which are, in ascending order: Kabinett, Spätlese, Auslese, Beerenauslese, and Trockenbeerenauslese. An Eiswein may be produced in any of the Prädikat classes.

Qualitätswein (quality wine)—A German wine that has been produced after July 1971, officially inspected, and awarded a certification number. The two basic quality levels are: Qualitätswein bestimmter Anbaugebiete and Qualitätswein mit Prädikat.

Qualitätswein bestimmter Anbaugebiete (quality wine from a designated region)—The lesser of the two types of Qualitätswein allowed to be produced in Germany. The wine must meet certain minimum standards in all stages of production, must be officially tested, and must be labeled in a particular way. This wine may be chaptalized (see *Anreichern*).

Qualitätswein mit Prädikat (quality wine with special attribute)—The superior of the two types of Qualitätswein allowed to be produced in Germany. The wine must meet certain minimum standards in all stages of production, must be officially tested, and must be labeled in a particular way. This wine may not be chaptalized (see *Anreichern*). There are five classes of wine within this category: Kabinett, Spätlese, Auslese, Beerenauslese, and Trockenbeerenauslese. Wine in this category is also sometimes called *Prädikatswein.*

Riesling—Germany's most famous white-wine grape variety. Grown in all areas, but most notably in the Rheingau and Moselle-Saar-Ruwer areas. Also grown in the United States, where it is often called Johannisberg Riesling. Accounts for 26% of the white-wine grapes grown in Germany.

Roseewein (rosé wine)—A pink wine made from the grape-must of red-wine grapes processed as white-wine grapes (prior to or shortly after the start of fermentation the skins are removed). *Weissherbst* is a rosé that must at least meet the requirements for a Qualitätswein bestimmter Anbaugebiete and is only made from one grape variety. *Weissherbst* may only be made in the Ahr, Rheingau, Baden, Franconia (Franken), Rheinhessen, Rheinpfalz, and Württemberg wine regions.

Rotling (reddish wine, rosé)—A wine with a pale to bright red color that is made by blending white and red grapes. Finished red and white wines, according to the German wine law, may not be blended together to produce a rosé. *Schillerwein* is a *Rotling* wine made exclusively in Württemberg and must be at least a Qualitätswein bestimmter Anbaugebiete.

Rotwein (red wine)—A wine made exclusively from red-wine grapes that have been processed for red wine (the skins are removed from the grape-must after fermentation).

Ruländer—A white-wine grape known as the Pinot Gris in France and grown mainly in the Baden, Rheinpfalz, and Rheinhessen regions. Accounts for 4% of the white-wine grapes grown in Germany.

Säure (acid)—Wine contains principally malic and tartaric acids. In an analysis the overall acidity is calculated in parts per thousand as tartaric acid. In a positive sense, one speaks of ripe, fruity, and pleasant acidity. In a negative sense, of green, hard, and sharp acidity.

Säureabbau (acidity reduction)—The drop in acidity, mainly during barrel aging, because of the precipitation of potassium tartrate or the bacteriological conversion of malic acids into lactic acids.

Scheurebe—A white-wine grape that is a cross between the Riesling and the Sylvaner varieties. S-88 is a popular type (clone) of Scheurebe. Mainly grown in the Rheinhessen and Rheinpfalz regions. Accounts for 2.5% of the white-wine grapes grown in Germany.

Schillerwein—See *Rotling*.

Schönen (fining)—The clarification of wine by the addition of such substances as kaolin, gelatin, or charcoal. The suspended particles causing a cloudiness are carried to the bottom by these substances, which precipitate and do not remain in the wine. The removal of iron is called *Blauschönung*.

Silvaner (Sylvaner)—A white-wine grape, which was previously the most widely grown grape in Germany. Grown mainly in the Rheinhessen, Rheinpfalz, and Franconia regions. Also grown in the United States, where it is sometimes called a Riesling. Accounts for 23% of the white-wine grapes grown in Germany.

Spätburgunder—A red-wine grape known in France as the Pinot Noir. Grown mainly in the Baden, Württemberg, and Ahr regions. Accounts for 26% of the red-wine grapes grown in Germany.

Spätlese (late harvest)—The fourth-highest Prädikat class. On labels of German wines produced after July 1971, the word *Spätlese* may only be used when the phrase *Qualitätswein mit Prädikat* appears. Such a label, which also must display an *Amtliche Prüfungsnummer*, indicates that the wine was made from fully ripened, late-picked grapes and that it has an alcoholic content in excess of a prescribed minimum.

Süssung (dosage)—A cellar technique by which wine is provided residual sugar. The proper amount of subtle residual sugar can round off and improve the taste of a wine.

Sylvaner—See *Silvaner*.

Tafelwein (table wine)—The legal designation, as of July 1971, for the group of light table wines, country wines, and carafe wines in the European Common Market. In France such wine may be called *vin de table* or *vin du pays;* in Italy *vino di tavola*. In the case of German (deutscher) table wine, the grape-must may be chaptalized (see *Anreichern*) when the grapes are insufficiently ripe. Official inspection of table wines is not required.

Tafelweinbaugebiete (table-wine production regions)—The five regions of origin for German table wines. The regions are: Moselle, Rhein, Main, Neckar, and Oberrhein. These regions are not the same as the Qualitätswein regions.

Traminer—A white-wine grape grown mainly in the Rheinpfalz region. Similar to the Gewürztraminer, but not quite as spicy. Also called Roter (red) Traminer because of its pink skin. Accounts for less than 0.5% of the white-wine grapes grown in Germany.

Trockenbeerenauslese (selected dry-grape harvest)—The highest Prädikat class. On labels of German wines produced after July 1971, the word *Trockenbeerenauslese* may only be used when the phrase *Qualitätswein mit Prädikat* appears. Such a label, which must also display an *Amtliche Prüfungsnummer,* indicates that the wine is made from shrunken, carefully selected grapes that have been subjected to noble rot (Botrytis). The ripe sweetness and concentrated acid supplied by the shrunken grapes allows these wines to be kept for extremely long periods.

Trollinger—A red-wine grape grown almost exclusively in the Württemberg region. Accounts for 17% of the red-wine grapes grown in Germany.

Ursprungsbezeichnung (statement of origin)—A statement, required for wine produced in the European Common Market, that gives the origin of the wine. For German table wines there are five regions; for German Qualitätsweins there are 11 regions, 32 subregions, about 300 Grosslages, and about 3,000 individual vineyards.

Weingesetz (wine law)—The current German wine law (called the "new" law) that has been in force since July 14, 1971. It applies to 1971 and subsequent vintages.

Weissburgunder—A white-wine grape known as the Pinot Blanc in France. Grown mainly in the Rheinpfalz and Baden regions. Accounts for 1% of the white-wine grapes grown in Germany.

Weissherbst—See *Roseewein.*

Weisswein (white wine)—Wine made exclusively from white-wine grapes.

Weitraumanlage (spacious planting)—A vineyard layout method that differs from the normal vineyard layout (4 to 7 ft between rows) in that it has widely spaced rows (8 to 11 ft between rows).

Zuckerrest (residual sugar)—The natural sugar that remains in a wine after fermentation is completed. Wine with very little or no residual sugar is often rated in Germany as suitable for diabetics. Fine wines usually have relatively large amounts of residual sugar to balance out their higher levels of acid and flavor elements. The words *Restsüsse* and *Süsse* are also used.

Wine Auctions

Wine auctions were recorded in Germany as early as the eighteenth century. In those days single estates auctioned their wines in casks, and the purchaser or merchant was responsible for bottling the wine. Later, cooperatives and auction associations offering bottled wines were established.

Today there are wine auctions in Rheinhessen, on the Moselle, on the Nahe, and in Rheingau, as well as nonregional wine auctions in the Kurhaussaal in Wiesbaden. The buyers are usually professional brokers who bid in their own names, but who are buying for specific clients. The auctions are held most often during the spring and autumn; a detailed schedule can be obtained from:

Bundesverband Deutscher Weinkommissionäre e.V.

6500 Mainz, Grosse Bleiche 29, West Germany

An auction of old German wines, similar to the famous wine auctions held at Christie's in London, was held recently as a novelty in Frankfurt. The auction was conducted by Auktionshaus Knut Günther (Körnerwiese 19, Frankfurt/Main), and museum rarities from the nineteenth century were offered. It is planned to repeat the auction on a regular basis.

Wine Festivals

Many German wine-producing communities have wine festivals to which the public is invited. The festivals differ from town to town; some have formal events with bands and entertainment, while others allow the participants to generate their own amusement. In every case, however, a large selection of local wines is always available, and the festivals provide an excellent opportunity to meet local citizens.

Wine festivals usually take place from April through October. If you're traveling in Germany during that time, you should plan to visit one of the major wine-producing regions, where you will be certain to find at least one *Fest* in progress.

You can obtain current information by writing to:

Deutsche Wein-Information
6500 Mainz, Fuststrasse 4, West Germany

Information may also be obtained from:

German National Tourist Office
6 Frankfurt/Main, Beethoven Strasse 69, West Germany

Useful Addresses

Wine Seminars in English

Moselle-Saar-Ruwer

Several two-day, weekend seminars are given each year. Information is available from:

Trier Wine Seminar, Volkshochschule Trier, 55 Trier, Palais Walderdorff, West Germany Telephone: (0651) 718330

or: Verkehrsamt Trier, 55 Trier, West Germany Telephone: (0651) 718446

Rheingau

The German Wine Academy conducts several five-day seminars each year. Lectures are given at Kloster Eberbach by Germany's leading wine experts and producers. Students taste, discuss, and evaluate about 150 different wines representing German wine regions, and visit most of the regions, see vines being cultivated, and observe wines being processed and aged. Lodging, meals, and transportation are arranged by the Academy. Information is available from:

Reisebüro A. Bartholomae, 6200 Wiesbaden, Wilhelmstr. 8, West Germany Telephone: (06121) 302004 or: German Wine Information Bureau, 666 Fifth Avenue, New York, N.Y. 10019 U.S.A.

or: German Wine Information Service, 15 Thayer Street, London, W1, England

or: Japan Public Relations, Inc., 765 Ohtemachi Building, 1-6-1 Ohtemachi, Chiyoda-ku, Tokyo 100, Japan

Wine Seminars in German

Baden

A six-day course is given at various times during the year. Information is available from:

Oberbadische Weinreise, Industrie- und Handelskammer, 7800 Freiburg (Breisgau), Wilhelmstrasse 26, West Germany

Franconia

A five-day course is offered. Information is available from:

Bocksbeutel-Weinseminar Volkach, Verkehrsverlin Volkach, 8712 Volkach, Rathaus, West Germany

Moselle-Saar-Ruwer

The same weekend seminar given in English is also given in German. For information, write to the addresses given under "Wine Seminars in English."

Nahe

A two-day seminar is given three times per year. Information is available from:

Wochenendseminar für Weinfreunde, Nahewein-Werbung e.V., 6550 Bad Kreuznach, Kornmarkt 6, West Germany

Rheingau

A series of five-day seminars designed for novice, intermediate, and advanced oenophiles is conducted. Information is available from:

Rheingauer Weinseminar, 6220 Rüdesheim am Rhein, Rheinstrasse 5, West Germany

German Wine Societies

Societies for the preservation of German wine culture:

Collegium Vini, 6000 Frankfurt/Main, Holzhausenstrasse 15, West Germany

Internationaler Hansenorden zu St. Goar, 5407 St. Goar, Heerstrasse 2, West Germany

Wine history society:
Gesellschaft für Geschichte des Weines, 6200 Wiesbaden, Amselberg 20, West Germany

German Wine Information and Publicity Offices

Ahr
Gebietsweinwerbung Ahr, 5481 Dernau, Hauptstrasse 55, West Germany Telephone: (02643) 263

Baden
Weinwerbezentrale Badischer Winzergenossenschaften eGmbH, 7500 Karlsruhe 1, Ettlinger Strasse 12, West Germany Telephone: (0721) 31308

Franconia
Vereinigung Frankenwein—Frankenland c.V., 8700 Würzburg, Juliusspital-Weingut, West Germany Telephone: (0931) 54465

Mittelrhein
Mittelrhein—Burgen and Wein e.V., 5400 Koblenz, Mainzer Strasse 602, West Germany Telephone: (0261) 33037

Nahe
Nahewein-Werbung e.V., 6550 Bad Kreuznach, Am Kornmarkt 6, West Germany Telephone: (0671) 27563

Rheingau
Rheingau Weinwerbung e.V., 6225 Johannisberg, Rathaus, West Germany Telephone: (06722) 8117

Hessische Bergstrasse
Weinbauverband Bergstrasse, 6148 Heppenheim, Königsberger Strasse 4, West Germany Telephone: (06252) 2101

Rheinhessen
Rheinhessen e.V., 6500 Mainz, 117er Ehrenhof 5, West Germany Telephone: (06131) 66162

Rheinpfalz
Rheinpfalz—Weinpfalz, 6730 Neustadt, Friedrich-Ebert-Strasse 11, West Germany Telephone: (06321) 3636

Moselle-Saar-Ruwer
Weinwerbung Mosel-Saar-Ruwer, 5500 Trier, Neustrasse 86, West Germany Telephone: (0651) 76621

Württemberg
Württembergischer Landesverband ländlicher Genossenschaften, Raiffeisen e.V., 7000 Stuttgart 1, Johannesstrasse 86, West Germany Telephone: (0711) 6611

Index of Estates, Locations and Vineyards

Abstatter Burg Wildeck 185
Abtswinder Altenberg 198
– Schild 198
Adelmann, Schlosskellerei Graf, Weingut "Brüssele" 179-180
Ahrweiler Rosenthal 3
– Silberberg 3
Alsheim 130-131
Alsheimer Fischerpfad 129, 130
– Frühmesse 129, 130, 136
– Goldberg 129, 130
– Rheinblick 129, 131
– Römerberg 129
– Sonnenberg 129, 130
Altenbamberger Kehrenberg 36
– Rotenberg 43
– Schlossberg 46
Annaberg 144
Anheuser, Weingut August 48-49
Anbeuser'sche Weingutsverwaltung, Rudolf 46-47
Assmanshäuser Höllenberg 94
Avelsbacher Altenberg 26
– Hammerstein 30
– Herrenberg 26
– Kupp 30
– Rotlay 30
Ayler Herrenberger 26
– Kupp 26, 34

Bad Dürkheim 140-145
Bad Kreuznach 44-53
Bad Neuenahr-Ahrweiler 3-4
Balbach Erben, Weingut Bürgermeister 110-111
Bassermann-Jordan, Weingut Geheimer Rat Dr. v. 152-154
Bayerische Landesanstalt für Weinbau und Gartenbau 197-199
Bechtheim 132-135
Bechtheimer Geyersberg 122, 132, 133, 136
– Gotteshilfe 132, 133
– Hasensprung 132, 133
– Heiligkreuz 132, 133
– Pilgerpfad 132, 133
Bechtheimer Rosengarten 132, 133
– Stein 132, 133
Bensheimer Kalkgasse 94
– Streichling 94
Bentzel-Sturmfeder'sches Weingut, Gräflich von, 181-182
Bermatinger Leopoldsberg 173
Bernkasteler Badstube 17
– Bratenhöfchen 13, 15, 32
– Doctor 15
– Doktor 17
– Graben 15, 17, 32
– Johannisbrünnchen 15
– Kurfürstlay 17
– Lay 13, 15, 17
– Matheisbildchen, 15
– Schlossberg 15, 17
Bernkastel-Kues 14, 15, 18
Beyer, Weingut Richard 132-133
Bingen 107
Binger Kapellenberg 107
– Kirchberg 107, 109
– Osterberg 107, 109
– Rosengarten 107
– Scharlachberg 107, 109
– Schlossberg-Schwätzerchen 107, 109
Birkweiler Kastanienbusch 159

Birnauer Kirchhalde 173
Bischöfliche Weingüter, Verwaltung 25-27
Bissersheimer Goldberg 139
Blankenhornsberg, Versuchs- u. Lehrgut für Weinbau 170-171
Blankenhornsberger 170
Bodenheimer Heitersbrünnchen 109
– Hoch 109
– Leidhecke 109
– Reichsritterstift 109
– Silberberg 109
Bosenheimer Paradies 52
Brauneberger Juffer-Sonnenuhr 17
Brenner'sches Weingut 133-135
Brentano'sche Gutsverwaltung, A. von 78-79
Bretzenheimer Hofgut 58
– Pastorei 44, 58
– Vogelsang 44
Bronnbacher Kemelrain 205
"Brüssele", Weingut, Schlosskellerei Graf Adelmann 179-180
Buhl, Weingut Reichsrat von 149-151
Bürgerspital zum Hl. Geist 200-201
Burg Hornberger Götzhalde 163
– – Wallmauer 163
Burg Layen 55, 59
Burg Layer Hölle 58
– – Johannisberg 55, 58
– – Rotenberg 55
– – Rothenberg 58
– – Schlossberg 55, 58
Bürgstädter Mainhölle 203

Bürklin-Wolf, Weingut Dr.
145-148
Castell 193-195
Casteller Bausch 194
– Feuerbach 194
– Herrenberg 194
– Hohnart 194
– Kirchberg 194
– Kugelspiel 194
– Reitsteig 193
– Schlossberg 193
– Trautberg 194
Castell'sches Domänenamt,
Fürstlich 193-195

Dahlem Erben KG, Wein-
gutsverwaltung
Sanitätsrat Dr. 127-128
Deidesheim 149-157
Deidesheimer Grainhübel
148, 150, 153, 154, 156
– Herrgottsacker 149, 150,
153, 154, 156
– Hofstück 142, 147, 150,
153, 155
– Hohenmorgen 147, 153
– Kalkofen 147, 153, 154,
156
– Kieselberg 149, 150, 153,
156
– Langenmorgen 147, 153
– Leinhöhle 147, 148, 150,
153, 154, 156
– Letten 150
– Mäushöhle 150, 153,
154, 156
– Nonnenstück 150, 157
Deidesheimer Paradies-
garten 150, 154, 156
Deinhard, Gutsverwaltung
14-16
Dettelbacher Berg-Rondell
203
Dhroner Hofberger 32
Diel auf Burg Layen,
Schlossgut 55-57
Dienheimer Falkenberg 46,
118, 119, 121, 123, 127,
129
– Güldenmorgen 122, 129
– Herrenberg 109, 129
– Kreuz 109, 121, 129
– Krötenbrunnen 129
– Paterhof 109, 120, 127,
129

– Schloss 129
– Siliusbrunnen 109, 129
– Tafelstein 46, 109, 115,
119, 121, 127, 129
Dirmsteiner Mandelpfad
139
Dorfprozeltener Predigt-
stuhl 198
Dorsheimer Burgberg 43
– Goldloch 43, 54, 55, 58
– Honigberg 58
– Klosterpfad 55, 58
– Laurenziweg 58
– Pittermännchen 55
– Trollberg 58
Durbach 164-169
Durbacher Josephsberg
165
– Ölberg 165
– Plauelrain 166
– Schlossberg 166
– Schloss Grohl 166
– Schloss Staufenberg 169
Dürkheim, Bad 140-145
Dürkheimer Abtsfronhof
142
– Feuerberg 142, 144
– Hochbenn 142, 144
– Hochmess 144, 153
– Michelsberg 142, 153
– Rittergarten 142
– Schenkenböhl 142
– Spielberg 142, 153
– Steinberg, 142

Ebernburger Schlossberg
43
Ediger Elzogberg 9
– Osterlämmchen 9
Eibelstadter Kapellenberg
196
Eitelsbacher Karthäuser-
hofberg Burgberg 19
– – Kronenberg 19
– – Orthsberg 19
– – Sang 19
– – Stirn 19
Einselthumer Klösterstück
132
Eitelsbacher Marienholz
26
Eller 9
Ellerer Bienenlay 9
– Calmont 9
– Engelströpfchen 9
– Pfirsichgarten 9

Eltville 90-99
Eltviller Langenstück 91,
98
– Rheinberg 98
– Sonnenberg 91, 94, 98
– Taubenberg 91, 94, 98
Eltz, Schloss 90-92
Engehöller Goldemund 5
Erbach 84-85
Erbacher Hohenrain 85
– Honigberg 85
– Marcobrunn 82, 85, 94,
98
– Rheinhell 85
– Schlossberg 85
– Siegelsberg 85
Erdener Treppchen 26
Erlenbacher Krähen-
schnabel 198
Escherndorfer Lump 203

Falkensteiner Hofberg 32
Filzen 36
Filzener Herrenberg 36
– Steinberger 36
Finkenauer, Weingut Carl
51-53
Fitz-Ritter, Weingut K.
142-143
Forst 148-149
Forster Bischofsgarten,
147, 150
– Elster 150, 153, 154, 157
– Freundstück 150, 153,
154
– Jesuitengarten 147, 148,
153, 154, 157
– Kirchenstück 147, 153,
157
– Mariengarten 149, 153,
155
– Musenhang 150, 153,
154
– Pechstein 147, 148, 150,
153, 154
– Schnepfenflug 147, 149,
150, 153, 155
– Stift 150, 153
– Süsskopf 150
– Ungeheuer 147, 148,
150, 153, 154, 157
Frankenberger Schloss-
stück 198
Frankfurter Lohrberger
Hang 102

Freiherrl. von Gemmingen-Hornberg'sches Weingut, Burg Hornberg 163-164
Freiherrlich Langwerth von Simmern'sches Rentamt 98-99
Friedrich-Wilhelm-Gymnasium, Stiftung Staatliches 32-33
Fürst zu Hohenlohe-Öhringen'sche Schlosskellerei 186-188
Fürst von Metternich-Winneburg'sches Domäne Rentamt, Schloss Johannisberg 69-72
Fürstlich Castell'sches Domänenamt 193-195
Fürstlich Hohenlohe Langenburg'sche Weingüter 188-190
Fürstlich Löwenstein-Wertheim-Rosenberg'sches Weingut 204-206

Gailinger Ritterhalde 172
Gebhardt, Weingut Ernst 195-197
Geisenheim 65-67
Geisenheimer Fuchsberg 66
– Kilzberg 73
– Kläuserweg 66, 68, 73, 80
– Mäuerchen 66, 82
– Mönchspfad 73, 82
– Rothenberg 66, 80, 82
– Schlossgarten 80, 82
Gemmingen-Hornberg'sches Weingut, Freiherrl. von, Burg Hornberg 163-164
Gimmeldinger Biengarten 156
– Kapellenberg 156
– Mandelgarten 156, 158
– Meerspinne 150, 158
– Schlössel 156, 158
– Gotteshilfe 136
Graacher Abtsberg 15
– Domprobst 13, 15, 24, 32
– Himmelreich 13, 15, 17, 24, 32

Gräflich von Bentzel-Stürmfedersches Weingut 181-182
Gräfl. von Kanitz'sche Weingutsverwaltung 63-64
Gräfl. v. Neipperg'sches Weingut und Schlosskellerei 182-184
Gräfl. Wolff Metternich'sches Weingut 166-167
Groenesteyn, Schloss, Weingut des Reichsfreiherrn von Ritter zu Groenesteyn 88-89
Grossheubacher Bischofsberg 198
Grünhaus 20
Guldentaler Honigberg 58
Gundelsheimer Himmelreich 185
Guntersblumer Autental 131
– Bornpfad 131
– Eiserne Hand 131
– Himmeltal 130
– Kreuzkapelle 127, 130
– Steig-Terrassen 131
– Steinberg 130
– Vogelsgärtchen 131
Guntrum, Weingut Louis 119-120
Güterverwaltung Vereinigte Hospitien Trier 27-28
Gutsverwaltung Deinhard 14-16
Gutsverwaltung Freiherr von Neveu 164-165
Gutsverwaltung Geh. Rat Julius Wegeler Erben 80-81

Haardt 157
Haardter Bürgergarten 156-158
– Herrenletten 158
– Herzog 156, 158
– Mandelring 156, 158
Hahnheimer Knopf 125
– Moosberg 125
Hahnhof, Weingut 154-155
Hallgartener Jungfer 82
– Mehrhölzchen 83
– Schönhell 80
– Würzgarten 82

Hambacher Feuer 156
– Kaiserstuhl 156
– Römerbrunnen 158
Hammel u. Cie., Emil 139-140
Hammelburger Burg 198
– Trautlestal 198
Handthaler Stollberg 198
Hattenheim 81-83
Hattenheimer Deutelsberg 83, 94
– Engelmannsberg 82, 94
– Mannberg 94, 98
– Nussbrunnen 82, 85, 98
– Pfaffenberg 82
– Schützenhaus 82, 98
– Wisselbrunnen 82, 85
Heppenheimer Centgericht 94
– Steinkopf 94
Hermannshof 113-175
Hessische Forschungsanstalt für Wein-, Obst- und Gartenbau 65-67
Heyl zu Herrnsheim, Freiherr, Weingut Mathildenhof 111-113
Himmelstadter Kelter 201
Hochheim 100–104
Hochheimer Berg 94, 100, 102
– Daubhaus 83, 94, 102
– Domdechaney 82, 94, 100, 102
– Hofmeister 82, 100, 102
– Hölle 82, 100, 102
– Kirchenstück 82, 94, 100, 102
– Reichesthal 98, 100, 102
– Sommerheil 82, 100, 102
– Stein 82, 94, 100, 102
– Stielweg 100, 102
Hoch'sche Güterverwaltung, Carl Jos. 156-157
Höfer Weingut Dr. Josef, Schlossmühle 111-113
Hofkammer-Kellerei, Württembergische 177-178
Hofstück 156
Hohenhaslacher Kirchberg 177
Hohenlohe Langenburg'sche Weingüter, Fürstlich 188-190

Hohenlohe-Öhringen'sche
   Schlosskellerei, Fürst zu
   186-188
Hohentwieler Olgaberg 172
Höllenpfad 139
Homburger Kallmuth 205
Hornberg, Burg, Freiherrl.
   von Gemmingen-Horn-
   berg'sches Weingut 163-
   164
Hörsteiner Abtsberg 198
– Reuschberg 198

Ihringen 170-177
Iphöfer Julius-Echter-Berg
   203
– Kronsberg 203
Ippesheimer Herrschafts-
   berg 198

Johannisberg 67-74
Johannisberger Erntebrin-
   ger 66, 68, 73, 82
– Goldatzel 68, 73
– Hansenberg 73
– Hölle 68, 73, 80
– Klaus 68, 73, 82
– Mittelhölle 73
– Schwarzenstein 73
– Vogelsang 68, 73, 80
Josephshöfer 24
Juliusspital-Weingut 202-
   204

Kallstadter Kreidkeller 144
Kanitz'sche Weingutsver-
   waltung, Gräflich von
   63-64
Kanzemer Altenberg 26,
   27
Kapellenhof, Weingut,
   Ökonomierat Schätzel
   Erben 124-127
Karthäuserhof Eitelsbach
   20
Kaseler Herrenberg 24
– Hitzlay 24
– Kehrnagel 24, 26
– Nies'chen 24, 26
Kauber Rossstein 5
Kesselstatt, Reichsgraf von
   22-24
Kiedrich 86-89
Kiedricher Gräfenberg 86,
   89, 94
– Heiligenstock 86, 89

– Klosterberg 86, 89
– Sandgrub 85, 86, 89, 91
– Wasserrose 86, 89
Kirchenweinberg 181
Kirchheim 139-140
Kirchheimer Geisskopf 139
– Kreuz 139
– Römerstrasse 139
– Steinacker 139
Kleinbottwar 179-180
Kleinbottwarer Oberer
   Berg 179
– Süssmund 179
Kleinkarlbacher Herren-
   berg 140
Klingenberger Schlossberg
   183
Königin Victoria Berg,
   Weingut 103-104
Kreuznach, Bad 44-53
Kreuznacher Breitenweg
   52
– Brückes 44, 48, 52
– Forst 44, 50, 52
– Gutental 52
– Hinkelstein 44, 46, 50, 52
– Hofgarten 48
– Hungriger Wolf 59
– Kahlenberg 44, 46, 50
– Kanzenberg 52
– Kapellenpfad 44, 50, 52
– Kronenberg 45, 52
– Krötenpfuhl 46, 48, 52
– Mollenbrunnen 50, 52
– Mönchberg 46, 48, 52
Kreuznacher Monhard 50
– Narrenkappe 46, 48, 52
– Osterhöll 44, 52
– Rosenberg 52
– Steinweg 50
– St. Martin 46, 48
– Vogelsang 50
Kreuzwertheim 204-206
Kreuzwertheimer Kaffel-
   stein 198, 205
Krötenbrunnen 136
Kurfürstenhof, Weingut
   Winzermeister Heinrich
   Seip 121-122

Lahrer Herrentisch 166
Landenberg, Weingut
   Freiherr von 9-10
Landgräflich Hessisches
   Weingut 67-68

Langenlonsheim 53-54
Langenlonsheimer Berg-
   born 54
– Königsschild 54
– Löhrer Berg 54
– St. Antoniusweg 54
– Steinchen 54
Langwerth von Simmern'-
   sches Rentamt, Freiherr-
   lich 98-99
Laubenheimer Hörnchen
   54
– Karthäuser 54, 58
– Krone 54
– St. Remigiusberg 54
Lauffener Kirchenweinberg
   185
Layen, Burg 55-59
Lengfurter Alter Berg 205
– Oberrot 205
Lindelberg 187
Lindenhof, Weingut, Eugen
   Spindler 148-149
Lorch 63-64
Lorcher Bodental-Steinberg
   63
– Kapellenberg 63, 82
– Krone 63, 82
– Pfaffenwies 63, 82
– Schlossberg 63, 82
Lorchhausener Seligmacher
   82
Löwenstein-Wertheim-
   Rosenberg'sches Wein-
   gut, Fürstlich 204-206

Mainz 108-110
Mariengarten 157
Marienthal, Kloster, Staat-
   liche Weinbaudomäne
   3-4
Marienthaler Klosterberg
   3
Marienthaler Klostergarten
   3
– Stiftsberg 3
Markgräflich Badisches
   Weingut, Schloss Stau-
   fenberg 168-169
Marktbreiter Sonnenberg
   196
Mathildenhof, Weingut
   Freiherr Heyl zu Herrn-
   sheim 111-113
Maulbronner Eilfingerberg
   177

- Eilfingerberg Kloster-
  stück 177
Maximin Grünhäuser
  Abtsberg 21
- - Brunderberg 21
- - Herrenberg 21
Max Markgraf von Baden,
  Weingüter 173-174
Meersburg 170
Meersburger Bengel 172
- Chorherrenhalde 172,
  173
- Fohrenberg 172
- Jungfernstieg 172
- Lerchenberg 172
- Rieschen 172
- Sängerhalde 172
- Sonnenufer 172
Meerspinne 157
Mehringer Blattenberg 32
- Goldkupp 32
- Zellerberg 32
Merler Adler 11
- Klosterberg 11
- Königslay-Terrassen 11
Mesenicher Goldgrübchen
  9
Mettenheimer Goldberg
  136
- Michelsberg 136
- Schlossberg 136
Metternich-Winneburg'-
  sches Domäne Rentamt,
  Fürst von, Schloss
  Johannisberg 69-72
Michelauer Vollburg 201
Mittelheimer Edelmann 80
- Goldberg 80
- St. Nikolaus 80, 82
Monzinger Gabelstich 46
Müller, Alfred 135-136
Müller, Egon, Scharzhof
  37-38
Müller-Catoir, Weingut
  157-158
Mumm'sches Weingut,
  G. H. von 72-74
Mundelsheimer Käsberg
  177
Münsterer Dautenpflänzer
  43
- Kapellenberg 43
- Königsschloss 55
- Pittersberg 43
Münster-Sarmsheimer
  Königsschloss 58

- Trollberg 58
Mussbacher Eselshaut
  156, 158
- Mandelring 156
- Schlössel 156
Muth, Dr. Reinhard,
  Weingut Rappenhof 130-
  131

Nackenheimer Engelsberg
  109, 121
- Rothenberg 109, 120
- Spiegelberg 122
Neckarzimmern 163-164
Neipperger Schlossberg
  183
Neipperg'sches Weingut
  und Schlosskellerei,
  Gräfl. v. 182-184
Nell, Georg Fritz von,
  Weingut Thiergarten 33-
  34
Neuenahr-Ahrweiler, Bad
  3-4
Neuleininger Sonnenberg
  139
Neumagener Rosengärt-
  chen 32
Neustadter Erkenbrecht
  156
- Grain 158
- Mönchgarten 156, 158
Neveu, Gutsverwaltung
  Freiherr von 164-165
Niederhausen 41-43
Niederhäuser Felsensteyer
  46
- Hermannsberg 43
- Hermannshöhle 41, 43,
  48
- Kerz 43
- Klamm 41
Pfingstweide 46
- Rosenberg 41
- Rosenheck 41
- Steinberg 43
- Steinwingert 41
Niedermenniger Eucharius-
  berg 24
- Herrenberg 24
Nierstein 110-124
Niersteiner Auflangen 109,
  111, 112, 115, 118, 120
  122, 123, 129
- Bildstock 110, 112, 115,
  121, 123

- Brückchen 123
- Brudersberg 112
- Findling 112, 119, 121,
  129
- Glöck 109
- Goldene Luft 121
- Gutes Domtal 121, 125
- Heiligenbaum 112, 115,
  119, 121, 123, 127, 129
Niersteiner Hipping 110,
  112, 114, 115, 118, 119,
  121, 123, 127
- Hölle 119
- Kirchplatte 121, 129
- Klostergarten 110, 119,
  121, 129
- Kranzberg 110, 112, 114,
  121
- Ölberg 109, 110, 112,
  114, 115, 118, 119, 121,
  123, 129
- Orbel 112, 114, 118, 119,
  121, 123, 129
- Paterberg 115, 119, 121,
  123, 129
- Pettenthal 110, 112, 114,
  115, 119, 121
- Rehbach 109, 111, 112,
  115, 118, 120, 122, 123,
  129
- Rosenberg 110, 112, 119,
  121, 129
- Schloss Schwabsburg
  112, 121
- Spiegelberg 111, 112,
  118, 120, 122, 123, 129
- Zehnmorgen 114
Norheimer Dellchen 48, 50
- Götzenfels 45
- Kafels 46, 48, 50
- Kirschheck 41, 50

Oberemmeler Agritiusberg
  24
- Altenberg 24
- Karlsberg 24
- Raul 24
- Rosenberg 24
- Scharzberg, 32
Oberwesel 5
Oberweseler Römerkrug
  5
- St. Martinsberg 5
Ockfener Bockstein 30, 36
- Geisberg 32, 36
- Heppenstein 30

Ockfener Bockstein (*cont.*)
– Herrenberg 30
– Kupp 36
Öhringen 186-188
Oppenheim 127–130
Oppenheimer Daubhaus
   127, 129
– Güldenmorgen 120, 129
– Gutleuthaus 129
– Herrenberg 109, 115,
   119, 127, 129
– Herrengarten 119, 127,
   129
– Herrenweiher 46
– Kreuz 119, 127, 129
– Krötenbrunnen 115, 122,
   129
– Paterhof 129
Oppenheimer Sackträger
   109, 118, 119, 127, 129
– Schloss 119, 121, 127,
   129
– Schützenhütte 119
– Zuckerberg 129
Ortenberger Freudental
   165
– Schlossberg 165
Osthofen 135-136
Osthofener Goldberg 136
– Hasenbiss 136
– Kirchberg 136
– Klosterberg 136
– Liebenberg 136
Oestrich 80, 81
Oestricher Doosberg 80, 82
– Gottesthal 83
– Klosterberg 80
– Lenchen 80

Pellinger Jesuitengarten 32
Pfeffingen, Weingut 140-
   141
Piesporter Domherr 24
– Goldtröpfchen 24, 26, 28
– Grafenberg 24
– Schubertslay im Gold-
   tröpfchen 28
Pilgerpfad 136
Plettenberg'sche Verwal-
   tung, Reichsgräflich v.
   44-45
Prüm, Weingut Joh. Jos.
   13-14

Randersackerer Ewig
Leben 198

– Marsberg 198, 201, 203
– Pfülben 198, 201, 202
– Sonnenstuhl 196, 198
– Teufelskeller 196, 198,
   201, 203
Rappenhof, Weingut, Dr.
   Reinhard Muth 130-131
Rauenthaler Baiken 82, 91,
   94, 98
– Gehrn 91, 94
– Langenstück 91, 94
– Rothenberg 82, 91, 98
– Steinmächer 83, 94
– Wülfen 82, 85, 91, 94
Rebholz, Weingut Ökono-
   mierat 159-160
Rebstöckel 157
Reichholzheimer Satzen-
   berg 205
Reichsgraf von Kesselstatt
   22-24
Reichsgräflich v. Pletten-
   berg'sche Verwaltung 44-
   45
Reinhartshausen, Schloss
   84-85
Reverchon, Weingut Ed-
   mund 36-37
Rheinblick 136
Rödelseer Küchenmeister
   203
– Schwanleite 203
Roxheimer Höllenpfad 44,
   46
– Mühlenberg 52
– Sonnenberg 52
Rüdesheimer Berg Rose-
   neck 73, 80, 89, 91, 94
– – Rottland 73, 80, 82,
   89, 94
– – Schlossberg 73, 80, 82,
   89, 94
– Bischofsberg 73, 80, 82,
   85, 89, 91, 94
– Burgweg 66, 73, 82, 89,
   94
– Drachenstein 73
– Kirchenpfad 89
– Klosterberg 66
– Klosterlay 89
– Magdalenenkreuz 66, 80,
   89
Ruppertsberger Gaisböhl
   147
– Hoheburg 147, 149, 150,
   153, 157

– Königsbacherweg 155
– Linsenbusch 147, 149,
   150, 153, 157
– Mandelgarten 154
– Nussbien 147, 149, 153,
   155, 157
– Reiterpfad 149, 150, 153,
   157
– Spiess 153

Saarfelder Schlossberg 27
Salem 173-174
Scharzberg 34, 38
Scharzhof, Egon Müller
   37-38
Scharzhofberger 24, 26, 27
Schätzel Erben, Ökono-
   mierat, Weingut Kapell-
   enhof 124-127
Schlossböckelheimer Burg-
   weg 45
– Felsenberg 43, 45, 48
– Heimberg 46
– In den Felsen 46
– Königsfels 48, 52
– Kupfergrube 43, 45
– Mühlberg 46, 48, 52
Schloss Eltz, Gräflich
   Eltz'sche Güterverwal-
   tung 90-92
Schloss Groenesteyn 88-89
Schlossgut Diel auf Burg
   Layen 55-57
Schloss Johannisberg,
   Fürst von Metternich-
   Winneburg'sches Do-
   mäne Rentamt 69-72
Schloss Johannisberger 70
Schloss Kirchberger
   Schlossberg 173
Schloss Michelfelder Him-
   melberg 163
Schlossmühle, Weingut Dr.
   Josef Höfer 57-59
Schloss Reinhartshausen
   84-85
Schloss Schönborn, Do-
   mänenweingut 81, 83
Schloss Staufenberg,
   Markgräflich Badisches
   Weingut 168-169
Schloss Vollrads 75-78
Schmitt, Weingut Franz
   Karl, Hermannshof 113-
   114

Schmitt'sches Weingut, Gustav Adolf 115-116
Schneider, Weingut Jakob 41-42
Schneider'sche Weingüterverwaltung 11
Schönberger Herrnwingert 94
Schönborn, Domänenweingut Schloss 81-83
Schozach 181-182
Schozacher Roter Berg 181
Schubert'sche Gutsverwaltung, C. von 20-22
Schuch, Weingut Geschwister 116-118
Schwaigern 182-184
Schwaigerner Ruthe 183
Schwarzerde 139
Seip, Weingut Winzermeister Heinrich Kurfürstenhof 121-122
Selzen 124-127
Selzener Gottesgarten 125
– Osterberg 125
– Rheinpforte 125
Senheimer Lay 9
Serriger Heiligenborn 30
– Hoeppslei 30
– Schloss 27
– Vogelsang 27, 30
Siebeldingen 159-160
Siebeldinger Im Sonnenschein 159
– Königsgarten 159
– Rosenberg 159
Sittmann, Weingut Carl 128-130
Sommerhausen 195-197
Sommerhäuser Ölspiel 196
Sommerhäuser Reifenstein 196
– Steinbach 196
Spindler, Eugen, Weingut Lindenhof 148-149
Staatliche Lehr- und Versuchsanstalt für Wein- und Obstbau 184-186
Staatliche Weinbaudomäne Kloster Marienthal 3, 4
Staatliche Weinbaudomänen Mainz, Verwaltung 108-110
Staatliche Weinbaudomänen Niederhausen-

Schlossböckelheim, Verwaltung 42-43
Staatliche Weinbaudomänen Trier, Verwaltung 30-31
Staatsweingüter Eltville, Verwaltung 92-96
Staatsweingut Meersburg 171-173
Staatsweingut Weinbaulehranstalt Bad Kreuznach 49-51
Staufenberg, Schloss 176
Steinberger 94
Stettener Brotwasser 177
Stiftung Staatliches Friedrich-Wilhelm-Gymnasium 32
Stromberg 178
Strub, Weingut J. u. H. A. 123-124
Stumpf-Fitz'sches Weingut, Annaberg 143-145
Stuttgart 177-178

Talheimer Schlossberg 185
Tesch, Weingut Erbhof 66
Thanisch, Weingut Wwe. Dr. H. 26, 35
Thüngersheimer Ravensberg 198
– Scharlachberg 198, 201, 211
Traisener Bastei 43
Trier 22-34
Trier-Eitelsbach 18-20
Trierer Augenscheiner 28
– Benediktinerberg 34
– Deutschherrenberg 27
– Kurfürstenhofberg 34
– Römerlay 34
– St. Maximiner Kreuzberg 27
– Thiergarten 28
– Thiergarten Unterm Kreuz 34
Trittenheimer Altärchen 26, 32
– Apotheke 26, 32

Ungsteiner Herrenberg 141, 142, 153
– Honigsäckel 141, 153
– Nussriegel 140
Untertürkheimer Altenberg 177

– Mönchberg 177
Ürziger Würzgarten 26

Veitshöchheimer Wölflein 198
Vereinigte Hospitien Trier, Güterverwaltung 27-28
Verrenberger Verrenberg 187
Versuchs- und Lehrgut für Weinbau Blankenhornsberg 170-171
Villa Sachsen, Weingut 107-108
Volkacher Karthäuser 203
Vollrads, Schloss 83, 89

Wachenheim 145-148
Wachenheimer Altenburg 147
– Böhlig 147
– Gerümpel 147
– Goldbächel 147
Königswingert 147
– Luginsland 147, 150
– Mandelgarten 142, 147
– Rechbächel 147
– Schenkenböhl 147
– Schlossberg 147
Walporzheimer Alte Lay 3
– Himmelchen 3
– Kräuterberg 3
– Pfaffenberg 3
Wartbühl 178
Wegeler Erben, Gutsverwaltung Geh. Rat Julius 80-81
Wehlen 13
Wehlener Abtei 23
– Klosterberg 13
– Klosterhofgut 11
– Münzlay 11
– Nonnenberg 13
– Rosenberg 13
– Sonnenuhr 13, 17
Weikersheim 188-190
Weikersheimer Karlsberg 189
– Schmecker 189
Weil, Weingut Dr. 86-88
Weiler, Heinrich 5, 6
Weinbaulehranstalt Bad Kreuznach, Staatsweingut 49-51
Weingut August Anheuser 48-49

Weingut August An-
heuser (*cont.*)
- Bürgermeister Anton
Balbach Erben 110-111
Weingut Geheimer Rat Dr.
v. Basserman-Jordan
152-154
- Richard Beyer 132-133
- "Brüssele", Schlosskell-
erei Graf Adelmann 179-
180
- Reichsrat von Buhl 149-
151
- Dr. Bürklin-Wolf 145-
148
- Carl Finkenauer 51-53
- K. Fitz-Ritter 142-143
- der Stadt Frankfurt am
Main 101-102
- Ernst Gebhardt 195-197
- des Reichsfreiherrn von
Ritter zu Groenesteyn,
Schloss Groenesteyn 88-
89
- Louis Guntrum 119-120
- Hahnhof 154-155
- Freiherr Heyl zu Herrns-
heim, Mathildenhof 111-
113
- Dr. Josef Höfer, Schloss-
mühle 111-113
- Königin Victoria Berg
103-104
- Freiherr von Landenberg
9-10
- Lindenhof, Eugen Spind-
ler 148-149
- Müller-Catoir 157-158
- Pfeffingen 140-141
- Joh. Jos. Prüm 13, 14
- Rappenhof, Dr. Reinhard
Muth 130-131

- Ökonomierat Rebholz
159-160
- Edmund Reverchon 36,
37
- Franz Karl Schmitt,
Hermannshof 113-115
- Jakob Schneider 41-42
- Geschwister Schuch 116-
118
- Winzermeister Heinrich
Seip, Kurfürstenhof 121-
122
- Carl Sittmann 128-130
- J. u. H. A. Strub 123-
124
- Erbhof Tesch 53-54
- Wwe. Dr. H. Thanisch
16-18
- Thiergarten, Georg Fritz
von Nell 33-34
- Villa Sachsen 107-108
- Dr. Weil 86, 88
- Heinrich Weiler 5, 6
- Weisses Ross 135-136
Weingüter Max Markgraf
von Baden 173-174
Weingutsverwaltung Sani-
tätsrat Dr. Dahlem
Erben KG 127-128
Weinsberg 184-186
Weinsberger Ranzenberg
185
- Schemelsberg 185
Weinsteige 178
Weisses Ross, Weingut,
Alfred Müller 135-136
Werner'sches Weingut
Domdechant 100-101
Wiltingen 37-38
Wiltinger Braune Kupp
27, 38
- Braunfels 24, 26, 27, 38

- Hölle 27
- Klosterberg 34, 38
- Kupp 26, 27
- Rosenberg 26, 27
Winkel 75-79
Winkeler Dachsberg 68, 73,
80, 82
- Gutenberg 68, 79, 80, 82
- Hasensprung 68, 73, 79,
80, 82
- Honigberg 73, 79, 83
- Jesuitengarten 68, 79, 82
Winzenheimer Berg 59
- Honigberg 59
- In den 17 Morgen 58
- Rosenheck 44, 52, 58
Wolff Metternich'sches
Weingut, Gräfl 166-167
Württembergische Hof-
kammer-Kellerei 177-178
Würzburg 197-204
Würzburger Abtsleite 198,
200, 202
- Himmelspforte 198
- Innere Leiste 198, 201,
202
- Pfaffenberg 198, 201,
202
- Schlossberg 198
- Stein 198, 200, 201, 202

Zell-Merl 11
Zeller Burglay-Felsen 11
Zeller Klosterstück 132
Zeller Kreuzberg 132
- Marienburger 11
- Petersborn-Kabertchen
11
- Schwarze Katz 11
Zeltinger Deutschherren-
berg 11
- Schlossberg 32
- Sonnenuhr 13, 32